LITTLE L

Jonny Steinberg was born and bred in South
Africa. He is the author of the critically acclaimed
Three Letter Plague, published by Vintage,
Midlands and *The Number*, which both won
South Africa's premier non-fiction literary award,
the *Sunday Times* Alan Paton Prize. Steinberg was
educated at Wits University in Johannesburg, and
at Oxford University, where he was a Rhodes
Scholar. He currently works at the University of
Cape Town where he is writing a book about
fear in South Africa past and present.

ALSO BY JONNY STEINBERG

Midlands
The Number
Three Letter Plague
Thin Blue

JONNY STEINBERG

Little Liberia

An African Odyssey in New York City

VINTAGE BOOKS
London

Published by Vintage 2012

2 4 6 8 10 9 7 5 3

Copyright © Jonny Steinberg 2011

Jonny Steinberg has asserted his right under the Copyright, Designs
and Patents Act 1988 to be identified as the author of this work

This book is sold subject to the condition that it shall not,
by way of trade or otherwise, be lent, resold, hired out,
or otherwise circulated without the publisher's prior
consent in any form of binding or cover other than that
in which it is published and without a similar condition,
including this condition, being imposed
on the subsequent purchaser

First published in Great Britain in 2011 by
Jonathan Cape

Vintage
Random House, 20 Vauxhall Bridge Road,
London SW1V 2SA

www.vintage-books.co.uk

Addresses for companies within The Random House Group Limited
can be found at: www.randomhouse.co.uk/offices.htm

The Random House Group Limited Reg. No. 954009

A CIP catalogue record for this book
is available from the British Library

ISBN 9780099524229

Penguin Random House is committed to a sustainable future for
our business, our readers and our planet. This book is made from
Forest Stewardship Council® certified paper.

Printed and bound in Great Britain by Clays Ltd, Elcograf S.p.A.

To Sheila

Contents

Part Three

Part Four

Exile immobilises to some degree the minds of those who suffer it. It imprisons them for ever within the circle of ideas which they had conceived or which were current when their exile began.

Alexis de Tocqueville

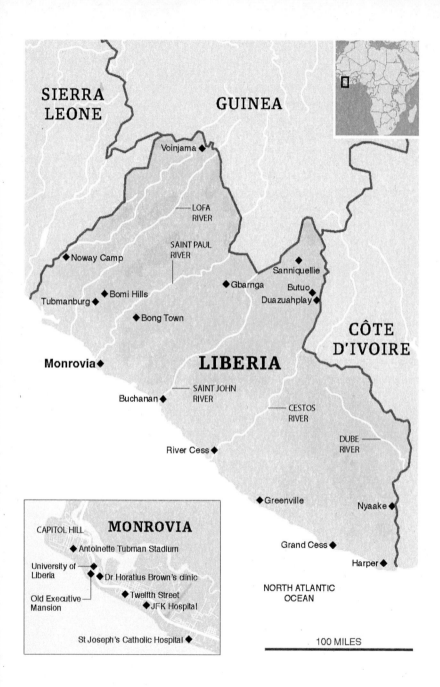

SIERRA
LEONE

GUINEA

Voinjama ◆

LOFA
RIVER

SAINT PAUL
RIVER

◆ Noway Camp

Sanniquellie ◆

◆ Gbarnga   Butuo
◆ Bomi Hills   ◆
Tubmanburg ◆   Duazuahplay ◆

◆ Bong Town

CÔTE
D'IVOIRE

Monrovia ◆

LIBERIA

SAINT JOHN
RIVER

Buchanan ◆

CESTOS
RIVER

DUBE
RIVER

River Cess ◆

◆ Greenville   Nyaake ◆

MONROVIA

CAPITOL HILL
◆ Antoinette Tubman Stadium

University of
Liberia ◆
◆ Dr Horatius Brown's clinic

Old Executive
Mansion
◆ Twelfth Street
◆ JFK Hospital

St Joseph's Catholic Hospital ◆

Grand Cess ◆

Harper ◆

NORTH ATLANTIC
OCEAN

100 MILES

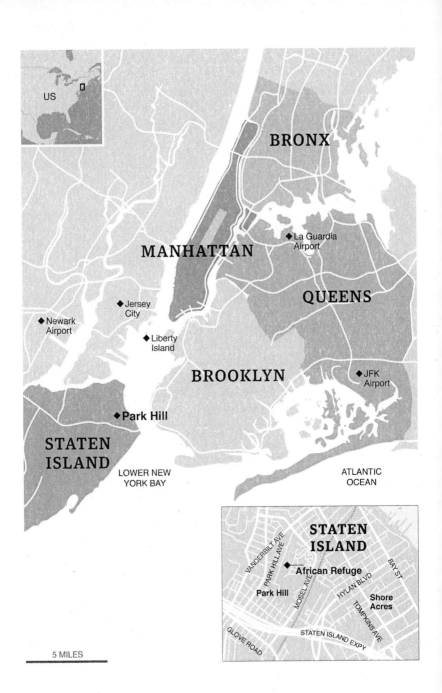

US

BRONX

MANHATTAN

◆La Guardia
Airport

QUEENS

◆Jersey
City

◆Newark
Airport

◆Liberty
Island

BROOKLYN

◆JFK
Airport

◆Park Hill

STATEN
ISLAND

LOWER NEW
YORK BAY

ATLANTIC
OCEAN

5 MILES

STATEN
ISLAND

VANDERBILT AVE

PARK HILL AVE

MOSEL AVE

◆ African Refuge

Park Hill

HYLAN BLVD

BAY ST

Shore
Acres

TOMPKINS AVE

GLOVE ROAD

STATEN ISLAND EXPY

Preface

The first time Rufus Arkoi walked onto Park Hill Avenue, in the summer of 1988, the very idea of it amused him: Liberians piled on top of one another, quite literally, from ground floor to sixth floor, in one building after the next. He had met many Liberians here in the United States during the last two years: in Newark, in Trenton, in Elizabeth. But they lived in a highly diluted state, barely discernible among the Ivorians, Nigerians, Ghanaians, Haitians and Jamaicans. In Elizabeth, you pass a black man on the street, you have no idea what will issue from his tongue: French, the whiny English of the Caribbeans, even Spanish. Here on Park Hill Avenue in New York, the Liberians were thick and unadulterated, like orange concentrate. You walked into the street and the women selling dried fish and chilli on the sidewalk were Liberian. Their customers were Liberian. His imagination ticked over. How many Liberians were there here? 200? Enough to field a soccer team of able-bodied men?

The last Liberian team he had seen take the field was very close to his heart: they were called the Sinkor Defenders. It was 20 September 1986, a Saturday, his very last afternoon in Liberia before leaving for the United States. He had woken a little after dawn in his bedroom in his father's house on Twelfth Street, Sinkor, and then gone to the stadium. Nobody who watched him going about his morning ritual would have imagined that by the following day he would be gone.

The Sinkor Defenders were to play the last match of the season at noon. Rufus was one of the men who had founded the club three years earlier. Their fortunes soared almost immediately, and he had become famous across the eastern suburbs of Monrovia. As he walked up Twelfth Street that morning, it is likely that everyone who crossed his path would have known him by face and by name.

The Defenders drew 1–1 that afternoon. Rufus had prepared the team with his usual pre-match talk, had spoken briefly about tactics at half-time, and then left soon after the game. At 5 p.m. he hailed a taxi and went to the airport. Only two people in the world knew where he was going: his childhood friend, Ben Richardson, who would run his soccer club, and a man named Dave Jackley in Newark, New Jersey, at whose house he would spend his first night in the United States.

His exit had taken many months of planning. Thanks to his growing influence in the city's soccer administration, he had managed to attach himself back in April to an official cultural expedition to Atlanta, Georgia. When the group applied for United States visas, he went along with them to the embassy and was duly granted one. They left for Atlanta in July without him. He remained at home, a valid United States visitor's visa in his passport. All he required now was an air ticket. He had savings. He could borrow a little without drawing attention to his plans.

It was clear to him from the start that he must tell nobody. Already, he was a fabulously successful young man. Most of the men his age on Twelfth Street were unemployed or in unskilled work. Rufus was in another league. He was his own boss, a dazzlingly successful tailor, owner of a soccer club, and increasingly respected in this section of the city. He had courted more than his fair share of envy. To have it known that he was going to America would be foolhardy. Although he had been educated at a fine Catholic high school in Monrovia, he had spent much of his childhood in the countryside, and he knew first-hand the power of witchcraft and sorcery. He was much too young and far too talented to die.

Now, two years later, the idea of Park Hill Avenue quickened his pulse. You go to America on a training basis, Rufus always said. You go because when you come home you have dealt in hard currency: nobody can offer you anything you haven't seen before; nobody has anything valuable enough to buy you.

But the danger, the risk you take, is that you drift, you dilute, you lose your touch: you come back to Liberia so rusty you can no longer function there. Here, on Park Hill Avenue, he thought, you can cheat geography. During the day you go and pick the riches of America. At night, the ferry takes you all the way home, as if a piece of Liberia had drifted across the ocean and docked in New York Bay.

Fourteen years later, almost to the day, another young Liberian arrived on Park Hill Avenue. His name was Jacob D. Massaquoi II. Like Rufus, he had left Monrovia quietly, although it was not envy he feared, but the anti-terrorism unit of President Charles Taylor. Shortly before his departure, an uncle of his, a senior figure in Taylor's administration, had come knocking on his door. 'Son, you gotta go,' he'd said. 'Don't stay here.' Staring at his uncle, imbibing his words, it had flashed through Jacob's mind that the world was guaranteed to surprise him; just as good people had once left him to rot, so a callous man in an evil regime had now taken the trouble to save his life.

Once he had dropped off his bags, he went downstairs and made his way along Park Hill Avenue leaning heavily on his wooden crutches. He imagined Liberian eyes watching him from the apartment block windows, watching closely, close enough to see that his right leg was several inches shorter than his left. He knew that they would draw fast conclusions, that in the length of his leg was an often-told story, one that could not easily be untold.

A curious man, he felt an urge to see the street on which he now lived in its context, preferably from a height. Over the following weeks, he caught buses; he got rides in private cars; sometimes, he set off with a cane, or on his crutches. One morning, he went to the summit of the ridge that stretches along the spine of Staten Island's North Shore. From there, he looked right across New York Bay onto downtown Manhattan, a huddle of skinny giants, it seemed, giggling at something they had spotted in the water. The houses up here were grand: they were three, four storeys tall, and they stood in large, manicured grounds.

As he made his way back down the ridge, the homes grew more modest. They were still utterly suburban: clapboard, two storeys, with wide driveways and basketball hoops above the carport doors.

In the valley, approaching the ocean, the suburbs vanished without warning and he was on Park Hill Avenue. Identical apartment blocks as far as the eye could see; fragments of hip-hop ricocheting from the cabriolets that cruised around and around. You crossed the street, went on another block, and you were back in the suburbs, the car stereos replaced by birdsong. It was as if Park Hill was a thin sliver of somewhere else spliced onto the surface of Staten Island.

Within a week, he had come to the conclusion that things were not right here. His visitor's visa would soon expire; he needed to apply for asylum. He was introduced to a Liberian who was said to be an expert in these matters, but after five minutes with the man, it was clear that he was a con artist. He looked around for more expertise. It appeared that there was none, not in all of Park Hill Avenue. Many of the Liberians on this street had immigration trouble. Could it be that between all of them and the Immigration and Naturalization Service stood one dodgy man?

The more he saw, the more troubled he became. There were unemployed people who knew nothing of the food stamps he had come across in Florida. There were sick people who had not stepped into an emergency room because it was two miles from Park Hill Avenue, and, for them, it may as well have been in a foreign city. And yet there were Liberians right here on Staten Island who had lived in America ten, twenty years; Liberians who were doing well, who knew the city like the backs of their hands, who knew everything there was to know about food stamps and health care and the INS. Why was this knowledge not being spread around?

Many of these well-off Liberians, Jacob noted, held positions on the Staten Island Liberian Community Association. Others, like the big man, Rufus Arkoi, ran organisations offering services to immigrants. Arkoi's outfit was well funded. It occupied much of an entire building down on Bay Avenue. When the newspapers wanted to know something about Liberians, they went to Arkoi. When the philanthropists came looking to save Liberian child soldiers, they knocked on Arkoi's door. Arkoi, it seemed, *was* Liberia.

Stepping off the bus at lunchtime one day, having spent the morning in Manhattan, Jacob looked up at the buildings of Park Hill Avenue, and it came to him in a flash that what was spliced onto the surface of Staten Island was a piece of Liberia. His countrymen and women had travelled across the Atlantic Ocean; they had settled in a metropolis littered with universities and hospitals and night schools and degrees by correspondence. Yet between them and the city stood big men with broad shoulders and loud mouths, just as, at home, the big men stood between Liberia and the world.

At first, he marvelled at this doubling, this little Liberia away from Liberia, and his thoughts turned to mental prisons. If his compatriots were to settle at the North Pole, would the big men monopolise access to the seals, to the fish, to the ice and snow itself? Soon it became a constant thought, living with him, tapping away at the inside of his head. By the time he had been on Park Hill Avenue a month, the idea that his street was a country had become quite familiar to him. What does one do in a country where things are not right? One contests power, of course. One gets busy.

PART ONE

1

Jacob

I walked into the Park Hill housing project in Staten Island, New York, on a stingingly cold afternoon in January 2008. The weather had chased everyone indoors, and the neighbourhood, so animated when I last visited, was perfectly still. Each building I passed was precisely like the last: a deadweight block of dark brown brick, sharp cornered and six storeys high.

I walked deeper into Park Hill Avenue, and still there was not a soul, and the buildings looked as if they might go on for ever. For some time I allowed myself the fancy that I could be walking anywhere, on any continent, that perhaps I was on the streets of some abandoned utopia, that this place had once been crowded, but that nobody lived here any more.

My reverie was broken by the sight of a pitch-black van parked on the side of the road, a satellite dish on its roof, a familiar sign emblazoned on its sides: 'ABC Eyewitness News'. As I drew nearer, the buildings on either side of the road at last came alive with sound: a disembodied voice, a reply, then another – a veritable commentary tossed from one window to the next.

'Where the TV man?'

'He in the TV van.'

'The fuck!'

'Say what? The Eyewitness Man?'

'Yeah. He in the van in his coat 'n tie.'

'Why he here?'

'Dunno, man.'

I passed the van and went into 185 Park Hill Avenue, walked along the ground-floor corridor, wide and gloomy and pungent, and knocked on the door of the African Refuge Walk-In Center. Feet scuffed and shuffled, and bolts were unlocked. The door opened. Standing before me was Jacob D. Massaquoi II. I had a one o'clock appointment with him; I was hoping to write his story.

Jacob smiled a wide, sweeping smile, one that involved most of his face, and opened his arms.

'My African brother,' he crowed. 'My *white*, *South* African brother.' He laughed very deliberately, a rapid cackle like a rusty machine gun, and squeezed and slapped my arm.

Jacob Massaquoi was in his late thirties and barely more than five feet tall, the only short man I have known whom one forgets is short, for he inhabits a self a good ten inches taller than the body he has inherited. He is an anti-Napoleon, I would come to learn, unthreatened to his very core.

We chatted. He brandished his knowledge of my country's politics, declaring with surprising passion his distaste for Jacob Zuma, the man who would soon be South Africa's president.

'What happened here today?' I asked.

'What happened?'

'There's a TV truck right outside,' I said. 'Eyewitness News.'

'You're serious? Where?'

'Right outside.'

He tugged at a window until it opened, perched on the ledge and poked his head through, his polished black shoes looping in the air. The ground floor of 185 is below street level, and he could see no more than I: car tyres and a pair of passing shoes.

He wriggled back inside and picked up his coat and hat. 'Let's go and see,' he said.

We made our way outside, and Jacob knocked politely on the window of the black van. It opened about halfway down, to reveal a man's face. He was Barbie's Ken to a tee, full-bodied hair scooped impressively behind his ears, his face chiselled-pretty and frozen in sincerity, his coat an immaculate black over a colourful tie.

'What's brought you here?' Jacob asked.

'Sexual assault,' he replied with troubled earnestness. 'In this building.' He nodded in the direction of 185.

'What happened?' Jacob asked.

'I don't feel comfortable talking about the details,' he replied, and to his sincerity was now added a grave professionalism. 'Have you read this morning's *Staten Island Advance?*'

'No,' Jacob replied.

'Go and get it. The story's all over the *Advance.*'

The window closed, and through the glass we watched Ken face front once more and pick up a clipboard.

We took a shortcut to Vanderbilt through the tiny park on Bowen Street and bought a copy of the *Advance*. It was on page three.

'Read it to me,' Jacob asked.

A Clifton father opened the door to his home and a horrifying scene Wednesday night – his eleven-year-old daughter and her thirteen-year-old friend naked with four older male teens.

Now the teens – one eighteen-year-old, two seventeen-year-olds, and one sixteen-year-old – face a variety of rape charges.

The younger girl alleges they held her down while they took turns having sex with her, and the older girl says the sixteen-year-old forced her into having sex with him.

The scene unfolded at about 3:30 p.m. Wednesday, in an apartment on the 100 block of Park Hill Avenue.

The youngest of the four teens, Patrick Gross, sixteen, also of Park Hill Avenue, is dating the thirteen-year-old girl, and has had sexual relations with her in the past, according to a law enforcement source.

The thirteen-year-old initially agreed to have sex with Gross Wednesday, but she changed her mind. He continued anyway, cops allege.

Jacob fumbled in his pocket for his cellphone. 'Patrick Gross! I know that boy. I know him. He has attended our youth activities at African Refuge.'

Now he was on the phone talking in rapid Liberian English, helping verbs expunged, consonants elided, leaving a thick soup of vowels I found utterly opaque.

Jacob hung up and put his phone back in his coat pocket and frowned and looked at the ground.

'Complicated,' he said, as much to himself as to me, as we walked back to Park Hill Avenue. 'One of the suspects is the victim's dad's stepson. Which means he has had his wife's child thrown in jail. She is not pleased. She turfed him out the house. He had to sleep outside last night.'

'So what do you do?' I asked.

He did not reply. He appeared to have forgotten my presence beside him. He stared at his shoes as we walked.

Somebody must have told Ken that Jacob was a community leader; by the time we got back to Park Hill Avenue, he was standing next to the van, snapping shut a silver business-card holder.

'You see now, sir, why I didn't want to tell you?' Ken said. 'I felt more comfortable you reading about it quietly and in private.'

'It's a very nasty business,' Jacob agreed.

'You run that centre in 185?' Ken asked.

'African Refuge, yes.'

'Will you comment?'

'Aaah, very busy,' Jacob replied bashfully.

'A quick comment on what has happened?'

'Sorry. Must go. Got to go home and eat.'

But no meant yes, really, which Ken immediately understood. 'It will just take a minute,' he said, tapping on the van's window and signalling to his cameraman. 'We'll do it right here, right now. It will be over before you know it.'

And to the cameraman now, who was shuffling out of the car. 'Let's be brisk, Mr, ah, the gentleman needs to get home to a late lunch.'

A minute later, Jacob and Ken were on camera.

'Sad! Sad! Sad!' Jacob was saying, staring at a spot just to the left of Ken's face. 'This leaves me sad, sad, sad. I know those boys. They are good boys. Really good boys. Parents in this neighbourhood must work all day to pay their bills. These kids are on the streets with nobody to raise them. In Africa, the villages were filled with adults during the day, and every adult was every child's parent. These kids should be coming to the after-school programmes we are providing.

We have interventions here, psychosocial interventions tailored to problems these kids have.'

'I understand that these children are refugees,' Ken said, 'from Liberia, right? From the civil war there.'

'Yes, they are. We concentrate on programmes for victims of trauma, as well as for kids afflicted by poverty.'

'Will you please tell us the name and address of your programme,' Ken requested.

'African Refuge. African Refuge at 185 Park Hill Avenue. We are open every afternoon to kids like the ones who are in trouble now.'

Ken lowered his mic, shook his head gravely and made a tut-tutting noise with his tongue.

'Thank you so much for your time, sir. You understand why I was uncomfortable telling you what had happened?'

'I understand, I understand,' Jacob muttered.

'You know,' Ken continued, 'I've reported on Sierra Leonians before, and there were even *child soldiers* among them. Is it the same with you guys? Are there child soldiers here?'

Jacob nodded again, this time with great concentration.

'That is not something I'll talk about on camera,' he said softly, staring at the ground.

'Of course not,' Ken replied. 'Yes, of course not.'

I marvelled at the economy of this exchange. These men had never met before, yet each knew precisely what the other needed. Between them lay the words 'refugees' and 'civil war'. With those words, Ken could file a report on a teenage gang rape transported across the ocean from some God-awful African Armageddon to a Wednesday afternoon in New York. And Jacob could be the one who knew how to heal these children, the question of what he himself had seen and done in that Armageddon lying unanswered in the background.

Late that night I sat in on a meeting of the Staten Island Liberian Community Association executive. It took place in a closed and windowless room on the ground floor of a Park Hill apartment block. The members of the executive, many of them heavyset men, crammed themselves into chair-desk contraptions designed for much smaller people. Opposite them sat the fathers of the two girls who had allegedly been raped.

It was 11 p.m. when the members of the executive began pressing the visitors to drop the rape charges. Both said no at first. Slowly, patiently, the members of the executive began to wear them down, quite prepared, it seemed, to go on until sunrise. By 2 a.m., one of the fathers had relented, while the other had walked out in protest and gone home.

As I was to learn later, in the subtext of the executive's urgings was a piece of knowledge common to everyone in the room: for four of our boys to spend a long stretch of time in a United States penitentiary is to turn them into African-Americans, and the worst sort, to boot.

I returned to Park Hill Avenue a few days later for a 4 p.m. appointment with Jacob. This time the street was busy, a steady flow of cars cruising slowly in both directions, disparate strands of hip-hop colliding briefly in the middle of the road.

Jacob and I arrived at his apartment building at precisely the same time. He was getting out of a taxi; a fidgety, hurried figure in an ankle-length checked coat and a checked hat. Once we were upstairs in his apartment, he took my coat hurriedly, made straight for a couch in front of his television set and invited me to sit with him. He turned to CNN, rewound to the start of the afternoon news programme presented by Wolf Blitzer, and then sat there transfixed for the next half-hour, his hand rubbing in constant agitation against his thigh.

It was 21 January 2008. The barely believable results of the Iowa Democratic primaries were less than a month old, and America was still new to the prospect that Barack Obama might beat Hillary Clinton and run against a Republican for the presidency of the United States. The two had debated the previous evening. Jacob had watched every moment, he told me. Now he wanted to absorb the commentary.

'He de-*stroyed* her,' Jacob pronounced. It was clear just from the tone of his voice that he was not talking about last night's debate; he had dashed ahead to the future and was looking back at the whole story.

'You see what is going on? You see what is happening in front of us? She has the whole Democratic establishment behind her, West Coast to East Coast. It is a machine, a huge, powerful machine. Her husband is *the* major figure, *the* dynasty man. Obama is taking them on.'

'Is it because he's black?' I asked. 'Is that what's exciting? Or because his dad was African?'

He looked at me dubiously for a moment, then threw his arms up in exclamation.

'One generation! Just one! Have you seen where his grandmother lives? Have you seen her place? One generation! And the man is taking on the *Clintons*; he is taking on the *machine*. And he has *poise*. He is *foxy*. He is *outwitting* them.' He let out a raw, uninhibited laugh, grabbed my thigh and shook it. 'I am suffering *badly* from Obama fever.'

In the half-hour we watched Wolf Blitzer, Jacob's cellphone rang half a dozen times. His calls were hooked up to his landline and routed through the speakers of his desktop computer, and so the ringing filled the entire apartment whenever he received a call. Sometimes he would frown at the screen and then ignore it. Other times, he took the call, fumbled for the remote control to turn Wolf Blitzer down, then paced about the apartment as he spoke and listened. I had not noticed it the other day, but he could not sit still; there wasn't a moment when each part of his body came to rest at the same time.

The housing project's apartments were all big and vinyl-floored. Jacob's displayed the inattention and practicality of a bachelor's home. The vinyl underfoot was naked, the large space of his living room largely unfilled: an old couch, two mismatching chairs, a coffee table, a dark-panelled television stand. His walls were empty save for a framed copy of a *Staten Island Advance* story about his life during the Liberian civil war.

A workspace was positioned in the corner of the room: a desk and chair; a large old desktop computer with the two speakers from which Jacob's phone rang; ill-sorted piles of papers spilling onto the keyboard and the floor and under the desk. This was clearly the centre of Jacob's home, the rest of the apartment just a backdrop.

As he took one phone call after an other, so his calendar for the following afternoon began to fill.

'Tomorrow was meant to be a schoolday,' he said to me between calls. 'I had cleared the entire day for schoolwork.' A look of panic briefly crossed his face, and then he banished it and returned his mind to Obama.

Schoolwork was a PhD in Leadership Studies by correspondence from the University of Phoenix. On an average day, he put aside the late-night hours for study; he'd start at about eleven, and end at two or three in the morning. Except, like now, when he was falling disastrously behind and needed to use part of the day to catch up.

The phone calls that echoed through his apartment were from politicians, administrators, non-profit organisations, members of the board of African Refuge, hospital directors, foster parents of Liberian children. Jacob, I was to learn, was neck-deep in Staten Island politics. He served on the District Community Board, was a board member of the local hospital, sat on Staten Island's Immigrants Council, and was invited incessantly to the cocktail and dinner parties hosted by Republican and Democratic grandees alike.

And he was penniless. African Refuge, the organisation he ran, began life in 2005 as a one-year project for survivors of trauma conceived by the staff of a programme at Columbia University's Mailman School. When the project was over, the organisation kept going, a fine and prestigious list of board members on its masthead, a wildly energetic Jacob in its director's office, but almost no money. When I met him, Jacob was drawing a pittance each month from the organisation's shallow coffers, sometimes no more than a few hundred dollars. He was Africa Refuge's only fundraiser, its only full-time employee, and he juggled running it with his Staten Island hobnobbing and his studies. The first time I slept over at his apartment, he was at his desk when I bid him goodnight at about one in the morning, and at his desk again, red-eyed and slouched, when I woke at half-past six.

As I walked away from his apartment in the darkness of early evening, it was the ferocity with which he stared at his television set that stuck in my mind. Obama's story was clearly his own: in what way, I did not yet know. It had been a long time since I had met a soul pointed so sharply and purely at the future. Every moment in his twenty-hour days was clearly a move in a very long game. Whether he was insane or formidably calculating I didn't yet have a clue. But I wanted to find out.

2

Rufus

I arrived at about 7 p.m. to a room in which there appeared to be no order. At least a dozen little children weaved their way between the furniture, under the tables, through Rufus's legs. They were shouting and screaming their faces off. A gaggle of them played with a dominoes set, quite nicely, it appeared, until one of them picked it up and threw it resoundingly to the floor.

Then there were the teenagers. All I saw were the backs of their do-ragged heads. Each was in his own digital world. I drew close, as discreetly as I could, to look over their shoulders at their monitors. Some were on YouTube, earphones wrapped around ears, heads bobbing and nodding, feet tapping. Or they were on Facebook, a big-toothed grin of a friend here, a group photograph of eight friends there.

At a long plastic table I counted seven elderly people, an exercise book open in front of each of them, pencils grinding paper, heads stooped low in concentration, some very low, ears touching the plastic table.

Somebody unplugged his earphones and there was suddenly poetry and percussion and expletive all over the room. The elderly did not bat their eyelids, except for one old man who lifted his head from the table, shook it with resignation, and stared into space.

Amidst it all there was Rufus Arkoi, a big man lumbering through the anarchy. He wore a black bowler hat on his head and a thick gold chain around his neck; he had just been out to collect his dinner from his wife and he still had on his knee-length winter coat, making him the largest figure in this room by far.

'Enough!' he bellowed. 'Enough! Before I beat you to smither-*eeeeeens!*'

He stared downwards, through thick eyelids and imperious lashes, and so one knew that it was the small children at whom he had shouted. They ignored him. They just kept on making their own noise. They did not so much as flinch at the sound of his roar. And I thought to myself: this must be a benign man, his space a comfortable space, for he is so big, the children so small, and yet his enormous voice elicits nothing from them.

I came again two nights later. The mood was different now, and in the gap between this evening and the earlier one it was apparent that what I had taken for anarchy was in fact deeply orchestrated, slowly matured.

There were no youths; the chairs at the computer terminals were empty. The little ones were sitting quietly around a square table, colouring in drawings with coloured pencils. The old ones were at work as before.

There was a knock on the door and a young man came in and made his way across the room. He was twenty-something, lean, powerful, carrying himself with the ramrod straightness one sees only in those who exercise many hours a day.

Rufus looked up at him and raised an eyebrow.

'Urgent email,' the younger man said in explanation. 'Home.'

Rufus nodded. 'Anyone try to follow you, close the door on him.'

'Where are the young people tonight?' I asked Rufus.

'They can come Tuesday night, Wednesday night,' he replied, 'between six and eight. For the rest, they are banished.'

'Why?'

'Complaints. Residents of this building say I am bringing *aaaall* the neighbourhood's criminals to my centre. They say: "Before you, the criminals were spread *out*. Now, they are all *in* here, in *our* foyer."

'I say: "Sure they are criminals. Of course. But where would you rather they be: out doing crimes, or in my centre on the computers? Because if you lock them out the buildings, you will meet with them in some other way."

'So we compromise: Tuesdays and Wednesdays, 6 p.m. to 8 p.m. Other times, no.'

'And the little ones?' I asked.

'Children of residents in this building. After-school care programme. By 8 p.m., they must be upstairs in their apartments.'

'And the old ones?'

'Literacy class. And thank you, Mr Steinberg,' he flashed a quick smile and hefted himself erect, 'for reminding me that I am ne-*glect*-ing my literacy students.'

He ambled over to the blackboard and began writing on it.

1 – great, 2 – winter , 3 – snow, 4 – coat, 5 – hat, 6 – January, 7 – cold, 8 – icy, 9 – freeze, 10 – food

He spun around with a flourish and smiled.

'Now, you are all, one by one, going to make a sentence with each of these words.'

And it went well, for all of them, with the exception of number nine.

'I frozen,' each of them said. 'Billy lock out his apartme' and he frozen . . . Aaron come to New York from Bomi County and every day he frozen.'

'No!' Rufus shouted. 'I am freezing! At home, I frozen. In Liberia, I frozen. Here, in the classroom, where the English is the Queen's, I am freezing.'

Rufus turned around again to write some more on the board, thought better of it, put his chalk down, and addressed his class once more.

'At work the other day,' he said, 'a man named Cory, he is from the Netherlands, he came to give a workshop on happiness.'

'On what?' one of the students asked.

'*Hap-pi-ness*. And you know what? I have read books, I have listened to preachers. And I have never, ever heard anything like this. I *begged* him to come to this community. He has agreed to do it for free. Starting February, every week for four weeks. I appeal to you. Come. I *urge* you. You will not be disappointed.'

One of the students snorted, loudly, a little rudely. He was well into his seventies.

'Happiness?' he announced to nobody in particular. 'I have not been happy for a day in my life.'

He looked up momentarily with a deadpan face, then stooped his head low over the desk. There was a Bluetooth device attached to his ear. It flickered and blinked like the light on the wing of an aircraft.

The youngster finished with his emailing, stood and walked out, giving Rufus a one-finger salute as he left, from temple to fresh air.

The elderly ones continued to scribble, heads down, and Rufus came to sit with me.

It was not always like this,' he said. 'Old, young, very young, crowded into one place.' His voice remained merry, as if he were still teasing his students about their struggles with American English. 'I once occupied a whole building and filled it with salaried staff. But Liberians do not like success. They would rather we all have nothing together.'

He turned to his students. 'Okay, ladies and gentlemen,' he said. 'Who is brave enough to share how he has used the word *freeeeeze*?' He smiled at me and winked, and then resumed his place in front of the blackboard.

3

Jacob

I slept over at Jacob Massaquoi's place for the first time on a week-night in early April 2008. We talked until about one in the morning, and when I woke at half-past six he was hunched over his monitor scrunching up his eyes. I greeted him gingerly, tiptoed around him and made my way to the shower. By the time I got out he was waiting impatiently for me.

'Doctor's appointment,' he said, a note of irritation in his voice. 'General check-up. If you don't arrive early, you're screwed. You want breakfast? I don't have time to give you breakfast. You're hungry? You shouldn't leave here without eating.'

He fed me toast and coffee and bustled me into a cab. By a quarter to eight, we had joined the back of a dispiritingly long line of patients in the basement of a North Shore hospital. Around us was a cross section of Staten Island's poor. A very obese white man had fallen asleep in his chair near the front of the line and was snoring loudly. A woman filed her nails nonchalantly in the chair beside him. Everyone else had gradually edged their chairs away, leaving the couple in a pool of empty space.

They were the only white faces in the line, and probably among a minority of American-born. The others were brown and black, the quiet murmurings issuing from their tongues Spanish and French and West African-accented English.

A woman in a wheelchair made her way down the corridor, and we all stood and picked up our plastic chairs to make room for her to pass.

Jacob stared after her.

'I was in a wheelchair like that a couple of years ago,' he said, almost to himself. 'I had reconstructive surgery on my leg. Several procedures, starting in 2004, ending in 2006. When I arrived here I was a disabled man. My right leg was several inches shorter than my left.'

'You'd been badly shot.'

He was still staring after the woman, his mind on other things, as it so often appeared to be when he spoke to me.

'I'd been badly shot. Lots of Liberians in this city used that to talk about my past.'

'As if you were a witch,' I said. 'As if the limp you brought from Liberia represented all the evil that had happened at home.'

My comment tripped a switch somewhere in his thoughts, and he snapped back into the present and made eye contact with me.

'No,' he said. 'You can't blame them. I am a Gio from Nimba County. So many Gio boys joined the rebels. I arrive on Park Hill from that terrible, terrible war, and I am limping. Nobody knows me here. I am a stranger. And I am loud. I make trouble. I am not one to stay quietly at home.'

The morning before our trip to the hospital, I had attended an HIV education workshop that Jacob had put considerable energy into organising. About half a dozen kids, all black boys ranging between about thirteen and sixteen, sat in two rows of chairs. The workshop facilitator was a large Latino woman, not much older than her charges, nineteen, perhaps, in a baseball cap and blue jeans. She sat no more than a yard from the first row of boys without the protection of a podium or a modesty board or a desk, her heavy thighs spilling over the edges of her chair, a Diet Coke in her hand.

For the boys she was a large, motionless target. They pelted her one after the other with talk of their cocks and their girlfriends' cunts, and their friends' girlfriends' assholes. She was magnificent. She did not blush or fluster. She responded to each question and comment with the utmost seriousness, skilfully sifting through the bravado for the substance of the enquiry buried beneath. In a steady stream of crisp and simple English, her considerable knowledge poured into the room.

Soon, there was a change in tone. The boys remained lewd, their rudeness as extravagant as ever, but in their questions there was now genuine curiosity, sometimes confusion. They were struggling to get their heads around the fact that a woman who is HIV-negative cannot give you HIV.

'What if her mouth is bleeding and she gives you head?' one of them asked.

'Doesn't matter,' the facilitator replied. 'She can't give you the virus if she don't have the virus.'

'What if I fuck her too long?'

'You mean, if your penis spends a long time in a vagina you'll get HIV, but if you get out of there quick you won't?'

'Yeah.'

'And the girl is HIV-negative?'

'Yeah. Even if she negative. What if I fuck her too long?'

Jacob came into the room. He stood in front of the two rows of chairs with his feet wide apart, the expression on his face grey and grave.

'You are making your educator feel bad,' he pronounced. 'You are interrupting her. I have been listening from the other room, and you are rude to her.'

She had been handling the situation just fine, I thought: it was Jacob who now threatened to puncture the bubble of communication into which she had enticed the boys.

'This workshop is not a licence. Talking about these things in the open is not a licence. Not a licence to have sex. You are in high school. You should not have sex in high school. You must wait. Wait for marriage. That is the only time for sex.'

And then Jacob said: 'Remember where you are from.'

He turned and went back to the adjoining room, and the faces of the boys looked like riverbed pebbles, the same old water flowing off their smooth surfaces.

Walking home with Jacob later, I brooded over his last comment: 'Remember where you are from.' The kids in the room all had American accents and dressed like gangbangers in their low-slung pants, their exposed underwear, and their Converse shoes.

'Was every kid in that workshop African?' I asked.

'They were all Liberian.'

'Why were there no African-Americans there?'

He said nothing, and we walked in silence a long time.

'I'm just trying to figure out how it works,' I said. 'You put up posters about this workshop on Park Hill Avenue, and because it says Africa Refuge only Liberian kids come?'

'No. No, let me explain. You saw back there, those girls we just passed? They were maybe twenty-five years old. They addressed me as uncle. I know their parents. I am an elder. The kids in the workshop: I know their parents too. I can discipline them. Their mothers will approve. In fact, they will be *happy*: happy to know that even when they are at work, there is an adult on the street with their values disciplining their children. That's how it is in Liberia. When the parents go away, everyone left at home is now a parent, a proxy parent. African-American kids: no. I'll get *sued* for disciplining them. You *talk* to one of them the wrong way, and all hell would break loose in this neighbourhood.'

I glanced over Jacob's shoulder down the length of Park Hill Avenue. The distinctions on this street were so strong, I thought, and so marked, but were nonetheless invisible to anyone who did not know Park Hill's residents by name, or at least by sight. I could not distinguish the kids in that room from anyone else in the neighbourhood. And yet across this street and its apartment blocks ran an invisible filigree of rules, one of which required that these children and these alone cross the threshold of Jacob's institution and into his care.

But the image Jacob had painted of an African village recreated here in New York in the midst of American strangers was certainly not right. The blankness in the boys' faces as Jacob spat out his lecture suggested that his authority over them did not run deep. And besides, the kids' mothers and fathers hardly saw Jacob as a benign uncle to their children. Weeks later, I walked with him through Clifton as he attempted to round up a gathering for another workshop. As we passed the sports fields at the back of Stapleton Houses, we saw groups of kids on the sidewalk, and others standing in jagged circles on the field itself. Jacob knew immediately who among them was Liberian, and he called over two or three boys. They came to us very obediently, and when Jacob began speaking to them, they stood very still and stared over his shoulder at nothing in particular. They waited respectfully for him to finish, and then left; none had uttered a word, or so much as made eye contact.

'This is such difficult work,' Jacob said, as we walked on. 'You can get people there, like to that HIV workshop a couple of weeks ago, but it takes hard, hard work. And I do not have money to employ people to do this work. It is me. I must go out personally. And then the kids go home and tell their parents that Uncle Jacob is organising this workshop, and they say to their kids: "Don't go. Uncle Jacob is just trying to enrich himself. He is trying to show the whites with the money that he is a leader in this community. He will walk over whoever he thinks is in his way. He destroyed Uncle Rufus that way."'

4

Rufus

On the day I met Rufus Arkoi, he was in the clothes of his day job, a maroon waistcoat and grey flannel trousers, and at first, his charisma did not show at all. The man from the post office, I thought to myself: knocking off from work, dying to get home and put his feet up. He showed me into his centre, which was quiet and empty. I took out a voice recorder and asked him to tell me who he was.

'I am Rufus Arkoi, Liberian immigrant. I came to America in 1986, September, to go to school. I did that a few years, engineering school, got an associate degree in electrical and chemical engineering. Then, in the early 1990s, the Liberian war caught up with this community. About 3,000 refugees came to Staten Island from the war in that year. I was in my final year studying engineering. I saw the community changing. So many young people, so many very old people. You go to church, you feel it. Their way of socialising was very different. Very loud. I was smaller at the time in size, I have a very strong athletic background. I used to go on the field. I used to see these kids with talent. With all the ups and downs in this community, I decided to use sports to attract them, to try to integrate them into this society.

'In February 1994, I established Roza here in America. Roza is a soccer club. Originally it was founded in 1981 in Monrovia. I left it in '86 to come here, and in '94 I started a branch here in America, to help these young people develop social skills. They were very much lacking a mannered approach, interacting improperly: everything was about *fight*. The strong survive. I started an under-sixteen team. I abandoned engineering and went back to school to study psychology and social work, to help me deal with these kids. My friend George Weah, he got me all the supplies, and I took on coaching. From 1994 to today, that's the formation of Roza in Staten Island.'

I liked his story immediately. A Liberian comes to America, makes good. Back home, an ungodly war breaks out: the world he had known explodes. Some of the shrapnel turns up here in Staten Island, in the form of troubled young men, men who are recognisably Liberian, but something else too, something he has never seen. They have brought war with them, in their mental lives, in their strange manners. He puts down what he is doing, and decides to live his life among them.

'The African-American kids in this neighbourhood were in for a shock,' Rufus continued. 'They see these African refugees arrive, washed up from a civil war, and the American kids think exploitation. They think: we can walk all over them.

'But the Liberian kids: they are *soldiers*. They have been shooting automatic weapons. They are fresh from the battlefield. They are too hardened for the local kids. They start getting a *reputation*. Many, many get incarcerated. Many others are deported. And so the cops on this street, they learn who is Liberian and who isn't, and they start picking on the Liberians. Round up a few every weekend. Just for *standing*. Just for being on the street. And I think, no man, this is going to end very badly. This is going to end *very badly*.

'So I walk into the police station, I ask to see the commander, and I say to him: What are you doing? These kids are *traumatised*. You are *retraumatising* them. You think they are tough, but they have witnessed a *war*.

'I could have got in trouble that day. I walked in and accused the commander to his face of making false arrests on the basis of nationality. But he was smart. He was sensitive. We talked. Next thing, the police came to Park Hill Avenue to shoot; not guns, but *hoops*. Get to know these boys. *See* them. *Feel* them. They are *boys*.'

The first time I saw Rufus at work with his boys was on an April evening. The members of his soccer team sat around a table at his centre talking. They were joined that night by two guests: me, and a reporter from the *New York Times*. The reporter was interested in writing about the Liberians in relation to the war they had left behind, and Rufus had agreed to broach the subject with his players.

Rufus spoke – 'We have suffered pain,' he had said, 'deep pain. What do we do with this pain?' – and then opened the discussion up to the floor. From nowhere a young man stood up and began to recount the day rebel soldiers slit open his father's belly in front of his very eyes. Before his story was finished, he had run from the room and out of the building into the street.

'We have known Isaac eight years,' Rufus told the *New York Times* reporter and me later. 'Eight years, every day, we have been playing soccer with Isaac. And this is the first time, *the very first time, any* of us has heard *anything* about this episode in the boy's life. It has been *inside* him all this time.'

After Isaac had fled the room, Rufus had had two things to say, one for the ears of the reporter, the other for his boys. To the reporter he had said: 'I do not have the expertise to deal with this. This is over my head. I need funding to pay a trauma therapist.' And to his boys he had said: 'Never, ever forget that the Americo-Liberians are the ones who did this. In all the years they governed Liberia, they never ever, not once, built a single school outside the capital city of Monrovia.'

He paused and looked down at his hands.

'And never forget who has been helping them.'

The young men around the table looked neither at Rufus nor at one another. They did not fidget or shuffle or stir. The room was absolutely still.

One had to know Park Hill Avenue very well to understand what it was that the young men had heard Rufus say. At the time, I had little idea quite how inflammatory his comment was, or how close to home the fire burned. To be sure, he was talking about why Isaac's father had been murdered; but he was talking too, in the same breath, using the same words, about people who lived on this very street, people who these young men greeted every day. He did not mention their names, or what they had done. But every boy in the room knew that he was accusing Jacob

Massaquoi of having brought him, Rufus Arkoi, to his knees in New York.

It was as if Park Hill and Liberia were twin voodoo dolls, every pinprick felt here drawing blood there, every stab back home wounding somebody in this exile.

PART TWO

5

His Great-Grandfather's Beard

Jacob Massaquoi tells me his story serially across a long stretch of Wednesday afternoons. He cannot simply speak of the past on tap, I soon learn; he needs to prepare himself over the course of a whole day. And so we soon adopt a weekly ritual. I arrive first thing every Wednesday, just as he is winding himself up – on caffeine, on CNN, on thoughts of his future – and preparing to throw himself at his morning.

His timetable is an ungoverned ensemble of meetings and phone calls and emails: some friendly, others hostile, none calm. An African-American woman on Park Hill Avenue wants to evict Jacob's walk-in centre from its premises and has sent a lawyer's letter; a prospective intern has been waiting since nine o'clock for an interview, and it is now after ten; the borough president's secretary is holding on the phone and cannot hold any longer. All the while, the office fills with elderly Liberians: they are here for blood pressure tests, for transport to the hospital, for advice on their green card applications. Jacob is a self-trained virtuoso, his batons spinning through the air around his office; any moment now, he will be distracted, and they will all clatter to the floor.

And then, without warning, he pulls down a screen between himself and the chaos of his office. His coat is on his back, his bag slung over his shoulder. He is waiting for me to follow. We amble our way back down Park Hill Avenue, two men with all the time in the world.

'I was waiting for my head to clear,' he says. 'I cannot talk about the past until the moment is right.'

Upstairs, we sit with our feet up and drink punch from Jacob's fridge. I put on my voice recorder. Sometimes he talks. Sometimes he doesn't. It is never easy.

Jacob was born in August 1971, nine years before his country began to fall apart. The memories of boyhood he chooses to share with me are stylised and slim; he hurries across the surface of his history in his urgent manner, stopping only briefly here and there, like a host impatient to lead his visitor on to more important things. At first I think that he speaks of the past in this way because he is an arrow aimed at the future, his childhood merely the quiver. He is interested only in those moments that explain who he might become.

'I grew up in the countryside,' Jacob tells me. 'I discovered the beauties of nature: green grass everywhere, coffee fields as far as the horizon. The coffee even grew between the houses. It was a rural life.'

He is quick to add that while the landscape was beautiful, he and his family were poor. 'We ate what we grew,' he recalled. 'We had little else.'

The village of Jacob's birth is in fact one of the remotest places in Liberia. It is deep in the interior, out on the eastern extremity of a hinterland county called Nimba, right on the border with Côte d'Ivoire. The nearest town is the sleepy provincial outlier of Butuo. The village itself is so remote that even its name is not firmly nailed down. Sometimes Jacob refers to it as Kaffeeglay – 'Coffee Town' in English – sometimes as Duazuahplay. Duazuah is a family name. The village is named after his father. Indeed, about half of its 500 or so inhabitants are Jacob's relatives.

One does not drive there, for the navigable roads end some distance away. When I visited, I walked the last miles through dense rainforest. There is neither electricity, nor plumbing. Homes are made from material sourced close by, and the cassava and rice are planted and harvested with much the same technology the Duazuahs used when the village was first settled more than a hundred years ago. To an untrained eye, this place may seem a slice of a still, unchanging past, mooning about incongruously in the present.

It is anything but. From his very first hours on this earth, the most intimate aspects of Jacob's life were shaped by Liberia's political history. The qualities he chooses to remember in his father, the question of whom he regards as his mother; these things are all awkwardly political. Jacob is living testimony that events in a nation's capital can mould the private lives of its most far-flung citizens.

Properly told, in fact, Jacob's story is tied up with one that begins a continent away, on a late summer afternoon in 1780, on a slave-owner's estate in Virginia. There, America's future president, Thomas Jefferson, put to paper a thought that, several decades later, would see fruition in the founding of Liberia. The passage Jefferson wrote that afternoon was affecting and haunted: it was about slavery and America's future.

> The whole commerce between master and slave is an exercise of the most boisterous passions: the most unremitting despotism on the one part and degrading submissions on the other. Our children see this and learn to imitate it.

And the wounds of slavery, he argued with great prescience, would never heal.

> Deep rooted prejudices entertained by the whites; ten thousand recollections, by the blacks, of the injuries they have sustained; new provocations, the real distinctions which nature has made; and many other circumstances, will divide us into parties and produce convulsions, which will probably never end but in the extermination of the one race or of the other.

Jefferson's answer was wholesale black emigration. The children of slaves, he argued, should be 'brought up, at the public expense, to tillage, arts or sciences'. Once they become adults

> they should be colonized to such place as the circumstances of the time should render most proper, sending them out with arms, implements of household and of the handicraft arts, seeds, pairs of the useful domestic animals, etc, to declare them a free and independent people, and extend to them our alliance and protection, till they shall have acquired strength.

Monrovia, which was to become Liberia's capital, was settled by freed American slaves more than forty years later. In the intervening years, the list of people advocating black American settlement in Africa had grown considerably, their respective reasons now an untamed orchestra of noise on how to heal America's soul. There was Paul Cuffe, son of a first-generation slave and a Wampanoag Indian, deeply involved in the project to found a black colony, who believed that 'blacks will never be a people until they come out from amongst whites'. To live out the truest values of American civilisation, Cuffe argued, blacks would have to leave America.

There was the Newport priest Samuel Hopkins, who suggested that in the founding of a black colony in Africa lay nothing less than America's redemption, for it was to be her way of repenting for the terrible sin of slavery, and until she did so, she would be eternally cursed.

And finally, there was what turned out to be the backbone of the movement that settled Liberia: white, slavery-supporting politicians and men of influence who believed that the future of slavery stood a much better chance if free blacks were taken from America's shores and deposited out of sight at the other end of the world.

And so the forces that pitched in to invent Liberia ranged across America's political spectrum. While the differences between them were vast, all held this in common: an understanding that the legacy of enslaved black labour would shape the fabric of American society for generations to come, and a belief that the problem could be worked out on African shores.

The black Americans who began to settle in 1822 never constituted more than 5 per cent of the Liberian population. And yet their descendants ruled Liberia from its inception in 1847 right until 1980, when Jacob was nine. They were called, alternatively, the Americo-Liberians, or the Congos, and for much of the time that they ruled Liberia, they claimed the right to do so on the grounds that they were not Africans but harbingers of Christian civilisation.

For outsiders, the position of the Americo-Liberians was easy to parody. 'The newcomers from America,' wrote the great Polish journalist, Ryszard Kapuściński,

unable to set themselves apart from the locals by skin colour or physical type, try to underline their difference and superiority in some
other way. In the frightfully hot and humid climate, men walk about
in morning coats and spencers, sport derbies and white gloves. Ladies
usually stay at home, or if they go out into the street . . . they do so
in stiff crinolines, heavy wigs, and hats decorated with artificial
flowers. The houses the members of these high, exclusive echelons
live in are faithful reproductions of the manors and palaces built by
white plantation owners in the American South. The religious world
of the Americo-Liberians is similarly closed and inaccessible to the
native Africans. They are ardent Baptists and Methodists. They build
their simple churches in the new land, and spend all their free time
within, singing pious hymns and listening to topical sermons.

When I visited Jacob's village, the oldest living soul there, a man
called John Duazuah, told me a story about Jacob's father, one intended
to explain the journey the family has travelled over the sweep of the
twentieth century.

Jacob's father was young, still a boy, perhaps in his early teens. It
was some time in the 1920s. His name, at this point, was simply
Duazuah. He was a Gio boy. Everyone from these parts spoke either
Gio or Mano. The only ones here who were neither Gio nor Mano
were the Americo-Liberian rulers, and there were not many of them,
for they ruled through local proxies.

Duazuah had a grandfather with a great, unkempt beard that
flowed over his chest. A government official visited the village inter-
mittently, an Americo-Liberian man, his arrival always the cause of
nervousness and consternation. On one of these visits, the official
pronounced that the great beard annoyed him, and he set it alight
on the old man's face.

His grandfather's humiliation branded itself into young Duazuah's
soul. There and then, he vowed that the same fate would never befall
him, nor, indeed, his unborn children. He left home and made his
way to the nearest town, Butuo, and went to the home of the most
powerful native Gio there. Her name was Gooh. She was married
to the most influential Gio in Liberia, an educated man who lived
in the capital city of Monrovia and worked for the government.
Duazuah told Gooh what had happened to his grandfather. 'I have

promised myself that the same will never happen to me or my future children,' he told her. 'I want to learn to read and write.'

On her next trip to Monrovia, Gooh took Duazuah with her. There, her husband spoke with a very powerful man in the Liberian government, a Vai man by the name of Massaquoi. Unlike the Gios, the Vai, a coastal people, had rubbed shoulders with the Congos since the earliest times of America-Liberian settlement. By the early 1920s, Vai aristocrats had long held positions of power and influence under America-Liberian rule. In the story the elders of Duazuahplay tell, Massaquoi was Liberia's Minister of Education.

I have scoured the records for this Massaquoi, but I cannot find him. Over the years, the story the Duazuahs tell has, it seems, been burdened with other memories. In any event, an influential man named Massaquoi took young Duazuah into his home, taught him something of the manners and customs of the elite, and gave him a rudimentary education. Jacob remembers his father reading from the Bible: 'He read slowly, with difficulty; he had been educated only a little.'

After several years, Duazuah left the Massaquoi household armed not only with his patron's connections, but with his very name. He was now Jacob Duazuah Massaquoi, primed to play his part in the theatre of America-Liberian rule.

First, he went to a town called Gbarnga, where he worked with the provincial government's agricultural administrator, and learned to grow cash crops, in particular, coffee. And then his story takes an interesting twist. If the village elders who tell the tale appreciate its irony, they certainly don't let it show in their faces. In Gbarnga, Duazuah was appointed to a very important job under the aegis of Bong County's Paramount Chief. His task was to collect taxes.

Now, in the story the elders tell, we do not know why the America-Liberian official burned Duazuah's grandfather's beard, other than that the sight of it annoyed him. But certainly the official would have been very concerned that the villages in his jurisdiction pay tax. It would not be too far-fetched to speculate that what annoyed the official was a certain stubbornness on the part of the bearded old man, a passive reluctance to part with his village's money.

Saying this out loud among the Duazuahplay elders would be

considered scandalous, but Jacob's father avoided the tax collector's wrath by becoming the tax collector's sergeant. Just one person I met in Duazuahplay is blunt enough to hint as much. His name is Dennis Duazuah; the patriarch's oldest surviving son, and thus Jacob's half-brother. Some forty-five years older than Jacob he was at his father's side when he went about his work in Gbarnga.

'The old man would put a list together, a list of who must pay tax,' Dennis Duazuah recalls. 'They would put him in a chair and carry him from village to village to collect taxes.'

'It must have been difficult work,' I suggest tactfully.

'No, it was not difficult for him,' Dennis replies. 'It was difficult for those who owed taxes. Sometimes they would scatter when they heard that he was coming.'

'Were people angry with him for collecting taxes?'

'Yes, they didn't like that he collected money on behalf of the Congos. But it was traditional practice during those days: if you can be a chief, your children will be free because your father is in power. You will not be a slave to anybody. I, for instance, was very happy. I never had to do forced labour because I was under the umbrella of my father.'

Jacob's father, Jacob Duazuah Massaquoi, circa 1985. He was wearing his nightgown when the photographer arrived and did not have time to change.

'What would happen to you if you couldn't pay your taxes?'

'You would have to do forced labour. You cannot pay, they suppress you until you pay. Sometimes, you run away. You run away as far as Ivory Coast so that you must not pay tax.'

The teenaged Duazuah who left his village to avoid his grandfather's fate returned Jacob Duazuah Massaquoi, his new name signifying his awkward place in the Liberian establishment. He brought home the agricultural knowledge he had learned in Gbarnga, and planted coffee all over the village. And he also brought with him connections to Congo families in three counties. Through these, he would find a way to educate as many of his fourteen children as he could.

Jacob was his father's twelfth child. He went to school, learned science and history, and grew to love these disciplines, because of a bargain his father struck with Liberia's Congo rulers.

He does not like it when I put it this way.

'The reason I work so hard,' he tells me one Wednesday afternoon, 'the reason I am getting a graduate education, a doctorate, is to protect myself against those people, the Congos. We must never be dependent on them again.'

The Duazuahs, it seems, are forever journeying to far places and educating themselves in trying circumstances in order to wrestle the Americo-Liberians from their shoulders.

6

The Americo-Liberians

'They all have high-sounding titles,' wrote William Nesbit of the Americo-Liberians. Nesbit was an African-American traveller who arrived in the Liberian capital at the end of 1853, less than seven years after the founding of the republic. '[N]early every man you meet is a General, Colonel, Major, Captain, Judge, and at the very least an esquire.' Yet the majority '*cannot read*, and are totally ignorant of the simplest duties belonging to their stations'.

It is a sham, a world built on nothing, for the Americo-Liberians do not *do* anything, cannot *make* anything.

'There is positively not,' Nesbit writes, 'nor ever has been, a plow, a horse, or a yoke of oxen, used in all the country . . . These miserable creatures are actually dependent on the naked natives for their rice and cassada'.

And herein lies their greatest perversity, for the colonists, according to Nesbit, enslave these naked natives, just as they themselves were enslaved in the South.

> As in [America, where] the slaves occupy small buildings near to their masters' residence, known as the 'negro quarters', so their imitators in Liberia, notwithstanding the masters live in bamboo shacks themselves . . . [are] never too poor to own slaves, and to have a hut for them at a short distance from [the main house].

The Americo-Liberians did indeed for many years rule like foreign aristocrats. They imported their clothes from New York, used indigenous children as house servants, and referred to those among them who had lived in America as 'been-tos', as if people who knew only Africa had never been anywhere.

Yet Nesbit's tale, repeated by many others over the years, doesn't adequately tell why Jacob got his name.

For the Nesbit-Kapuściński accounts describe something of a freak show. These clownish fellows sweating in their morning coats, blissfully belting out hymns from their Baptist hymn books: they are little more than Pavlov's dog. The master-slave relationship was drummed into the brains of their forebears, drummed so deeply and soundly, it seems, that it became a genetic inheritance. These people, were they to be expelled to Mars, would search the red planet for material from which to build antebellum mansions, and enslave whatever life form they were to find. That is all they know.

There is a more plausible story about them.

Imagine the people who settled Monrovia in the 1820s. Their leading citizens are black freemen from America's north-eastern seaboard. They are Baptists and Episcopalians, steeped in Enlightenment values. Their aspirations are profoundly and unmistakably American.

'We the people of Liberia were originally the inhabitants of the United States . . .' they were to write in the document founding their republic. 'We were everywhere shut out from all civil office. We were excluded from participation in Government. We were taxed without our consent . . . All hope of a favorable change in our country was thus wholly extinguished from our bosoms, and we looked with anxiety abroad for some asylum from this deep degradation.'

Indeed, some among them believed that it was they, and not whites, who truly understood the meaning of the English language, of Christianity, of the idea of equality. God gave these precious values to Europeans, but their racism twisted and perverted them. It was only black-skinned Christians who understood that the civilisation God bequeathed to them was intended for all men and women.

Not once did the word 'Africa' appear in the document that founded the Liberian republic. The settlers were tied to the West Africans around them by skin colour, and, in the broadest sense, by common ancestry, but by little else. The first groups they met, the Kru, the Gola and the Vai, had for generations been slave traders. There wasn't a Christian among them.

And yet neither were the Americo-Liberians agents of some

Western empire, for their skins were black. As late as 1908, a Liberian delegation to Washington led by President Arthur Barclay was refused an official audience with the United States government because of the colour of the delegates' skins.

Marooned on a foreign continent, and yet without a home, how do such people set about the business of living? Do they face inward or outward? Do they lay their foundations here in Africa, or do they try to build a bridge across the ocean? Within a generation, some among them were increasingly attracted to the idea of Liberia as a democracy of independent farmers, much like Thomas Jefferson had once imagined America. Liberia would be sustained by the soil and by hard work. And the democracy built here would be an exemplar to the whole continent: Liberia would lead a renaissance of black civilisation.

And yet the settler families gaining power in Liberia were not farmers, they were merchants. And their aversion to farming was an expression of the most existential of their fears. They worried that a country of small landholders out here on this forgotten continent would be cut adrift from the world. Liberia could only exist if it was *seen*. And to be seen, it must trade. They wanted standing among the great nations of the West. They wanted to have commerce with France, with Britain, with Germany and Holland and with the United States; they wanted to trade their way to the centre of the world.

The more far-sighted among them saw that this could only end badly. How does one build a country that makes nothing, produces nothing, is uninterested in its own soil, in developing its own people? From the start there was a rift among the settlers: between the black nationalists who envisaged building an inward-turned, African civilisation; and those who believed that salvation lay in brushing shoulders with the great powers. The former were mainly darker skinned, the latter largely mulatto.

And so Liberia traded, and while it did well here and there, nothing, it seemed, was destined to last. The greatest blow to Liberia's future as a trading nation was the arrival of the steamship. With its capacity to cheapen transportation and to carry massive loads, it soon changed the Liberian trading environment into one dominated by highly capitalised outsiders. The major European commercial houses operating in Liberia invested in their own shipping lines. Liberian merchants did not have the capital to acquire steamships, and they could not compete with these new colossi. Foreigners began buying up Liberian commercial interests one by one. By the last quarter of the nineteenth century, the Liberian government was a tenant in its own national courthouse, which was owned by a German company. Liberian merchants were squeezed to the sidelines of international trade. In the 1890s, shipping lines were refusing to load Liberian-owned cargo.

Liberia never had a chance of competing in so capital-intensive an industry. Its own national coffers were far too paltry to invest in steamships. Maintaining a Western identity on the African coast was a very expensive business, and it sapped much of Liberia's savings.

'[M]ost of the income earned from trade,' Liberian scholar and one-time interim President Amos Sawyer writes,

> was used to support an opulent lifestyle. For example, in 1864, 66 per cent of the total value of imports represented expenditure on food items, spirits and tobacco ... 11 per cent ... represented purchases of cosmetics such as beauty powder, perfumes and accessories such as handkerchiefs and 'fancy goods'. Less than 5 per cent ... accounted for purchases of tools such as cutlasses, hoes, and other implements of production.

By the beginning of the twentieth century, the Liberian state was bankrupt, its economy owned and controlled primarily by Hamburg-based commercial houses. Without productive enterprises of its own, and unable to trade, Liberia's settler society was left with one remaining avenue of income: its legal sovereignty. It could sign concessions for the use of Liberian land; it could collect customs duties for commodities traded through its ports; it could charge a fee to recruit Liberian labour. In other words, it could try to make money by manoeuvring among the foreign entities that had taken over its economy, and turn the government itself into an enterprise from which settler society could feed.

That is how the Americo-Liberian elite came to survive in Africa, and how their relationship with families like Jacob's was shaped. In the coming decades, there would would be plenty in Liberia for the settler elite to rent out to foreigners – vast rubber farms were to be planted, copious deposits of iron ore were to be found, much timber was to be harvested – but in the early 1920s, when Duazuah witnessed the burning of his grandfather's beard, much of this was in the future. The Liberian government was broke. Members of the Congo elite were making a living using pieces of their fragile state machine to coerce people to work and to pay tax.

The Liberian interior, where Jacob's father came of age, was divided into districts, each run by a district commissioner, and, under him, an indigenous chief. Among their primary functions was the collection of tax from the indigenous people: first a hut tax, then a poll tax. As an incentive, chiefs received a commission of 10 per cent on all tax they collected.

This system could never have worked without muscle. Along with indirect rule came the establishment of a Liberian Frontier Force. The historian James Campbell describes it as a system of 'semi-official banditry':

> Frontier Force soldiers, their salaries years in arrears, periodically appeared at villages to demand hut taxes, food, and labor. Hostage taking became endemic, especially of women, who were claimed as wives by soldiers or simply raped. Villages were torched, traditional authorities were humiliated, and young men were conscripted into the ragtag army.

As a very young man, Jacob's father watched this world taking shape, and he saw things in stark terms: he could either watch his family being smothered and strangled, or he could join the Congos and take his 10 per cent.

7

Duazuahtay

Jacob D. Massaquoi II. That Jacob's father chose to give his twelfth child his own name was a sign of prosperity and of satisfaction. And yet also, perhaps, it was an intimation of death.

'When Jacob was born,' Dennis Duazuah told me, 'life was good enough for the old man to sit back and think: "Well, I'm actually getting old. And my name is such that it ought to remain on this earth when I am gone."'

As if imbibing the ascendancy vested in his name, Jacob was born with congenital ambitiousness. That, at least, is how his infancy is remembered now. Duazuah Massaquoi's third wife, today well into her eighties, recalls the first words baby Jacob uttered.

'I had taken him on my back to the town of Butuo,' she recalls. 'We watched a car drive past us. I think it was the first car Jacob had ever seen. He watched with open mouth.'

And then Jacob spoke. Astoundingly, the words that came from his mouth were not Gio, the language he had heard every day since his birth, but the language of the elite, Liberian English.

'Motor come, motor go,' he pronounced.

Later, when he could speak full sentences, Jacob told the old woman that he had already travelled the whole world, that he had done so before his birth, and that he would do so again.

'Next time,' she recalls him saying, 'I will take you along.'

Jacob's own memories of early childhood, in contrast, are not all about triumph. Some are sad. He has two vivid recollections of his mother. In the first, it is dinnertime. She is young and very beautiful, and she is eating, while Jacob and his father both watch her. Each is besotted.

In his second memory of her, Jacob is five or six years old. He is sitting on a mat together with a younger sibling. His mother is feeding them. She is pregnant, and she is in excruciating pain. 'The other women came,' he recalls. 'They took her away. That was the last time I saw her. One of my father's other wives brought me up, my mother's sister. And then, later, my two older sisters raised me: Judy and Willett.'

In sharing this memory with me, Jacob is, I think, making a pointed comment. His father may have been doing well, but what did it really mean for a Gio villager to be doing well under Americo-Liberian rule? His household remained a place where a young woman got sick and died, like an animal.

Nonetheless, Jacob's father's success was measurable in a hundred ways. He had five wives and twelve children, a patriarch if ever there was one. His legacy was such that it had renamed the ground beneath his feet. His village was alternatively called Duazuahplay, a tribute to his influence, or Kaffeeglay, a recognition of what he had done to reshape it. Most of his children had been, or were being, educated. The humiliations of the early 1920s were a world away.

If the Duazuahs' fortunes had changed, it was in part because Liberia's fortunes had changed too, quite dramatically so. The days of chronic fiscal crisis belonged to another time. Indeed, Liberia believed itself to be stinking rich. Swathes of the countryside were now covered in rubber trees, and the largest producer on earth, the Firestone Rubber Company, farmed great plantations. Whole towns had sprung up around the country's new iron ore mines. In the years before Jacob's birth, the national economy grew as much as 15 per cent a year.

Liberia had been saved by the long global boom that began after World War II. During this quarter-century of prosperity, the world's thirst for commodities seemed unquenchable. And Liberia was covered in them.

In villages like Duazuahplay though, the signs of Liberia's fat days were not what you might think. The government did not build a good road to connect the village to the rest of the world. Nor did it provide a decent school. Modern health care remained as remote and inaccessible as ever. In fact, Liberia's great boom happened in a parallel world sealed off from villages like Jacob's. If a man like

Duazuah Massaquoi wanted his children to taste Liberia's new fat, he would have to send them off into this parallel world, and to do so he would need to know powerful people.

Here is how the system worked. Foreign companies were welcomed to tracts of the Liberian countryside to extract its natural resources. These companies created vast enclaves of economic activity almost entirely disconnected from the Liberian environment. They imported their own managers and technicians, their own machinery and tools, their own accountants and bookkeepers. In exchange, they would pay taxes and concessions to the Liberian government. Much of the country's national earnings thus flowed directly into the president's office, making him a very powerful man indeed. For he, in turn, would distribute his country's earnings across Liberia through a vast network of patronage and connections.

From the time they settled Monrovia, the Congo elite battled to hit upon an agreeable relationship between work and dignity. First, it was the idea of farming that troubled them. Manual labour brought echoes of slavery, and the idea of a community of farmers evoked isolation. And so they traded. But when Europeans forced Liberians out of trade a generation later, the very idea of commerce became sullied. By the time Jacob was born, a dignified Americo-Liberian gentleman was either a lawyer or a civil servant, preferably both. Economic production was left to foreigners. The elite clustered around the state and fed off the taxes and concessions the foreigners brought.

This national system of patronage turned Liberians, Congos and natives alike into a fawning and obsequious people. To get anything, you had to know somebody more powerful than yourself, a patron to whom you ought to show great deference. And so the trappings of power and office were greatly exaggerated in Liberia. There was much self-aggrandisement and pomp, for these were the currencies in which influence and power were traded.

Duazuah Massaquoi might have been the king of his own realm, but in this system he was just a local powerbroker in a far-flung district, and charting a course was not easy. Tapping every connection he had made among the elite over half a century, he plotted to get each of his children out of Duazuahplay and into the home of an Americo-Liberian family, where they would get an education, and, hopefully, a patron.

It was tough, to say the least.

'My father didn't have enough connections to get everyone into a different family,' Jacob recalls, 'and he didn't have the money to make our lives comfortable when we were away. He'd improvise; the older ones would go and get educated, sometimes under comfortable conditions, sometimes under not such comfortable conditions. And then, when the younger ones turned six or seven, he would send them to live with one of the older children. He had this tradition. Every December it was compulsory for all the children to come home to usher in the new year. Then he'd take a seven-year-old, give him to an older sibling − now take the young one with you.'

That is how Jacob ended up in Sanniquellie, the capital of Nimba County, at the age of seven, shuttling between the homes of two older sisters, Judy and Willett. It was the sort of childhood one does not envy. His mother had been dead a year or two. And neither of his sisters, if his memory serves him right, was especially warm. In fact, one of the reasons his father sent Jacob to Judy was to be something of a domestic labourer for her. She was pregnant, and she would need somebody to help her with house chores while she raised her child.

'When I was with Judy,' Jacob remembers, 'she was quite hard with me. I was severely chastised for every mistake I made as a child. I had to fill several drums of water every night. I had to serve three people their meal. I waited for them to finish eating, then washed their dishes. Only then was I permitted to dish up food for myself. This was Judy.'

Jacob is close to Judy now and loves her deeply, and when he looks back he is grateful for the discipline she taught him; he doesn't believe that he would have survived the coming war without it. But at the time, her hardness made him feel all the more the difficult transition from the warmth of Duazuahplay to a strange city.

Nor was the school Jacob attended in Sanniquellie what you might imagine. It was not a place for children, not exclusively so, at any rate. People enrolled for school when their circumstances allowed, even if they were twenty or thirty years old. And so most of Jacob's classmates in first grade were fully grown adults.

And schooling was in English, a language Jacob hardly knew. He was a Gio boy from a remote Gio village. Several times a week, he would go over to the house of his sister Willett, a schoolteacher, to receive English lessons from her. It is from this ritual that his earliest and nastiest memory of Sanniquellie comes.

He was walking between Judy's and Willett's house, on his way to an English lesson. Sanniquellie was still new, and still alarmingly big, for he had never lived anywhere remotely this size. He was about seven years old.

His mind wandered; he cannot remember today where to. But once he had shaken himself awake, he had lost his bearings. He no longer knew whether the way to Willett's house was left or right. He would have to ask.

It was only then that it came to him that he did not have the language to ask directions. The street was full of people, but everyone passing him by spoke either English or Mano, the language of the local Sanniquelliese. He walked and walked, unsure of where he was going. Soon, he did not recognise the streets at all.

He broke into a run, his cheeks and chin wet with tears.

Jacob did find a proxy for his mother's love during his time in Sanniquellie. But it is difficult, unacknowledged love; its traces are concealed in the folds of the story he tells.

Not once does he mention her by name. She was Willett's husband's grandmother. She had come to live in Willett's household in Sanniquellie to manage her grandson's home while he was studying in college. Young Jacob had never met anyone like her before. She was doubly exotic; first, because she was a pious Muslim, and Jacob had never heard of Muslims until now; and second, because she was fluent in but one language, Kissi, and Jacob did not understand a word of it. The way he tells it, he got close to this woman of strange customs and tongue for strictly tactical reasons; he was after her food.

'I loved to eat,' Jacob tells me. 'And this grandma would make separate food for herself: Muslim food. Her grandson didn't like her very much. I liked her a lot. I saw my father through her. When he came to visit he saw her moving about the house. He advised me to treat her well, to treat her like my grandma.'

In all the stories Jacob tells of his childhood, this is the only one in which his father, who looms so large over everything, actually comes to life. He has sent his children off to live among strangers under difficult circumstances. He has little control over how much they will be loved. On a fleeting visit, he scans Jacob's home, and his gaze fixes immediately on the most likely source of warmth: Make her your grandma, he says.

'My Muslim grandma and I used to go to the mosque together to pray,' Jacob remembers. 'The other Muslims there called me Yakooba. They made a little kufi for my head. I became a little Muslim boy. For the forty days of Ramadan, I would pretend to fast. But I did not fast. I liked food too much to fast. My Muslim grandma laughed at me. Said I was a bad Muslim, a hypocrite Muslim. Then she would give me a second bowl of food.'

They must have become very close, far closer than Jacob cares to remember. Much later, when he is discussing his adulthood, he tells me that he speaks enough Kissi to pass for a native speaker, at least during a superficial interaction.

'Where did you learn Kissi?' I ask.

'From my Muslim grandma,' he replies.

'She taught you not just a few words here and there, but how to speak the language?'

'When I left Sanniquellie at the age of eighteen,' he replies, 'I could speak the language.'

8

School

Some high-school students are indifferent to their schoolwork and get through it because they must. Others enjoy it. A rare category of student discovers that he has entered an enchanted world. He had no inkling of it before he got there, and yet, once he has found it, he feels that it has been hibernating deep inside him all his life. His experience is sublime. He has been given spectacles to see beneath the surface of things, to see why things are as they are, and he will henceforth never be able to do anything else but wear those spectacles and *see*.

That was Jacob's experience of school.

'I wanted to become a scientist,' he tells me. 'A physicist. I was really thrilled, thrilled and inspired, by Albert Einstein's theory of relativity, and Sir Isaac Newton's laws of motion, and Galileo Galilee's laws of universal gravitation. They were my source of inspiration. At home, when we were eating a meal, I wanted to know the science of what had happened when something fell off the table; the relation between its weight and the velocity of its fall, the sound it made as it dropped and the way that sound travelled to my ears. I wanted to debate these things with my family. I was a very argumentative guy.'

Jacob was an oddity at school. He was younger than most of his classmates, decades younger than many. Intellectually, though, he was way ahead of them.

'There were many older women in my class,' Jacob recalls. 'Some were in their thirties. They needed me to do their homework for them. I came to their houses to tutor them. I was the elite in my class, the cleverest. And I was a virgin. I had no time for girls. I was working too hard. My sister told me that if I had sex I would not pass school. And I saw that the people having sex were doing badly in school. So the evidence . . .'

'You were already so driven,' I comment.

'Jonny, I was so . . . I was very into science. I read it every night. I read about the Concorde jet and linked it to the laws of movement and the laws of gravity. I was very excited by the idea of becoming a physicist. But I was also very excited by social science and politics, particularly by the ideas of the pan-Africanist movement inspired by Ghana's former president, Dr Kwame Nkrumah.'

'You were politicised by a schoolteacher?' I ask.

'Mr Obakwe. He was tall, a seven-foot man, one of those inspired by Dr Nkrumah. He was Ghanaian. All my teachers were Ghanaian. When Nkrumah was dethroned in Ghana, when he was toppled in a coup, his supporters in the schools left the country. And so we got them: these militant pan-Africanists, so full of ideas.

'Obakwe really took me through my political journey. Through history: World War I and II, and the Cold War; the French Revolution, the American Revolution, the transatlantic slave trade. He taught us a bit about Liberia's formation, some Liberian history. Then segregation, Martin Luther King. I was deeply, deeply excited. You see . . . You must understand the natural laws of creation, that way you will understand more about history and politics. They are interconnected. Why, for instance, did London produce Isaac Newton? Political forces, environmental, cultural: these forces led him to become curious about his environment, to ask why things move.'

'Obakwe spoke to you about contemporary Liberia?'

'Yes, about how [Liberian president William] Tubman was America's proxy in Africa, about how Tubman, with the West behind him, sabotaged African unity, while Nkrumah and Emperor Selassie from Ethiopia wanted to bring Africa together. Wow, Jonny! At a young age, I began to understand the world!

'And the economic dimension. When you study the economic dimension, you understand the whole thing. It's the laws of natural selection. Darwin comes into play. You understand why America used Tubman to divide Africa, why Europe colonised Africa. Education is a powerful tool. You understand the reasons underpinning people's actions. That is the beauty of education.'

The physicists and the pan-Africanist revolutionaries Jacob was discovering appeared to him to be in league with one another. Science and revolution were coupled. To ask why an object falls down rather than floats up seemed a wildly radical question, born of a mindset that took nothing for granted. And if one is to question the basis of everything, then surely political power ought not to be spared. To understand the laws that shape a political system is to understand how to topple it. An activist, in Jacob's milieu, was a scientist, and a scientist was an activist.

Jacob relives his excitement every time he describes his discovery of ideas, as if he is discovering them all over again, and the image his enthusiasm draws is of a lone boy on a singular journey. In fact, his experience was not especially atypical. Students across Liberia had begun to speak of science and revolution a generation before Jacob, in the early 1970s. At high schools and colleges and at Liberia's two universities, young men talked in newly acquired Marxist jargon about the internal contradictions of Americo-Liberian rule and the logic of late imperialism. On the school playgrounds, they were creating revolutionary councils and action committees and rival political parties. As many as four or five parties would form at the bigger schools, each with its own constitution and officeholders. They would hold elections for the student governing body. The winning party would appoint ministers of finance and foreign affairs, a prime minister, a cabinet secretary, and, of course, a president. The opposition parties would appoint a shadow minister of finance, of foreign affairs, and so forth. They drafted student government constitutions, tore them up, and redrafted them. They fought about what policy they should adopt towards school management, the Liberian government, the Organisation of African Unity, and the United Nations.

Invariably, there would be coups. Many who became president of a student body in the 1970s have memories of waking up one morning to discover that they had been overthrown. Indeed, coups became so fashionable that they spread beyond the schools. Neighbourhood soccer clubs would overthrow their managers. Debating societies would unseat their secretaries. Among students, no structure, committee or organisation was small or insignificant enough to avoid being usurped. A committee formed to hire a bus for an outing could be toppled on the grounds that it did not consult the student body about which bus company to use. Young, educated Liberians understood that every sphere of life, no matter how petty, was organised around a centre of power, and centres of power could be stormed, their personnel driven into the wilderness.

These strange goings-on among the young were surface ripples; beneath them stirred a deep, wild current, one that was slowly, imperceptibly unmooring the system William V. S. Tubman had built.

By the early 1970s, Liberia considered itself to be rich. But for a place like Liberia, wealth heralds problems. Economies need to be governed. And bigger economies need bigger governments. As the country flourishes, more people must be recruited into the white-collar jobs of expanding state departments. Bureaucracies must be staffed by people with technological know-how. Who, in Liberia, would fill these functions? The elite made up only some 5 per cent of the population. The country, in other words, was growing too big to be run by the Congos alone.

And so the Americo-Liberian regime began educating and hiring more and more native Liberians. Yet they were extremely reluctant to create equal opportunities for them. Indigenous people who rose to the top might bring indigenous followers with them, and thus constituted a political threat. Native Liberians entering state service found that the ceilings above their heads were very low indeed. And there was nowhere else for them to go. Commerce was out: the rubber plantations and the iron-ore mines, from which Liberia was gathering her riches, accounting for more than 90 per cent of the country's export earnings, were foreign domains largely unconnected to the local economy. An ambitious young indigene looking to the state for a career was likely to find only frustration and disappointment.

Unsettling ideas permeated Liberia, arriving through its schools and universities. The regime was always anxious that this might happen. If the education of indigenous Liberians was to expand, who would teach them? There certainly weren't enough elite members to go around. Indigenous schoolteachers were dangerous, for who knew what ideas they harboured? And foreign teachers from elsewhere in West Africa were dangerous too, as the spell Mr Obakwe cast over Jacob testifies, for the ideas seeping across Liberia's borders

from the capital cities of its neighbours were not the sort to give an
Americo-Liberian a peaceful night's sleep.

For the elite, it was a worrying time. By the late 1960s, much of
West Africa had acquired independence from its colonial masters.
No longer the only independent republic on the African continent,
the idea of Liberia as a beacon of black hope had fast become
anachronistic. The teachers pouring in from Nigeria and Ghana,
especially those from Ghana, came with very different ideas about
Africa and Liberia's place in it. Ghana's first president, Kwame
Nkrumah, had spoken of Africa uniting against an exploitative West,
and of the Liberian regime as little more than a bunch of black
lackeys in service to greedy Western corporations. This was a story
that fell on receptive indigenous ears in schools throughout Liberia.

Ironically enough, the ideas were coming, not only from Ghana,
but from the Americo-Liberian elite's motherland: the United States.
In the late 1960s and early 1970s, a generation of ambitious young
indigenes, frustrated by the limitations of Liberia, went to America
to study. They came home with the entire plethora of radical ideolo-
gies that shook American campuses in 1968. Among them was the
idea that their leaders were living parasitically off a world system
that kept them poor and powerless.

On a Sunday afternoon in the early winter of 2008, I knock on
the door of Jacob's apartment on Park Hill Avenue.

Several locks unlock and chains unchain, and Jacob stands there
in the doorway, wearingly an outlandishly large white T-shirt, the
shoulder seams falling about his elbows, the hem dangling around
his bare knees. He grabs my wrist eagerly and drags me across
his apartment. With my free arm I wave to his older brother,
Ignatius. Ignatius has been living in New York less than two years.
I have met him only fleetingly; this is to be my first substantial
conversation with him.

Jacob offers me a seat in the lounge. On the coffee table, mid-
distance between him and his brother, is a large jug of deep red punch,
heated on Jacob's stove. He and Ignatius have already worked their
way through one jug. A third awaits in the kitchen.

As afternoon becomes evening, Ignatius and Jacob are to remin-
isce about many things, some of them harrowing and horrible, and

I will discover in Jacob a relationship with his past I had never imagined. But at first, they speak about high school. Ignatius, through his father's connections, got into one of the best institutions open to indigenous Liberians, William V. S. Tubman High, located in the Monrovia neighbourhood of Sinkor. His last year at school was 1979, which was also the last year of Americo-Liberian rule.

'I got very involved in student politics,' Ignatius recalls. 'I was a member of the Uhuru Party. Tubman High was a vocational school. Everyone was specialising in a practical subject. I was doing book-keeping. So, when the Uhuru Party got into government, I was made Finance Minister. Alaric Topka' – who was to become a prominent Liberian intellectual – 'was foreign minister.'

'Foreign minister?' I asked. 'What exactly was his job?'

'To liaise with any body or organisation located outside of Tubman High: the student bodies of other schools, the organisations at the university. It was a very important position, because it was the inter-face with the outside world.'

'And I guess you had a Minister of the Interior, too?' I asked.

'Yes. Also a very important portfolio. That ministry was respon-sible for writing laws for what happened on school grounds, in the student body. It was the most contentious ministry because it governed our opponents: the other political parties on campus.'

Jacob at high school in Sanniquellie, 1989. Jacob is in the centre of the photograph, his face turned from the camera.

'Did they fight you?'

'Fight us? They overthrew us. There was a coup. They marched into our office one day and seized it. They said: "The Finance Minister must make the announcement." They made me stand in front of the entire school body and announce that there had been a coup, that we had been overthrown.'

Jacob slapped his thigh and then thumped the arm of his chair. 'Ha! You were a coup victim. I was a coup *instigator*. In Sanniquellie. In 1987. A classmate died. A committee was formed to raise money for his funeral. They were corrupt. They stole some of the money. It was the last straw. We *cleansed* the place! We *swept* them out!'

He roars with laughter, the punch and the memory of coups making him as merry as I have ever seen him.

Thinking about that afternoon with Jacob and Ignatius, I feel great sadness. What brings it on, primarily, are the unspeakable horrors to which both of these boys will bear witness in the years after high school. These memories of coups and counter-coups are of the last days of their innocence.

But they are memories of something else as well. From its inception, Liberia has been located at the other end of the world. Real people lived elsewhere, and Liberians fantasised with props borrowed from afar. First it was the morning coats and the derbies. Then it was the coups and the revolutions. These were the pretend worlds of a place that felt forever half-formed, that had always to mimic in order to be. There is nothing so dangerous as a world of fantasists, all the more so when the recurring fantasy is of the capturing and recapturing of power.

9

Coup

In the end, it was neither students nor intellectuals who ended Americo-Liberian rule, but a group of junior army officers with barely a high-school diploma between them. At about one o' clock on the morning of 12 April 1980, seventeen young Liberian soldiers entered the Executive Mansion. One of them was Samuel Doe, a twenty-eight-year-old sergeant from the hinterland county of Grand Gedeh. On their path to the bedroom of President William Tolbert, the man who had ruled Liberia since 1971, they slew several members of the Mansion's security staff. How they killed Tolbert himself is up for grabs: by some accounts he was stabbed fifteen times; others say that he was disembowelled. By dawn, Doe was on national radio, declaring that 133 years of Americo-Liberian rule were over.

12 April was a Saturday. That weekend, the streets of Liberia's cities and towns played host to a haphazard carnival. Storefronts were smashed and goods looted. Through cheering crowds, the mutilated bodies of Tolbert and the others killed at Executive Mansion were carried through the streets of Monrovia, taken to the edge of the city's Palm Grove Cemetery, and then dumped in a nearby swamp. Ninety senior members of Tolbert's administration were arrested. Ten days later, thirteen of them, mostly cabinet ministers, were shot by firing squad on a beach in central Monrovia. Their houses, in the meantime, had been looted by bands of soldiers and civilians. The old elite had all been Freemasons, their masonic temple an austere, neoclassical building on a hill overlooking the ocean. That weekend, soldiers looted the temple before making their way to the home of its caretaker and shooting him dead.

The successful coup plotters had made a mighty show of lopping off the old regime's head. The question of what they would do next was unknowable, perhaps not least to themselves.

Jacob was nine years old then, a student at a Baptist school in Sanniquellie. Einstein, Nkrumah and pan-Africanism still lay ahead of him. The coup's impact upon his life was both immediate and intensely personal.

Jacob had lost his village just two years earlier, his mother a year before that. He had received a stern form of love from the older sisters responsible for him. Among his quests in Sanniquellie was a source of warmth and affection. He had found one in an elderly Muslim woman whom he adopted as his grandmother. It seems that he perhaps found another source, too, one that he will scarcely acknowledge, and that he lost in the coup. It spills out of him, almost by accident.

Duazuah Massaquoi had sent Jacob's older sister, Willett, to Sanniquellie several years before Jacob, to live with a Congo woman who ran a government guesthouse in the city. Her name was Nora Ricks. She had adopted Willett some time in the mid-1970s. Indeed, Willett's surname had become Ricks. Now, Jacob tells me, hurriedly and in passing, that Nora Ricks adopted him too, just months before the coup. He went to live in her household, and he did so as her foster son.

'Willett and I were treated like royalty,' Jacob tells me. 'There were other indigenous kids living on the property and they were treated very badly. They were there to work. They were just slaves.'

'It must have been awkward for you,' I say. 'You must have identified with these indigenous kids because you were also indigenous. And yet you were almost like an Americo-Liberian kid. A strange position.'

'You didn't notice these things,' he replies coolly. 'It was the way things were. Only later, after I was politicised . . .' and then he trails off.

Jacob will not refer to his foster mother by name. He calls her 'the Americo-Liberian woman', or 'Willett's mother'. Only when I ask does he tell me flatly, disinterestedly, 'Miss Ricks'. It is as if she was a nondescript matron who ran a boarding house at which he happened to live, a person he passed in the corridor from time to time.

Yet when I probe his memories of 12 April 1980, the day of the coup, the recollection takes down an old guard, and something comes out.

'My mom was thrown out of the government compound where she lived and worked,' he replies. 'That very day, 12 April, the soldiers came to her house: "This is government property. You must leave. Today." So my mom lost her house. And we lost ours. We left her then; we went to live with Judy. My mom was never the same after that. Life was hard. She spent the 1980s cussing.'

Of course it is hard to acknowledge, this Americo-Liberian mother. Jacob sits at the dinner table while the other indigenous kids work in the yard. He is her son by virtue of a difficult bargain his father made long ago. This is not part of the life story he tells now.

Back home, in Duazuahplay, Jacob's family's views of the coup were conflicted.

'I had several brothers in the army,' Jacob remembers. 'They came home from Monrovia jubilant. They were going to get higher rank, higher pay. They were now indigenous Liberians in an indigenous-led army. Their brother-sergeant, Doe, was leading the whole country.

'But even among my brothers, it was mixed. One of them was the chauffeur of the colonel who was head of security at Executive Mansion. That colonel was killed during the coup. And as chauffeur to this man, my brother was nearly killed too.'

Jacob's village was a victim of Americo-Liberian rule, and yet his family owed what it had to his father's connection with its functionaries. They could not know how they would fare after the fall of their patrons. Would Duazuah Massaquoi finally be permitted to shed his fawning, subordinate status under indigenous rule, or would he simply lose his ties to men of influence? Would his sons prosper in an indigenous-run military, or would the fact that they owed their jobs to their father's links with Americo-Liberians count against them? Jacob does not say how his father greeted news of the coup. He probably doesn't know; he was just nine years old, and was living in a city more than a hundred miles from his father's village.

One can speculate, though, that the old man was anxious. He had spent half a century cultivating a relationship with the

Americo-Liberian regime. I doubt whether he was the sort of man to beckon uncertainty.

The young soldiers who took control of Executive Mansion on 12 April declared that power now lay in the hands of a junta called the People's Redemption Council. Samuel Doe was appointed council chair. Not yet thirty, poorly educated, and a newcomer to Monrovia, he was wise enough to know that neither he nor his fellow coup plotters had sufficient knowledge to run a country. And so Doe invited onto his Council a motley assortment of educated people. Some of them had been junior members of the regime Doe had just overthrown, and had managed quickly to ingratiate themselves with their new patrons. Also invited into government was a range of student activists, professors and left-wing intellectuals who had spent the 1970s in Monrovia and the United States plotting to overthrow Americo-Liberian rule.

Scores of young indigenous Liberians, frustrated by their limited prospects at home, had gone to study in America. Between them they imbibed the entire spectrum of radical ideas suffusing post-1968 American campuses, from various strains of Marxism to pan-Africanism and Third Worldism. They had formed a host of organisations, some in America, others based at the University of Liberia campus in Monrovia, to fight Congo rule. Now, Doe invited a cross section of them into his government.

Overnight, Liberia's cabinet was filled with men with American PhDs. Bacchus Matthews, who had a doctorate from the City University of New York, and had in fact lived on Park Hill Avenue for some time, became Foreign Minister. George Boley, the first member of the Krahn tribe to receive a doctoral degree, was appointed Minister of State. Amos Sawyer, who had a doctoral degree from Northwestern, was appointed chairman of a commission charged with drafting a new constitution for Liberia. Togba-Nah Tipoteh, who had a doctorate from the University of Nebraska, Minister of Economic Planning.

Meanwhile, Doe prepared himself for his new role. According to one observer, the new chairman spent his time 'taking regular lessons in English grammar and pronunciation, spending hours to know where Peking was and why, despite her strong dislike for communism, the USA was friendly with Peking, or having long briefing sessions on complicated problems involving the IMF and the World Bank'.

The intellectuals Doe had invited into his government observed how the chairman was spending his time, and they were very excited indeed. While their soldier bosses were learning English grammar and pronunciation, the course of the new regime, they believed, would be theirs to steer.

They could not have been more wrong. The professors and junior technocrats Doe had cobbled together were too incoherent a mix to move in the same direction at once. They were China-supporting Marxists, Moscow-supporting Marxists, African socialists, as well as staunch free-marketeers. Doe, uneducated as he was, was canny enough to realise that, in the Cold War, West Africa remained of strategic importance to the United States, and that he could take control of the disparate new Council if he had American support. Among his daily lessons he received instruction in what the United States government would like to hear, and he quickly mastered this language very well.

The Council soon split over the question of Liberia's international allegiances. Things came to a head when it had to decide whether to establish friendly relations with Libya. Five members of the Council were especially dogged fans of Libya. Doe stuck to his pro-American line. Neither side would budge. The impasse dragged on for weeks. In August 1981, Doe solved the matter by having all five of the Libya supporters executed, setting the tone for the remaining nine years and eight months he would spend in office.

Doe, it turned out, was both highly paranoid and prone to extreme violence. Utterly unable to hold together the diverse array of soldiers and intellectuals he had gathered in his Council, he began packing the upper echelons of the government and army with members of his own ethnic group, the Krahn, one of Liberia's smaller linguistic groups that hailed from the south-east of the hinterland, among the remotest parts of the country. Doe trusted only those beholden to him, marginalised everybody else, and dealt with real and imagined threats with seemingly whimsical violence.

In 2008, many years after his death, Doe's former Deputy Information Minister, Emmanuel Bowier, told me what it was like to work with him.

'Thank goodness for soccer,' he declared. 'It was Doe's only source of relaxation.'

Yet the problems of the 1980s extended well beyond the proclivities of one person, no matter how influential. The Americo-Liberians had ruled Liberia by lending the country to foreign companies, filling the state coffers with commissions and taxes, and distributing the proceeds to networks of clients. The president's office was a trough at which various constituencies came to feed. Politics became the art of fashioning oneself into the sort of person who would receive a place at the trough. Chiefs emphasised ethnicity and solidi-fied the boundaries of ethnic groups, because to represent a people entitled one to receive a share. To be a Krahn or Gio or Kissi leader meant that one could become a patron in one's own right, and dispense resources in turn.

A system of patronage is awfully deceptive. On the surface, its signature style is supplication. Everyone fawns at the feet of whoever is standing a little closer to the centre of power. Men are lionised and exulted. Concealed beneath the flattery is the managed plunder that is in fact the essence of the system. People exult those at the centre in order to take from it. And if the centre no longer gives, then people stop fawning and descend on the centre and grab.

That is pretty much what happened in the 1980s. For all that the soldiers and intellectuals in Doe's Council spoke of Marx and Gaddafi and other ideological lodestars, they came to Monrovia as Liberians had always done; they represented various regions and clans and ethnic groups, and they were expected to bring home jobs and devel-opment and money. The old system under the Americo-Liberians had been carefully calibrated; successive presidents made sure that each region and power bloc in Liberia got a piece of his patronage. Doe's arrival ruined these calibrations. He was a parochial young man from a Liberian backwater. He soon became paranoid, and locked out those he did not trust. And when Doe locked people out, they went to war.

This is no exaggeration. Almost everyone who became a warlord in the 1990s had a senior position in Doe's government in the early 1980s. The men who came to conduct the fighting had all been on first-name terms. They came to Monrovia for power and wealth, and when it was denied them, they took up arms for it. A handful of American-educated intellectuals armed and equipped vast swathes of the Liberian population to storm Monrovia and strip it bare.

Within three years of coming to power, Doe fell out with the most influential among his fellow coup plotters, Thomas Quiwonkpa. Quiwonkpa, very popular among Liberia's rank-and-file soldiers, and widely respected among civilians, had become commanding general of the Armed Forces of Liberia in the days after the coup. Fearful of Quiwonkpa's level of support, Doe removed him from the army and appointed him to a civilian position in October 1983. Quiwonkpa refused the new post, and soon went into exile in the United States, where he began planning a campaign to topple Doe.

Quiwonkpa was a Gio from Nimba County. When he was iced, so was the entire county. Gios found it harder and harder to get government jobs, to receive promotions, especially in the army: the resources of Monrovia were increasingly shut off to them. In 1985, Quiwonkpa returned to Liberia with an armed force and attempted to overthrow Doe. The coup failed. Quiwonkpa was captured by Doe's soldiers, mutilated and killed.

Doe declared war on Nimba County and its Gio speakers. Jacob was a Gio speaker from Nimba County. He was fourteen years old.

Taylor

When Jacob first spoke to me of his high-school days, the picture he painted was bright with Einstein and Nkrumah and his own bursting intellectual excitement. In the background were any number of older women: classmates having too much sex and doing too little schoolwork; two sisters; a Muslim grandma. Only later, when he began speaking of the war and its long preface, did it become apparent that something very important was missing from this image: a constant sense of menace.

'My family had been jubilant after the coup,' Jacob told me, 'but the conflict between Doe and Quiwonkpa began early, and once it started, there was tension all over Nimba. The county was flooded with Krahn soldiers. Suspicion of Nimbians ran very high. Then came the 1985 coup and it shattered the relationship. The day news of the coup reached us, people expressed jubilation on the streets of Sanniquellie. Some of those dancing in the streets were my class-mates. The Krahn soldiers noted who was celebrating. When the coup was put down, the celebrators were punished. What I mean is that people from my class were arrested: some were beaten, others were imprisoned, and some were taken away and executed. That is how they were punished.'

My face must have gone ashen, for Jacob pointed at my cheeks and laughed. When he had spoken of Newton and Marx and his radical questioning of the world, I had identified with him. For I, too, had been a student activist, and I knew what it was to sit in a lecture theatre and pick away at the foundations of the world while, not far away, soldiers patrolled the streets. But casual executions of classmates by low-ranking soldiers: what do the laws of motion and gravity mean in this context? From where did Jacob find the motivation to go home and read about the physics of supersonic travel?

'Personally I got on extremely well with the Krahn soldiers,' he continued reassuringly, evidently enjoying my surprise. 'I hung out with them in high school. Because I had beautiful chicks in my class, and I was the middleman between the beautiful girls and the soldiers.'

'You were young to be selling sex,' I commented.

'Yes, and a virgin myself. I had no interest in the older women in my class. But the military guys did, and I was in the middle.'

'You were a pimp,' I said.

He roared with laughter and slapped his thigh. His white teeth flashed in the gloom of his shuttered apartment.

'Don't you dare write that,' he said. 'You will ruin the friendship. *Completely ruin* the friendship.'

'Did they pay you?' I asked.

'Sometimes a few cents. I was, I am, a sociable guy. I made friends with them.'

In Duazuahplay, Jacob's family's situation was growing increasingly dire. Three of his brothers and several uncles were in the army, but they were not sure whether their positions helped or hindered them. They still received their salaries and reported for work every day, but the suspicion under which Gio soldiers were held darkened. They, too, were living among people who they feared could turn on them at any time.

As for Jacob's home village, it was now under siege from what amounted to a foreign army.

'After the Quiwonkpa coup in 1985,' Jacob recalled, 'there were army checkpoints on the road all the way from Sanniquellie to Butuo. To travel by road was to be harassed by Krahn soldiers every few miles. "Hey, Gio boy! What's in your pocket? Give me!" And there were constant patrols in my village. The army would deploy soldiers along the river. They would come and shoot in the air. "Where is the chief? He must provide us with food!"

'My father suffered very badly. He had a lot of cattle and other domestic animals: goats, sheep, chickens. Soldiers came constantly and took them away forcibly. In some instances, it is just common respect that when a government official enters town, you feed the person. But this was not on the basis of courtesy. They took by force.

'So people hid their cattle. My father secretly had what was left of his herd taken over the border to his family in Ivory Coast. Everything else he lost to the soldiers. By the time I finished high school in 1989, he had nothing. Graduation is a very big thing in a village like mine. How many people from there get to finish high school? When I got home after my graduation, my father was unable to provide a goat or a sheep for the celebration.'

Jacob's father had spent more than half a century putting distance between his family and the burning of his grandfather's beard. His life's project had been to shelter his village from the prospect of armed men who might come to pillage and steal. It was as if the last sixty years had fallen away from beneath his feet.

I have no way of knowing whether Jacob's father caught wind of, or even encouraged, some of the clandestine activities that began to take shape in the late 1980s. I would be surprised, though, if he had been entirely unaware. Several dozen men in the villages of Butuo, some of them esteemed and influential, would steal across the river into Ivory Coast, where they fell under the leadership of a man named Charles Taylor. They were among 166 Gio and Mano men Taylor recruited at that time. They would all receive military training in a camp outside Tripoli so that they might invade Liberia and overthrow Samuel Doe.

Charles Taylor's life until this point had not been without colour. Son of an Americo-Liberian father and an indigene mother, he was studying at a university in Massachusetts in the late 1970s, and from there led an organisation of American-based Liberians in fierce opposition to the Liberian government. After the April 1980 coup, he was appointed head of procurement in Doe's government. Unfortunately for him, his patron in the Provisional Revolutionary Council had been Thomas Quiwonkpa. When Quiwonkpa fell out with Doe in 1983 and was forced to leave for the United States, Taylor went too. Doe accused Taylor of taking nearly a million of the Liberian government's dollars with him and sought to have him extradited. He was arrested pending extradition and held prisoner for fifteen months in a Massachusetts prison before escaping and leaving the country, right on the eve of Quiwonkpa's botched 1985 coup. His intention had been to join the coup; in the event he was lucky to have missed it.

Here and now, more than two decades later, I have not met a Liberian who does not believe that Taylor escaped with the clandestine help of a United States security agency. America, they say, had finally realised that in Doe they had backed a dud, and that Quiwonkpa was their new client. The police would claim that Taylor and four cellmates sawed through the bars on their cell window and lowered themselves to the ground on knotted sheets.

Taylor and his 166 Gio and Mano fighters finally invaded Liberia in the last week in 1989. It was a ramshackle affair. Poorly armed, they divided into three groups. Each crossed the border and made its way to separate Armed Forces of Liberia facilities. It was a harebrained gamble to seize enough of Doe's own guns and ammunition to mount an insurrection against him.

Two of the three groups were overpowered almost immediately. The third, which consisted of just sixty men, crossed the border between Ivory Coast and Liberia on 24 December 1989, some seven or eight miles from Jacob's village. None, as far as I can ascertain, were from Duazuahplay, but all were from villages close by, and would have known Jacob's father by name and reputation, if not by sight. They moved quickly through the rainforest on paths they had known since childhood, towards the district capital of Butuo. There, they quickly took control of the Armed Forces of Liberia post and raided its armoury. Doe's soldiers scarcely put up a fight; most dropped their guns and fled.

Taylor's men now moved from village to village, where they were greeted as heroes. Within a week, they had amassed almost a thousand volunteers. More than a dozen of them were Duazuahplay men. Several were members of Jacob's family.

Taylor called his movement the National Patriotic Front of Liberia (NPFL). At the time, many Liberians had never heard of the NPFL, and only those familiar with the inner workings of Doe's government knew much about Taylor. That would quickly change. In the coming weeks and months, as Taylor's army fought its way westwards, thousands upon thousands of Liberians from several counties would join its ranks. By July, the NPFL would be on the outskirts of Monrovia, planning an assault on the Executive Mansion. On its way to the city, it had armed an untold number of ordinary people, many of them prepubescent children.

As for Duazuahplay, there can be little doubt that many villagers celebrated their fathers' and brothers' decision to join Taylor on his march to Monrovia. For several generations now, Liberia's capital city had been the source of all the wealth in their world. During better times, the more enterprising among them had struck up alliances with Congo families to get a place in Monrovia's schools, a job in its army, or ownership of one of its famous surnames. Then Doe took over, and Monrovia closed its door. Now, Duazuahplay men were finally going to the capital to loot its riches. Some would come home with wire fencing for their farms, zinc for their roofs, even a press for their sugar cane.

11

To Monrovia

News that war had begun reached Jacob over Christmas lunch, and his first response was one of deep denial. He had graduated from high school six days earlier, and was going to train to be a scientist; that is the future that every fibre in his being demanded. He had passed the entrance exam to the University of Liberia. In the new year, he was headed for Monrovia.

And so when he heard that war had started, his first thought was that he must leave for Monrovia a little earlier than planned.

'I was at my sister's home in Sanniquellie,' he recalls. 'Somebody came in and said, "Oh, there is a message from Butuo: the soldiers have come from over the border and attacked Butuo." We were not sure what to think.

'That evening, on the streets of Sanniquellie, Doe's soldiers came out in full force. They were arresting every young man from Butuo. We were hearing gunshots. We were told that some of the young men they identified were being executed. I was very scared. I knew I must get out of town.

'I wasn't widely known to be from Butuo. I used to hang out with people from all sorts of backgrounds. So I could move in the streets. I had some time. Between Christmas and New Year I managed to get money from my sister to go to Monrovia. I escaped to Monrovia.'

'You ran towards Doe,' I said. 'A young Gio boy ran to Doe's headquarters. That is hardly an escape.'

'I wanted to start university,' he replied. 'Do you understand? My head was full of ideas, scientific and political ideas. My dream was to go to university. I didn't want to think that this fighting would get in the way of my dreams. So I went to Monrovia. I took my high-school diploma, and my ID card. I would need these things to get into university.

'I was in a taxi, a minibus taxi, headed for Monrovia. At the very first gate, at the exit from Sanniquellie, we were stopped by soldiers. They told all the men to get out and line up in single file. "Where are you from? You, where are you from?"

'They started speaking in Krahn among themselves, discussing who to pick out of the line. I did not understand what they were saying.'

As Jacob spoke, his eyes drooped, his speech slurred, and his head began to tilt forward. He was on the brink of sleep. Soon, I would be alone in his apartment with the silent CNN images on his television screen.

The moment his head hit his chest, he jolted awake.

'They took a young man from the group,' he continued, as if nothing had happened, 'and they began to beat him. Because he had jeans and a red T-shirt they suspected him. It was believed at the time that the rebels attacked Butuo in jeans and red T-shirts. So everyone wearing that was targeted.'

He was battling against sleep. He tilted his head up a little and slanted his eyes, the pupils revolving upwards and disappearing, leaving his eye sockets full of white.

'So they took him away.' His eyes were suddenly wide open now. 'There was a house next to the roadblock. They took him behind the house. There was a gunshot. One shot. They came back without him. We drove off. Those were some of the things I saw.'

A long silence.

'Actually, we didn't drive off immediately. Our response to the boy's murder was this: the driver came around to us one by one and took money from each of us and gave it to the soldiers, and *then* we drove off. But every ten or fifteen miles, a new checkpoint, and we go through the same exercise. "You! Where are you from?"'

His eyes rolled once more, and his chin dropped, very gently, not enough to jolt him. This time, he slept.

In Monrovia, Jacob had two older brothers. Peter was an officer in the Armed Forces of Liberia and lived in an army barracks downtown. Ignatius had recently qualified as an engineer and worked at the American embassy. Jacob sought out Peter first, but his soldier-brother shooed him away. The men in his barracks were mainly Krahn. They knew that in months their city was to be invaded by a largely Gio army. Peter felt scared for himself; his fellow soldiers tolerated his presence for the moment, but they might turn on him at any time. He did not fancy the chances of his eighteen-year-old brother, fresh from the countryside, the city utterly foreign to him, in this dangerous, mercurial environment. So, he sent Jacob to live with Ignatius.

'Oh, Jonny,' Jacob said the next time we spoke of the war. 'My memory is . . . I'm so sad because, um, so I came to town with a view to going to university. I'd passed the entrance exam. I did not go to Monrovia to be caught in a war.'

Jacob did not fall to sleep again while talking about his wartime experiences, but he would never speak of them for long. A great weariness would come over him, sometimes only ten or fifteen minutes into our interview, a little longer on a good day, and he would ask me to turn off the recorder. The moment I stopped it he would spring to his feet, as if the button I just pressed had recircuited his wiring.

Nor could he talk about the war at will. On some Wednesdays, I would shadow him all day and go home late in the evening, neither of us having mentioned the prospect of a formal interview. At other times, African Refuge would empty in the late afternoon, the office would grow still, and Jacob would still with it.

'Now is a good time to talk,' he would say. 'It's a good time.' And I would turn on my voice recorder.

'Ignatius and I lived with a family on City Bypass,' Jacob tells me. 'We rented two bedrooms in their house. The man's name was Wilfred Duailu. We lived in his house with him like family. He was a Krahn. His wife spoke Gio, so we all spoke Gio in the house. His nephews and his wife's brothers were all in the army. They made terrible statements about Gio people. But they were not living with us. They were not a threat.

'Wilfred Duailu grew to love me, Jonny. I believe that part of him truly loved me. I got close to his children. I am a friendly man. His children became very fond of me. His son was useless. I tutored him. I sat with him for hours, taking him through the sixth grade. Duailu had a daughter, too. She was about fourteen. I got on well with her, too.

'Duailu would take me for a ride in his car. Just the two of us alone. He told me he was very proud of me, getting to university having come from this small village. He said he was proud.

'We would read the newspaper together. He'd read it, then he'd give it to me and I'd read it, and then we would discuss politics. I knew he was dangerous. I was getting close to the neighbours. They were saying that he had killed many people in the army. I was very cautious. I didn't tell him my mind. I only told him things he wanted to hear.

'We stayed there three months. Until April, I think. I was going to the university most days, meeting fellow freshmen, getting orientated. Monrovia was waiting for the war to come. The NPFL wasn't in Monrovia yet. But everyone knew they were on their way.

'Wilfred Duailu came to me one day and he said there is a war coming to this city, my family is no longer secure here, I want to move to the outskirts of the city.

'He said: "I want you to stay here and look after the house. You have been so nice to my children; you have given them free tuition all this time; you and your brother need not pay rent if you choose to stay."

'We thought it was a good opportunity.

'He gradually started moving his things out of the house. I saw the expressions on his children's faces. They were not very happy. His children were very sad that they were moving. They came and said, "Jacob, we will miss you." I told them to hold tight.

'The man and his family moved on the Saturday. On the Sunday I was alone in the house listening to BBC "Focus on Africa". It is what you listened to if you wanted to know what was happening in Liberia. I heard a bang on the door. Bang! Bang! Bang!

'"Jacob! Go! They are coming to kill you! We saw the death squad! They're having a drink around the corner! They're planning how to kill you guys! Don't stay here! You must get out!"'

'I was so scared. I took my brother Ignatius's diploma. We had discussed it. If the time came that we needed to run, I would take my brother's engineering degree, nothing else. I went next door, to my informer. She was a woman from the Sappo tribe, almost like a Krahn. She was a little older than me. We were friends. I am a sociable person. A social butterfly, so to speak. I am not shy to start relationships with people.

'I spied through her window. After ten minutes, they came. My landlord was leading the troop. Wilfed Duailu. Personally! He was the head of them! We could see clearly from the window. They were outside my landlord's house shouting:

'"Come outside! Bring yourself outside! You damn rebel! You Gio man!"

'I left through the back door of my informer's house. There is just a narrow path going down the slope. As I was leaving, I saw my brother, Ignatius, come. He was tipsy. He was coming back from drinking.

'I said: "Don't go to the house! They have come to kill us!"

'He started arguing with me. "I don't owe anyone! I work for the American government! I am an engineer!"

'He was so indignant. He wanted to fight me. He wanted to keep walking and go home.

'Fortunately for him, someone from the neighbourhood came towards us, someone who had seen what was happening at our house. They had forced open our door, looted our food, looted our bedrooms. Ignatius saw it was serious. We sought a taxi and ran back to Peter's house in the army barracks, the very place we were meant to avoid because it was not safe.'

'What was your landlord's motivation?' I asked.

'He was an evil man.'

'But he was close to you.'

'People who are close to you can kill you, Jonny. He praised me. He always praised me. A part of him loved me.'

12

The Sergeant

After that awful Sunday afternoon at City Bypass, Jacob and Ignatius took refuge with their brother, Peter, at the military complex in which he lived. It was hardly safer than the place from which they had fled. Doe's soldiers were feeling as if the apocalypse would soon descend upon their city. Taylor's army had now split into two, one led by Taylor himself, another by his erstwhile subordinate, Prince Johnson. They were in a race to get to Monrovia: each wanted to be the one to overthrow Doe's regime and take Executive Mansion. With two Gio-dominated armies closing in on the city, it was not a good time for a family of Gio brothers to be moving in with AFL soldiers.

'Peter did not stay there,' Jacob recalled. 'He was in hiding. He considered it too dangerous to stay among his fellow soldiers. But there was nowhere else for us to go, so *we* stayed there, Ignatius and I. Which meant that I was there alone most of the time because Ignatius was working long hours. I didn't know Monrovia very well. I was young. I was eighteen. I had to negotiate that place alone.

'It was a big compound, a little like Park Hill. There were maybe 100, 160 people living there. In our house there were five or six rooms, and this was Africa, so you had whole families of four or five people living in each room. And it was a menacing place. The children walked around armed: the teenaged children of the adults walked through the passages of this house with automatic weapons slung over their shoulders. That's how it was in Monrovia on the eve of the invasion. Every child of my age belonging to the Krahn and the Grebo [an ethnic group from the south of the country] had guns. The militias in the house were walking around carrying their weapons saying they were going to kill those bastard Gio people.

Can you imagine? And I was living in that house. Jonny, I was new to Monrovia at that time. I did not know how to move around the city.'

Peter was well aware that he was leaving his younger brother in grave danger. In the two or three hours they were together in the house before Peter spirited himself away to his girlfriend's place, he left Jacob two instruments with which to defend his life.

The first was guns.

'Peter was in Armed Military Intelligence,' Jacob recalls. 'He had an army-issue handgun, a .45 calibre weapon with a twenty-bullet magazine. He showed me how to assemble, disassemble, shoot. He showed me how to take position if someone comes into the house.

'He also had an Uzi, an Israeli submachine gun, which he left with me and showed me how to use. For the Uzi he had about five or six magazines filled with ammunition. He put duct tape around them so they could all hook together and I could therefore spray bullets continuously at whoever came into the room.

'And then he said something to me, Jonny, he said something I have never forgotten. He said: "Do not die like a coward. If they come to kill you, spray them with bullets."

'He was looking at me, his younger brother, looking at me in the eye, and he was seeing my death. He was instructing me how to die. I will not forget that moment, not ever.'

But Peter left Jacob with a second weapon: friendship.

'He had been in the army a long time,' Jacob recalls. 'There were people he was very close to. He thought maybe he can protect me through the friendships he has built.'

Before leaving, Peter introduced Jacob to two men. The first was the sergeant in command of the house, a Kru. He almost certainly saved Jacob's life, and when I ask Jacob his name he is embarrassed that he cannot remember. Days later, I ask him again, and still the sergeant's name eludes him.

Jacob knew instinctively that he must come to mean something in this man's life, and that it needed to happen soon.

'I used my intellectual development to make myself interesting to him,' Jacob says. 'All the discussions with my Ghanaian high-school teachers about world history, it all came to use now. We discussed politics, history, global affairs: everything except the war. He liked that. I think I helped to take his mind off the grave danger he was in. I stimulated him.

'In the three weeks we lived together in that house, he grew very fond of me. He knew me to be an early bird. He would knock on my door at 6.30 a.m.: "Jacob, come up to the roof with me." I would join him. It was peaceful up there so early. We would talk about this and that.'

The second man to whom Peter introduced Jacob was a corporal named Augustus. He was half Gio, half Krahn, and at least a decade older than Jacob. Jacob describes their friendship as intimate. 'If we had come to know one another for longer we would have become like brothers,' Jacob says, 'like blood brothers.' But when I press for details – what August looked like, what they spoke about, why they become so close in so short a space of time – Jacob falls silent for a moment and then changes the subject. Perhaps what happened later has emptied the Augustus preserved in Jacob's memory, leaving him a simple shell.

Despite the protection of the nameless sergeant and Augustus the corporal, the house remained extremely dangerous. As Monrovia waited for the rebels to arrive, the compound's residents grew increasingly capricious.

'Everyone else in the house was a hardcore Doe supporter,' Jacob remembers. 'When I listened to BBC "Focus on Africa" to find out what was happening in my country I had to close the door and turn the volume very soft. They disliked the idea of people listening to BBC "Focus on Africa". The station was considered the enemy of the state. It was thought that the BBC spread the propaganda of the rebels.

'There was one particular guy in the building who persistently threatened to kill me. One morning, we were on top of the building, on the roof. He looked into my eyes and he said: "Today is the day I am going to kill you. When I see you tonight, I am going to kill you." He told me that.

'I went straight to the Kru sergeant, the one with whom I would watch the dawn break from the roof. The sergeant immediately confiscated this man's rifle. When I saw him the next day, he lifted up his shirt and showed me a handgun tucked into his waist. He said: "I can kill you now." He drew the weapon and pointed it at me. Someone in the house saw this and came to us and said: "Hey! What are you doing?" They were divided. Some were advocating our death. Others were saying: "They've done nothing to us. Leave them."

'It became clear at some point that one day soon the rebels would take over the city. Taylor's forces had taken Robertsfield Airport and were headed for the eastern districts of the city. Prince Johnson's soldiers were on Bushrod Island, just west of the city centre. The government divided Monrovia into blocks and established checkpoints everywhere. Some of the men in my building were responsible for guarding the checkpoints. And then right at this time, there was the first atrocity Monrovia would experience during the war, the atrocity at the UN compound in Sinkor. Various people were hiding there: opposition politicians, Nimbians, student activists. The soldiers came in there one night and killed several innocent people.

'The next morning, there was an outcry. The papers were saying that Doe was involved. The civil society organisations of Monrovia were outraged. They decided to protest to bring the war to an end. Several thousand people took over the streets of Monrovia. They were planning to march to Executive Mansion to call on Doe to resign for the sake of the future of Liberia. They wanted to say to Doe: "By continuing in this office, you are endangering us all."

'What the protestors did not know is that the day before the demonstration, it had been decided to give the army an order to shoot. I knew that. I knew that because I was living among the soldiers. I knew that people were going to get killed the following day, many of them. People I met at university over the last few months were going to be there, student activists who I had met and considered my colleagues.

'In that dreadful house I was staying, everyone knew that tomorrow might be the last day they would control Monrovia. They were all packing their bags. They were getting ready to abandon the compound and move to the main army barracks at Barclay Training Center. Everyone was putting spare gas in their car. Monrovia was now thoroughly an outlaw place.

'The Kru sergeant came to my room late on the night before the demonstration: He said: "It will be hard for me to protect you in the house from tomorrow. I will not have sufficient control. I want you to pack a bag, just your essential things. Tomorrow, Augustus and I will take you somewhere safe."

'The shooting began at about ten o'clock the following morning.'
He imitates the sound – 'blah . . . blah-blah-blah-blah-blah . . . blah'
– and with each 'blah' he throws his head to the side, carelessly,
imperiously: the brutal swagger of an armed soldier among civilians.

'Shortly after the shooting started, the Kru sergeant came into
my room. He said: "Jacob, get the *fuck* out."

'That's the language he used. I had never heard a profanity from
his mouth before. And he was right. Because of what happened that
day, my presence in the house would no longer have been tolerated.
I would have been killed.

'The sergeant and Augustus, they put me and my little bag in a
car, and they drove me across town. Augustus had his rifle pointed
out of the window. He was ready to shoot. The sergeant drove. He
was speeding. He was not going to stop, except for army checkpoints.
It was too dangerous.

'They drove me to Sinkor, to the Lutheran church on Tubman
Boulevard. That is where everyone was going to take refuge. We
made it through many checkpoints. By the grace of God, we got
there. I was like a son to him.

'He said, as he was dropping me off: "I am going to bring my
family here too. You will see me again later today."

'I didn't ever see him.'

'Until this day?' I asked.

'He may have died. Most of the military personnel in that house
died after Prince Johnson took Monrovia.'

13

St Peter's

The church Jacob walked into that morning was chaotic. In the histories of Liberia's civil war that have subsequently been written, it is said that more than 2,000 people had taken shelter there by the last week of July 1990, the time Jacob arrived. But that is surely a rough guess; there was no way of counting. Many of those who had taken refuge were Gio and Mano, for Doe's troops were killing their kin at will. But there were many others besides. Ordinary Monrovians, too afraid to take to the streets, or, indeed, to stay in their homes, aware that open warfare would erupt in the heart of the city the moment the rebels arrived, were using the church as a shelter from which to see out the fighting.

Jacob walked through the church looking for members of his family, and found none. This pleased him. Three months earlier, on the day he and Ignatius had moved into Peter's quarters at the military compound, the Massaquoi brothers had come to an agreement.

'We decided that whenever there was a situation of mortal danger,' Jacob tells me, 'we would split up and care for ourselves. Because if we were together, the chances of all of us dying were too great. It was a question of family preservation.

'So, with half an eye, I looked for Peter and Ignatius and other family members. And I when didn't see them, I thought: good; I will see them when I see them.'

The church was not equipped to house so many people. There was nowhere to defecate, and little to eat. What rudimentary organisation that did exist was devoted to the task of separating the genders: men in one large room, women and children in another. People were reasonably respectful of one another, but each was on his own.

Keeping themselves and their children healthy and nourished took up much of the refugees' time.

'A supermarket on Tubman Boulevard not far from the church was looted,' Jacob recalls. 'There was stuff strewn all over the street. It was there for the taking. Once or twice, I was among the people who went out to pick up some of the food.

'On 29 July Charles Taylor announced on the radio that he was the President of all of Liberia. The AFL soldiers were panicking. They thought that an invasion of Monrovia was imminent. They started pointing fingers at the church and saying that as a place of Gio refuge it was too dangerous. There were rumours. It was said that the army was going to come into the church.'

The Doe government had established a curfew in Monrovia at that time. At six o'clock each evening, Tubman Boulevard emptied. That night, the refugees locked the gates of the church behind them and put extra people on guard duty to sound the alarm should anyone try to enter. By nightfall, all 2,000 or so of them had bedded down.

'At about nine that night,' Jacob tells me, 'there was commotion at the gate. Then I heard guns go off. Ba! Ba! Ba! Everyone scrambled. Everyone was trying to get out of the church. We were like sheep in a pen.

'I found my way out. It wasn't easy to choose where to run to; the gunshots sounded like they were coming from everywhere. I ran onto an embankment with another guy. We had hung around together the last couple of days. We had spoken. We were aiming to scale the top of the embankment and escape. Next thing I knew, blood was splashed all over my body. I did not know whether the blood was his or mine. I fell to the ground and lay there. I thought I might be dead. I wasn't sure. I was trying to figure it out.

'I knew I was alive when I heard a soldier coming. He was shining a flashlight at us to see if we were dead. I stayed still. The guy I was with had been shot. It was his blood all over me. I could feel his body shaking against mine. So the soldier with the flashlight, he kicked this man so that he was even closer to me now, almost on top of me, and shot him again, in the back. Twice. Ba! Ba!'

Jacob frowns, and on his face there is a peculiar expression: shy, almost embarrassed.

'I'm sure you will want to ask,' he says, 'how would I know that

they shot him in the back? My eyes were closed. I was pretending
I was dead. But, you know, when you're in that state, you see things
in your vision. You imagine your surroundings. You capture what
goes on around you through your imagination.'

I ponder for some time the significance he draws from the fact
that his eyes were closed.

'Where were you in your imagination?' I ask. 'Were you watching
from above?'

He is puzzled. 'No, I was lying there. Right there by the guy. He
was lying almost on me; the soldier had pushed the guy right up
against me. The soldier pushed him up against me and shot him
again to be sure he was dead. Ba! Ba! And then the soldier cursed
him. My eyes were shut; I was pretending to be dead; it was my
imagination telling me that these things were happening.'

I still do not understand. Defeated, I soon forget and think of
other things. And then, several months after this conversation, Jacob
tells me of a series of events that took place nearly six years later,
in April 1996. What he describes is very gruesome indeed, almost
unbearably so, and when he is finished describing, he comments: 'It
was my worst hour, Jonny. For all that the war was six years old, it
was the first time I had *seen* it. After all, at the church in 1990, my
eyes had been closed.'

It dawns on me for the first time. His eyes had been closed; he
had thus witnessed nothing but the conjurings of his imagination.
It is a most childlike and sympathetic form of self-protection. His
eyes shut, he had been saved, not just from dying in the slaughter,
but from experiencing it.

What happened that night is now remembered with capital letters
– the St Peter's Lutheran Church Massacre – and there surely isn't
a Liberian who doesn't know of it. Just as it can only be guessed
how many living souls bedded down behind the church's locked
gates that night, so the question of how many died can only be estimated. The figure that has been settled upon is 'more than 600'.
For several hours that night, the church became a slaughterhouse.
It emerged later that the soldier who led the attack, Captain Tailey
Yonbu, had been recruited into the Armed Forces of Liberia just a
few months earlier, by President Samuel Doe himself, and had had

no formal military training. He was among the countless Krahn civilians the Doe government armed during its last months in power.

The Lutheran Church Massacre would be among the last events associated with Doe's legacy. He was to survive little more than a month. In the early hours of 10 September Prince Johnson would capture him and have him tortured and his ears dismembered, in front of a video camera.

As for Jacob, he had no idea at the time how many had been murdered, or the place the massacre would come to occupy in Liberian history. His world had just narrowed considerably. His only concern was his survival.

Early the next morning, he found himself in a very large crowd, more than a 1,000 strong, he believes, on the streets of Sinkor. Many were survivors of the massacre, some of them badly wounded, but among them were countless people who had simply taken flight from their homes and were seeking safety in numbers. Safe they were not. The objective of the soldiers had been to murder as many people as they could, and a crowd on the streets, especially one known to have many Lutheran Church survivors in their number, was vulnerable to attack.

Amidst the people, Jacob caught sight of his brother. Not Peter or Ignatius, but a much older half-brother.

'He was an army officer,' Jacob says. 'He had thrown away his uniform and had joined the refugees. His name was Kruo.'

In the crowd, the talk was about where to seek refuge now that the church had been breached. People were speaking of the Americans. A compound occupied by the United States Agency for International Development was in spitting distance, on Tubman Boulevard, mere blocks from the church. It would not take long to get there, ten minutes at most.

Jacob and Kruo walked side by side. They barely exchanged a word.

The crowd arrived at the USAID compound to find that its gate was bolted. The crowd waited. There was not so much as a stir from inside. Eventually, those at the front began to heave themselves against the gate, and then those behind them joined in, and it was not long before the weight of the crowd had torn the gate from its hinges. The people poured into the American government compound.

'We stood there inside the grounds and waited,' Jacob says. 'Nobody came in and nobody came out. Some of the American staff watched us from the windows. Rumours started going around the crowd: they are not going to take us in; they are not going to protect us.

'The rumours were right. They came out and told us to go away. We are a risk to the facility, they said. We are a reason for them to be targeted. We must go. And they lowered the American flag from their flagpole and left us alone.

'You must understand,' Jacob says, 'there were American helicopters flying over us. At one point, there was a C30 flying low. They were taking pictures. They were apprised of the situation. They obviously knew that the army wanted to kill off the survivors of the massacre, and they didn't want it to happen in their facility.'

At the time, 2,000 US marines were stationed just off the Liberian coast. They were there should it become necessary to come to shore to defend American government officials and civilians, not to protect Liberians. In any event, two days later something happened at the other end of the world that distracted American attention and immediately put paid to any thought of an intervention: Iraq invaded Kuwait. By the end of the month, the marine contingent was gone, and Liberians were left to their deepening war.

It is a source of enormous bitterness to many Liberians. Doe had been an American proxy in the 1980s, America's Cold War ally. And yet when it was time to clean up the mess he had made, the Cold War was over, and America no longer gave a damn. And so, as the refugees from the church watched the American flag go down while AFL soldiers waited to kill them, the disappointment they felt in the United States was bitter indeed.

Once the flag had been lowered and taken away, it became clear to the refugees that they must leave the compound fast. As in the church the previous night, they were penned in, and thus vulnerable to another slaughter. And so they poured out once again onto Tubman Boulevard. The Massaquoi brothers walked side by side.

'We headed towards the rebel-held areas. Paynesville. Charles Taylor's NPFL held Paynesville. It was not that far. We were over 2,000. We said we will go. You can kill all of us. We are going to Taylor's side.

'We thought we'd be safe there. Especially Gios. And I knew that there would be family amongst the NPFL forces. There would be people I knew.

'But getting there was a terrible ordeal. We had badly injured people among us, maimed people. We were carrying people in wheel-barrows. We did a detour past JFK hospital to drop the injured off. Then we kept marching towards Paynesville.'

Somewhere along Tubman Boulevard, a truck full of AFL soldiers stopped in front of the refugees. The troops jumped off and fired their rifles into the air and screamed instructions. They wanted the men to separate from the women; two lines, both single file, on either side of the road. Once this was done, they instructed the crowd to keep moving.

'They were looking for Gios,' Jacob recalls, 'looking for rebels. They were pulling this one and that one out of the crowd, arresting them, interrogating them. Kruo and I were walking together, not in single file, but side by side.

'"Hey! Hey, hey hey! You! Rebel man! Come here." You heard that, you just kept your head down. You hoped it wasn't you. "Hey! You!" It was Kruo they wanted. They pulled him out of the crowd. I did not stop. I did not turn around. I kept walking. To be associ-ated with him was to share in whatever was going to happen to him. I had walked maybe ten feet, maybe twenty feet, and I heard two gunshots. Ba! Ba! I put my eyes to the ground and I kept walking.'

I have asked Jacob several times what went through his mind then, what goes through his mind when he speaks of Kruo now. At first, he does not answer. He cocks his head to the right and stares for a moment at the empty space on the couch next to him. And then says: 'We had decided as a family that we must not die together; we must look after ourselves.'

I cannot imagine that Jacob managed to hold Kruo in his mind for long, for five or ten minutes after his death, another group of AFL soldiers intercepted the refugees. This group was not going to bother separating men from women; it simply began to fire.

'We scattered. We all ran between the houses, everyone fleeing in different directions. Some were getting shot down. Others were escaping. I went inside an abandoned building. I climbed into the eaves of the roof. There was a little platform where the roof meets the wall. I saw that there were three other men who had done exactly the same. We could not be seen from below. We lay there in absolute silence, not daring to say anything to one another.

'An hour passed, maybe two hours: the four of us saying nothing. And then one of them whispers: "Jacob! Jacob!"

'I said nothing.

'"Jacob! It's me!"

'"Augustus? Is that you?"

'It was incredible. Augustus had thrown away his uniform and taken refuge in the church. He was one of the people I was closest to in the world, he had risked his life for me earlier that week. And here he was with me hiding in the eaves.

'We stayed there, the four of us, for a long time, nobody speaking in more than a whisper. It grew dark. The new morning came. We were still lying there.

'At about eight o'clock, the other two decided to climb down to the ground. Augustus and I deliberated. We did not think it was safe. Throughout the night we had heard soldiers, gunfire, shouting. Early in the morning we had heard them again. We stayed where we were.

'So the two went down and left, and just a few minutes later, we heard shouting, then pleading, then gunshots. And then silence; we were sure they were dead. We heard men cursing in Krahn.

'And so we just stayed. On and on and on. Augustus and I. In the end, we stayed in those eaves three nights. At no point did it seem safe to come down. The gunfire was always too near. But on the third morning, we could not take it any more. We had both dehydrated. We had both become sick.

'So, we came down. Augustus was our point guy. He was checking around to see where the soldiers were. We had gotten a block, maybe just a block from the building where we had hidden, when the soldiers saw Augustus, and we both ran.

'I ran into a house. I was very, very fortunate. It was one of those houses you call a "straight": you know those buildings where the front door leads straight to the back down a passage. I ran through the front door and closed it, through the back door and closed it. They thought I was in the house, they searched it, but I was still running. Ideas were just flowing to me: do this, do that; ideas were just flowing to me. I threw myself in the long grass. Lie down.

I heard people scream in the house. They were beating them. Then I heard my friend Augustus. He was crying: "Don't kill me! Don't kill me!" They said: "Where's the other rebel? Where's the other rebel?" "I don't know." And then Ba Ba! Ba Ba! I didn't hear his voice again.'

As he speaks, the expression on Jacob's face is as blank and as hurried as his words. I want to ask him to slow down, to remember more, to try to resurrect something of what he was feeling. But I sense the considerable weight of his pride crouching low over this experience, sheltering it from my eyes. It is as if he has turned on a tape recorder, replaying words he formulated long ago, words he has not thought about or listened to in a long time.

It was around midday. He kept to the shadows, not sure what he was going to do next, when he heard voices. He listened. They were speaking in Kissi, the language of his Muslim grandmother in Sanniquellie.

It had not been long since he had spoken Kissi. Could he remember? Could he keep the conversation simple enough to pass?

He stood up, strolled towards the sound of the voices, saw that they belonged to a man and a woman. He greeted them in Kissi.

'They asked me what happened. I said I am a displaced person. They said: "Oh, no." They were very sympathetic. They asked me my name. I said it was Sahmomo, an obviously Kissi name. I said I needed clothes. I had about $25 on me. They gave me clothes and breakfast. I ate. They said there was a Kissi guy in the neighbourhood who was part of a death squad. I must find him; he will keep me safe. They gave me the whole rundown of the neighbourhood. There were several checkpoints. I then went out to find this Kissi death-squad man. His house was behind JFK hospital. I was on Seventeenth Street. It was a dangerous walk, a dangerous one-hour walk. I found his house and knocked on the door, I actually saw him and sat with him, the leader of a death squad.

'I spoke to him in Kissi. I tricked him. I said I needed to stay with him. He said no, he cannot protect me; he is out all the time on operations, and the soldiers are coming always knocking on the doors of all the houses, and if they knock when he is not there, and they see a stranger, they will shoot the stranger.

'I obviously did not tell him I was from the church. I told him

I was from a district the NPFL had taken. I said they had taken my house, my food, that I had fled with the clothes on my back.

'He said: "Brother, you need some help." He gave me $10, and he told me of a Kissi family living on Old Road. He gave me directions how to get there.

'I started walking. My name is Sahmomo. My name is Sahmomo. I was talking to myself in Kissi.

'Everyone I passed I addressed in Kissi. There were all sorts of people on the streets: displaced people, fleeing people, people looking for shelter, people looking for food. I crossed paths with a young woman. When I greeted her in Kissi she greeted me back in Kissi.

'She felt sympathy! She gave me a *warm* reception! She took to me. I told her I was a university student. She was Bassa but she spoke Kissi, good Kissi. She took me in. I went to her house. She introduced me to her mom, her grandmom; she said if any military personnel come, I'm her brother.

'After a few days, she wanted to be physical with me. You know what I mean, Jonny? She wanted to be physical. Thing is, she had a military boyfriend. She didn't *tell me* she had a military boyfriend. She said: "I have a drunk who brings me food at night. Around twelve or one, when he comes, he shoots in the air, that's how I know he is here."

'And just at that moment, we heard shots being fired. He and his friend arrived with looted property. It was the first time I'd eaten dog. They brought dog meat. When we heard the gunshots, we walked out together to meet them.

'His name was Joe. Immediately, he said: "Who's this? You a Gio man?"

'The girl said: "Get the fuck out of here, he's my brother, why you call him a Gio man?"

'She used profanity on him. She did not know I was Gio.'

'I noticed he had a small Bible with him, a pocket-sized Bible. I have a deep and broad knowledge of the Bible, from when I attended a Baptist school in Sanniquellie. I used it to counsel him. We began to read the Book of Psalms. We started reading Psalm 91.

'I said: "That's a very powerful psalm. King David was a warrior; he used to read it."

'He said: "You know any good prayers and verses?"

'I said, yes, and we became prayer partners. I built an alliance with him. He gave me intelligence, how the rebels were reaching around us, how they may take over at any time.

'In the end, the NPFL took over in less than a week. On 8 August, the eve of my nineteenth birthday, the rebels attacked the Nigerian embassy. A lot of soldiers took off their uniforms and buried them. Because if the rebels come into your home and see a uniform they can kill everyone there. So Joe, my Bible study friend, was making plans to bury his uniform.

'The next day, the government brought a Katyusha forty-barrel missile onto the street. This is what Hizbollah used to fire rockets into Israel. When I saw it in the photographs I knew it was exactly what the Liberian government was using. It is a gun mounted on the back of a truck, with forty rocket-launching barrels. The government brought that thing in, and they fired it indiscriminately, fired maybe twenty-five times, into Congotown. That calmed down the rebels for a while. The next day around eleven o'clock the rebels started attacking again. This time they took over.

'We were in a zinc house. We all had to lie on the hot, zinc floor. I heard the rebels coming. Lying flat on my stomach, I heard cursing in Gio outside. They were using profanities in Gio, "Look at those fucking cowards running away."'

14

Taylorland

'Among the first rebels who walked into the zinc house were class-mates from high school in Sanniquellie. You have no idea the relief, how comforting it was. I shouted to them in Gio. It seemed a long, long time since I had spoken Gio. And soon I found out that my name went a long way. Not Massaquoi, that is a colonial name. Duazuah. My father's name. My father was a big man in Butuo. There were Butuo people of the highest rank in the NPFL. When I said my name was Duazuah, it meant something.

'I was given a house to stay in. And I met my brother, Peter. He had thrown away his AFL uniform and had crossed over to rebel lines. And I found out that a man from our village, a relative of my mother's, was now an NPFL general. And not just any general, but the most feared general in the NPFL. His name was Sam Larto.

'So at this point, I was a very happy man. I believed I was in the hands of the force that was to liberate Liberia from Samuel Doe. And it was not just me. It was not just Gios. At that point, in early August 1990, much of the country thought of the NPFL as liberators.'

The illusion did not last.

'Even on that first day, it was clear that something was very wrong,' Jacob recalls. 'Nobody was in control. There was a sense of wildness. People would drive through in trucks and shout and shoot their weapons in the air. The person with the most soldiers in his truck would be the one in command.'

In mid-August, Jacob prepared to leave Monrovia and walk into the hinterland, under the protection of an NPFL unit.

'We had not even left Monrovia, we were marching through

Congotown, when the rebels stopped two men and questioned them. One was apparently military personnel, the other was Krahn. They executed them there and then. Ba! Ba! Ba! Ba! They're both lying dead on the street. That moment, I knew I was not saved. The NPFL was the same as the ones I had fled. It was a lawless environment. Wherever you went in Liberia you'd be in this wild, crazy place. There was no escape, nowhere. Not in Nimba, not in Monrovia. Nowhere.'

The scenes Jacob witnessed as he journeyed through NPFL territory towards Nimba were to become notorious. Charles Taylor's army spent much of the second half of 1990 establishing control over swathes of the Liberian interior. The roads were soon littered with NPFL 'gates', usually no more than a rope thrown across the road, staffed by gun-toting teenagers who demanded loot from whomever passed. Untold numbers were killed after hasty, careless interrogations.

Many of the gates were adorned with macabre decorations such as human skulls and limbs. The more infamous were christened with names. 'No Return' was among the most well-known gates; the United States embassy estimated that more than 2,000 people were executed there in 1990. The bodies lay exposed at the sides of the road; anybody seen attending to them risked the ire of those staffing the gate.

'Something I enjoyed during that time,' Jacob remembers, 'thanks to my name, I managed to save three people.

'One day, the rebels arrest these three guys. They interrogate them, and interrogate them, and they finally conclude that these guys were Krahn. They were going to kill them.

'But it was bullshit. They were Nigerian. I *knew* them.

'I said: "Listen to me. You don't know what you're doing. These guys are okay."

'They said: "Fuck off and leave us to do our jobs."

'And then I said to them: "Do you want me to tell General Larto? He has known me since the day I was born."

'They backed off immediately, *immediately*.

'Sam Larto. Go to Liberia and ask about him. They are still talking about him now. General Sam Larto. He does not play. He just kills for fun. Just that name, General Larto, all the commanders, they were afraid of me.'

He laughs raucously, his heavy cackle echoing through his empty apartment.

'I said, "I will tell General Larto."' He laughs again, even louder this time. 'He used to kill his men, just like that.'

As he walked into the hinterland with the NPFL, the things Jacob was discovering – about his people, his family, his village; about the ease with which they turned to looting and killing – finds expression in his hollow laughter. He will not put this knowledge into words. 'My people were tricked by devious men,' is all he will say when I press him.

By November 1990, Jacob was installed in a small Nimbian town under the protection of a distant uncle.

'My uncle was part of the NPFL establishment,' Jacob tells me. 'I lived with him. It was quite interesting. He was illiterate. Couldn't read or write. And he couldn't understand the English on the radio. By default I became his assistant. He asked me to write his letters for him. I would listen to the news for him. But if what I heard was against the NPFL I wouldn't tell him.

'I was getting good sources of news, listening to BBC "Focus on Africa", listening to the government's broadcasts from Monrovia, to Taylor's broadcasts. And there was a lot of bad news for the NPFL towards the end of 1990. First, they had failed to take Monrovia. They were in retreat. I didn't tell my uncle that. And second, evidence was being broadcast about the brutality at the NPFL gates. I didn't tell him about that either.

'Some of the horrible crimes of the NPFL I witnessed living there. I saw people being tortured under my uncle's command. It gives me shame to relate this to you. If I were to write about the NPFL, how they operated . . . it was a very ruthless organisation where people lied. Nobody was safe. It didn't matter who you were. Everyone had enemies. People were set up to lie on each other. It was an organisation without trust, without camaraderie. It was very vicious place.

'People weren't trained. Commanders weren't properly in control. They were looking for numbers. They were looking for quantity, not quality. Most of the people had joined along the road: some joined the fighting forces for survival, some for revenge, some recognition.

But the overwhelming majority of child soldiers joined for survival. The greatest victims were the women because they were used as sex objects. The child soldiers, young men in the town, their parents made them join, so that they can support the family. So what did the war do? It reversed the social hierarchy. Children supporting parents by bringing home booty.'

Jacob was in a remarkably privileged position to witness the war. He had lived among the Armed Forces of Liberia in their own barracks, and was now observing the NPFL from within. And if what he saw at close range was both varied and intimate, he was also, thanks to his radio and to his official position as taster of his uncle's daily doses of news, beginning to see something of the bigger picture.

Throughout July, while Jacob was holed up in a hostile army barracks in Monrovia, it looked very much as if Taylor was going to win a quick and decisive victory. He was racing towards the capital, his army was swelling, and the swathe of politicians and professionals who had fled into exile under Doe was largely behind him.

By late August, however, much had changed. Prince Johnson had split off from Taylor, and was soon to capture and execute Samuel Doe. More importantly, perhaps, a West African peacekeeping force, Ecomog, dominated by Nigeria, landed in Monrovia on 24 August. In mid-September, deploying a squadron of warplanes, Ecomog forces drove Taylor's NPFL from the capital city. It then confined AFL soldiers to barracks, appointed an interim government of neutral Monrovia politicians, and ran the capital city. Monrovians would live without warfare for almost two years.

Taylor was now caught in a kind of limbo. In terms of sheer landmass, he controlled much of Liberia. But Monrovia, which housed the bulk of the Liberian state and the lion's share of its personnel, remained closed to him. Taylor quickly set up a parallel state, which he called Greater Liberia, with its own currency, and located its capital in Gbarnga in Bong County, close to the border with Guinea. It is here that the true nature of his project began to show itself.

Nominally, Taylor did run a state. He appointed ministers to various departments, and they appointed director-generals. Some even had makeshift offices in Gbarnga. But they were little more than a thin façade. What Taylor really had was personal control over commodity-rich territory, and once they knew this, foreign companies of all stripes began dealing with him. Firestone was keen to restart rubber production as soon as possible; the Liberian Minerals Company wanted the same for their iron ore mines in Nimba. Soon, logging companies were also knocking on Taylor's door. He would grant an operating licence and receive payment in US dollars. With the proceeds, which, as early as the end of 1990 had already grown sizeable, he would purchase arms for his ongoing assault on Monrovia, and fill the pockets of chiefs and local notaries in the territories he controlled. No doubt, many of Jacob's 'distant uncles', as he called them, who occupied places in Butuo's petty aristocracy, did very well under Taylor.

Soon, Taylor's nose for business took him across Liberia's borders. In March 1991, he would send several army units into Sierra Leone, to band together with the rebels of that country's Revolutionary United Front (RUF), in a joint initiative to seize mines and sell the country's diamonds. When Taylor finally came to stand trial a decade and a half later, it was for crimes committed in Sierra Leone, rather than in Liberia.

The extent of Taylor's commercial reach was considerable. The United States government estimated that in the early 1990s, about $75 million a year passed through Taylor's hands as a result of taxes levied on diamonds, rubber, timber and iron ore.

As for Taylor's troops on the ground, they saw very little of his newfound fortunes. Their primary income-generating tools were their automatic weapons, and the positions they occupied at the various NPFL 'gates' strewn across Liberia.

It was not just Taylor who saw the country this way. As the NPFL descended on Monrovia in the summer of 1990, an array of its potential victims fled into exile: AFL commanders, Krahn and Mandingo businessmen and professionals. Now, from their safe havens in Sierra Leone and Guinea, many began plotting how to fight their way back home. Initially, they formed one unified organisation, the United Liberation Movement for Democracy in Liberia (ULIMO). But ULIMO soon split into factions, based on ethnicity, on personal loyalty, on calculation. The factions fought one another over who was to command the remnants of Doe's exiled army, and, not least, over who would control access to the diamond and hardwood trades along the Sierra Leonean border. The line between politics, warfare and business, it seemed, had entirely collapsed.

And so the era of Liberian warlordism was born. In the capital city, a foreign army managed the heart of what remained of Liberia's civil service and state machinery. Out in the countryside, and along Liberia's borders, various military-political entrepreneurs fought one another for control over foreigners' access to Liberia's riches, and they armed untold numbers of young Liberians in the process.

Neither man remembers precisely when, but some time after Jacob had settled with his uncle, Ignatius Massaquoi travelled from Monrovia to Nimba. He was looking for his younger brother, for he had something he wanted to say.

'I was worried about Jacob living behind NPFL lines,' Ignatius told me eighteen years later. 'It was a dangerous place for a man with an education. Very uneducated people were running the show, and they had weapons on their hips, and they were using them. Monrovia was peaceful under Ecomog and the interim government. The University of Liberia was opening its doors again. It was time for Jacob to come and resume his studies.'

Ignatius had lost his job as a civil engineer at the United States embassy, for the Americans had left town. He was now employed by the Monrovia city administration as a senior manager at Robertsfield, Liberia's international airport, the funds for his salary in all likelihood drawn from Nigerian state coffers. Out in the hinterland there was war; in the capital, Ignatius woke up every morning and reported for work.

And he was right that in the rabidly paranoid world of the NPFL Jacob lived in constant danger.

'One night, I was in my room,' Jacob tells me, 'fiddling with the radio, tuning it. I found the government station broadcasting from Monrovia. Some rebel boys came past my room and overheard. "What are you doing listening to the enemy? You're a University of Liberia boy? Who's paying you? What's your agenda?"

'In that atmosphere, one of them could have just pointed his gun at me and pulled the trigger. You have to think very fast on your feet. You have to talk down crazy people.'

Aside from being scared, Jacob was bored. Among his uncle's businesses was a motel, and Jacob was assigned the task of running it.

'As a university boy, as somebody who could keep an account book and understand how a business worked, I was very valuable to him,' Jacob says. 'He was going to squeeze me for everything I was worth. I was desperate to get back to Monrovia. The university was opening again. The comrades I had only just begun to get to know were there. I wanted to study physics. I was hungry, *ravenous*, for an education.

'When I told my uncle I wanted to return to Monrovia to study, he dismissed the idea out of hand. *Treasonous*, he said. What is in your head is *treasonous*.'

In the end, an entirely unexpected turn of events directed Jacob back to Monrovia.

'We were not far from the border with Guinea. There was a Guinean town on the other side; I would go there from time to time to replenish supplies for my uncle's inn.

'One time, my uncle's sons gave me a ride. They said they'd take me there and bring me back. They were going because they were selling scrap metal in Guinea. When we got to the border, one of the guys spoke French very well, and he started negotiating with the Guinean official. The Guinean officers opened the gate. We drove the truck into the Guinean town. This was very unusual. They did not usually allow us to drive into the middle of town. And then, my God, they were exchanging money.

'My uncle's sons came to me and said: "The deed is done. We have sold our father's truck."

'I said: "I've got nothing to do with this. I played no part. I am going to go home."

'They said: "You can go home, but they will execute you. They will never believe that you had nothing to do with it."

'So, I had to make a plan. They gave me some money, I think a little less than a thousand dollars. We all went back to Liberia, to Ganta, we slept at a hotel, one night. Five o'clock the next morning, my uncle's people were looking for us all over Ganta. Everywhere, there was talk of this stolen truck.

'Immediately, before dawn, I paid a guy $100 to take me to Monrovia. When I got there, I went straight to Ignatius's house.

He was staying in a house on the Old Road with my sister, with Judy. We lived together a long time, maybe eighteen months, until Charles Taylor attacked Monrovia again. Then we split up. By now it was the family philosophy; when war breaks out, don't stay together.'

15

Nassa's Mother's House

When Jacob enrolled again at the University of Liberia in early 1991, he joined SUP – the Student Unification Party – the most radical of Liberia's student organisations. Formed in the early 1970s, it was aggressively oppositional during the final decade of Americo-Liberian rule, its membership consisting largely of young indigenous men from the countryside who had come to Monrovia to study. During the 1980s, it soon became an outspoken opponent of Samuel Doe, and several of its members were detained, tortured, and executed. Others fled into exile. Now, in the early stages of Liberia's civil war, its leaders were already speaking of establishing tribunals to try those fuelling the war, or, at the very least, to ban them from running in the democratic elections that they demanded must come at the war's end.

'What was your political programme?' I ask Jacob.

'We developed NGOs,' he replies, 'rallying people, talking about the war, having discussions off campus. I was a freshman. I was not fully equipped intellectually. I attended everything. We were there chanting back and forth. We went home and read, formed reading groups, developed our own intellectual skills. We learned to dissect information, to separate trickery from the facts.'

In October 1992, Charles Taylor tried, and failed once more to take Monrovia. He called his invasion Operation Octopus. Today, when Monrovians discuss the warfare that besieged their city for the duration of that month, they refer, simply, to Octopus. Following what had become a faithful wartime family tradition, the Massaquois split up when the fighting began. Jacob would not share a roof with his family again, not on Liberian soil.

When Operation Octopus failed, it finally became clear to Taylor that he was incapable of taking Monrovia by force; indeed, that he would never rule Liberia from its capital city without the consent of militarily dominant Nigeria, which controlled the Ecomog forces in Monrovia. And so he began to negotiate.

As for the Nigerian army, the senior officers running Monrovia had by now entered into commercial relationships with all of Liberia's warlords. Ecomog controlled both of Liberia's ports, one in Monrovia, the other in Buchanan, and its generals charged premium rates for armed factions to export their booties of timber, iron and rubber. So, the Nigerians, too, were open to negotiating.

Between early 1993 and late 1995 no fewer than thirteen peace accords were signed between Liberia's armed factions. The result of all of these negotiations was a veneer of peace, the longest Monrovia had known since the outbreak of war, under which accumulating layers of skulduggery formed. As talks proceeded, so the various armed factions returned to Monrovia. They were now invited to share in the governing of the Liberian state. And yet they did not surrender their arms. Each came to Monrovia accompanied by fully fledged armies, and all were prepared to use their armed forces to defend the section of the state they had won at the negotiating table, and to encroach on the turf of others. Monrovia entered a period of extreme instability. Leaders ostensibly running the city together would plot to kill one another when backs were turned. The capital was brimming with armed men, all now employed by one state agency or another, with fighting liable to break out between them at any time.

This state of affairs left the likes of Jacob immensely vulnerable. An unarmed movement of students and a handful of professors calling for accountable government, free and fair elections, and a tribunal to put warlords on trial would be foolhardy enough in a country run by a strong dictator. In the opaque and treacherous conditions of Monrovia, where seemingly everyone was armed and nobody was in control, left-wing activists took their lives in their hands.

Jacob spent these years in a flurry of activity. He was, he tells me, deeply involved in the Student Unification Party, a diligent student whenever the university was open, an active participant in an array of political, philosophical and scientific reading groups. To support himself, he found a job as a teacher.

'I was teaching maths at a junior high school on Old Road,' he tells me. 'The school is still there. It is still running today.'

'Where did you find time for it all?' I ask.

'I was busy, busy, busy,' he replies.

It is hard to get him to remember precisely when, but some time during that period, Jacob was crossing a busy road near his brother's house, in the eastern suburbs of the city, when he saw a familiar face, one he hadn't laid eyes upon in years.

'His name is Nassa Jabal,' Jacob tells me. 'I knew him from Sanniquellie. He had been a mentor to me. We were student militants together, although he was quite a bit older. He was from a wealthy business family, his father Lebanese, his mother Mano. When the war started, he went to live in Europe, in Switzerland. Now he was back. He had many, many business ideas for wartime Liberia. He wanted to do this, he wanted to do that. I don't think that any of his ideas ever materialised.

'We hooked up. We moved together. We started discussing politics. You know how I am, Jonny. I find someone. I move with him for a time. Nassa hated Taylor. He had many terrible things to say about Charles Taylor. We discussed politics until we were exhausted.

'He invited me to come and live at his house with his mother. That's how it was; we were moving together. His mother adored me, she really adored me; I became like a foster son to her. I have happy memories of living in that house. I was there for more than two months, I think.'

Late one night in early October 1994, close to midnight, as he remembers, Jacob was sitting alone outside Nassa's mother's house. In the distance, he heard the agitated voices of a group of men. He sat. Their talk grew louder. They seemed to be making their way to the house.

He went out to confront them. Walking briskly through the night, something stopped him in his tracks: the glint of metal, he thinks he recalls; they were armed.

He rushed inside, locked the front door, and ran through the house shouting at the top of his voice, dragging everyone from their beds.

'Everyone in the house woke up. We tried to prevent them from opening the door. We all stood at the door and pushed against it. There was an Ecomog checkpoint right around the corner. It was right there, so close. We thought they would never shoot. They would be arrested straight away. But that did not deter them. One of them put the barrel of his gun in the gap between the floor and the door and opened fire.'

The surgeon who attended to Jacob later that night, Dr Horatius Brown, counted seven entry wounds in his right leg, the lowest just above the ankle, the highest just below the knee. None of the other occupants of the house were hit.

'It felt as if they had cut me in two,' Jacob tells me. 'I dragged myself to the other end of the house. There was a large closet in the furthest room. I was in the closet by the time they entered.'

From the menacing commands of the invaders and the replies of his housemates, Jacob understands that these men are robbers, that they have come to take what they can.

But then, from his position in the cupboard, he hears this:

'"Where is Jacob!"

'"He is not here. He slept out."

'"I am warning you; where is Jacob?"

'"I said he's not here."

'Ba! Ba! They have shot Nassa's mother in the foot.

'"I told you Jacob is not here. Do you want to kill me?"

He pauses.

'If they were robbers,' he says, 'why were they asking for Jacob? How did they know Jacob? Somebody had told them that this Jacob man lived in the house.'

'Who do you think they were?' I ask.

'I don't know. Soldiers pretending to be robbers? I was deeply involved in advocacy work. And I had a big mouth. That very day, on campus, we had been handing around flyers calling for war tribunals. This was 1994; the government was being run by a coalition of warlords. They didn't want to hear about war tribunals. And you know me, Jonny, I am not one to hand out a pamphlet silently.'

16

Azariah

A day earlier, about fifteen miles from the house where Jacob was staying, another man was crippled by gunfire. His name was Azariah Sirleaf. Jacob had neither met him nor heard of him. Before the year was out, the two men would come to love one another dearly.

When I visit Azariah at his home in New Jersey in the summer of 2009, he knows very well that I wish to talk about 4 October 1994, the night he was attacked. But he is a man who believes in starting at the beginning of a story.

Azariah was shot while carrying out his duties as mayor of Clay-Ashland, a hamlet on the right bank of the St Paul River, just beyond the outskirts of Monrovia. He is very particular in telling me the story of how and why he became mayor.

He grew up in a well-to-do family. His father was Mandingo, his mother Americo-Liberian. He graduated from the College of West Africa, the best high school in Monrovia, then studied at the University of Liberia, before going to live in his parents' home town, Clay-Ashland, in the late 1980s.

'I got my first job there,' he tells me. 'I was serving as clerk of the city corporation of Clay-Ashland when the war broke out. Shortly after the commencement of war, the then Lord Mayor of Clay-Ashland, the late Vanjah Richards, was murdered.'

Aside from running Clay-Ashland, Richards was Liberia's most famous sculptor, his work still visible in many of Monrovia's public spaces. He was executed by government troops at the beginning of the war, for reasons that remain unclear to this day.

'When he died,' Azariah continues, 'I was appointed mayor, because by virtue of the city ordinance, which serves as the constitution of the city, in the absence of the mayor, whether by death, sickness or travel, it is the clerk of the city who represents the city.'

Azariah is a big man. He sits very still on his living-room couch, speaking in slow, fastidious sentences. Listening to him, watching him, one can imagine the sort of mayor he was. During the course of the war, every single armed faction at some stage fought to control Clay-Ashland: Taylor's NPFL, Johnson's INPFL, later MODEL (the Movement for Democracy in Liberia) and both ULIMOs. Through it all, Azariah insisted that he had mayoral duties: fiduciary, constitutional, and, not least, moral. And so, from mid-1990, right through to 4 October 1994, every time he heard reports of rebel activities, or the cough of gunfire, or news of an armed assault, he took himself off to Monrovia and the headquarters of Ecomog, the foreign peacekeeping force, to report what was happening, and to request peacekeeping intervention.

The first time he did this, the Ecomog field commander sent troops to Clay-Ashland and flushed the rebels out of town. From then on, all armed factions regarded Azariah as a foe.

Returning on an early October afternoon from one of his many trips to Monrovia, Azariah stopped at a home on the outskirts of Clay-Ashland. He had attended an important peace conference in the capital, and, as darkness fell, a crowd began slowly to gather to hear his news.

At some point in the early evening, three young rebel soldiers, all of them teenagers, made their way through the crowd. They were menacing, demanding rice from the gathering's host. She said she did not have any, and asked them to leave.

Still, Azariah was thinking only of his duties as mayor. Against the wishes of his host, he invited the boys to stay and talk. He urged them to come into town and to hand over their weapons. In exchange, he said, they would be trained in a trade, or sent to school, depending on what they chose.

'I felt for them,' he recalls. 'They were dirty, hungry; they were living in the bush. I said to them: "Look at me. I am mayor. It is because I am educated that I am mayor. You, too, can rise."

'They said: "That's a good idea, but if we go into the centre of town, people will recognise us and accuse us of killing their relatives."

'I said: "Well, if you cut your hair, instead of growing it like a wild man, have decent clothes on, they would not even recognise you."'

The boys said they would think it over. They shook hands with Azariah and left. Two hours later they returned, this time with a large group of heavily armed men, their commander among them. The commander began shooting sporadically. People fled. Azariah was suddenly alone with the rebels. The commander stared into his eyes and began speaking of him in the third person. 'Here is the man who is going to Ecomog to say we are harassing people. This is the man sabotaging our operations. And now he wants to lure three of our men into town to be arrested.'

'They wanted me to go with them,' Azariah recalls. 'I knew that if I went they would have slaughtered me. So I resisted. They hit me in the face with a flashlight. They began kicking me, punching me, in my back, in my stomach. I fought back. If they had over-powered me, they would have killed me.'

The commander yelled: 'Fire him!' And one of them, one of the original three who had sat with Azariah a couple of hours earlier, shot him twice in the right foot with a semi-automatic assault rifle, shattering his tibia and his phalanges. They turned and left, presuming that out here on the outskirts of Clay-Ashland, far from medical attention, Azariah would bleed to death.

It so happened that there was one car in the hamlet that night, and it was there by chance. A taxi driver from Monrovia, anxious to get early morning custom from commuters leaving Clay-Ashland the next day, had decided to spend the night there. Azariah was taken to this car in a wheelbarrow, and the man was woken; he drove Azariah to Monrovia.

But that was just the start of the ordeal.

'The nearest hospital in Monrovia,' Azariah tells me, 'was the Médecins Sans Frontières hospital on Bushrod Island. When we arrived there I had been bleeding profusely for quite some time. But they sent me away. They said they had no suitable doctor; the nearest orthopaedist was at the Catholic hospital in Sinkor, on the other side of Monrovia. When we got there, they said the orthopaedist is on call, but he is performing surgery at JFK hospital. So, on we went. I did not get seen until 10 a.m. the following morning. I did not get to the OR until 2.30 p.m.'

Azariah spent the first few days after his surgery at a ward in JFK. But his family soon decided to move him for it was common knowledge that rebels were finding their way into hospital wards and looking for patients to kill, particularly those with bullet wounds. It was the easiest way to track down and kill wounded enemy soldiers. So, Azariah was moved to the private clinic of the man who operated on him, Dr Horatius Brown; the clinic was a few miles closer to the centre of town, just opposite the Monrovia City Hall.

Jacob was admitted to Brown's clinic on the same day. He was there because Nassa Jabal's family was paying his medical bills. Feeling responsible for the fact that Jacob had been shot in their house, they insisted that he receive the best medical attention available.

For more than three months, Jacob and Azariah lay a few yards from one another, separated by a thin wall, without ever meeting face to face. Each was trapped, motionless, by virtue of his shattered leg. Day in and day out, they listened to one another's voices.

'At first, I was blacked out for so much of every day,' Azariah recalls. 'They were always sedating me. A lot of people were dying from bullet wounds. They were very worried about lifting the sedation. Every now and again I would come round and I would hear this lively guy, this very lively guy – you know Jacob, always laughing, always talking. When you are sick, the people who come and visit try to console you; they are always making fun, trying to take your mind from the pain and the agony. People would come to him: his friends from the university, laughing and talking. Other people, too: you know, his relatives. I would listen to the laughter. Different voices every day, but always, his voice. So lively.

'One day, it struck me: just as I am hearing him, surely he is also hearing me. What is he hearing? I asked myself. Every day I had a singing group, a "sing-spiration", where people would come and sing, make the whole place lively. Sometimes, while singing, I thought of Jacob listening to us.

'The first time I saw him was the very day he decided to come out of his room. You know, he's active. He jumped on his crutches. He wanted to get out of there. My door was open, he passed, he looked.

'"O! You the guy who in here! My name is Jacob." This, that and that.

'I said: "Jake, good to meet you."

'But I couldn't get out of bed. I could not use crutches. There was no wheelchair. They had something called an anti-rotational bar on my ankle. My situation was very severe. Everything in my foot was dismantled, shattered. They had to keep it in this cage. All I could do was sit up and look into the street. I was in constant pain. I was always sedated.

'So, Jacob came past and spoke to me and we just got on. And then he would come and visit me again. I could not go to his room. He would explain to me how he got shot. I would explain how I got shot. We were close. My family would bring food; we would eat together. His family would bring food; we would eat. And when I was able to go onto the patio, we would sit on the patio together. It was like being released from prison. We would sit there and play cards. Our family would come and visit. That's how our time went.'

Listening to Azariah describe an effervescent, gregarious Jacob, I am taken aback. This is not how Jacob remembers the first months of his convalescence. Indeed, for a long, long time — more than a year from the day he agreed to speak to me about his life — he will not talk about it at all. When he finally does allow himself to speak into my voice recorder about this period, and to do so with candour and emotion, his motives are complicated. He is trying to write a record of that time; he believes it will do him good, and he wants to show it to others. But he is stuck. Whenever he tries his hand at it, a welling anger turns him from his keyboard. He finds that he is distracted, cannot work on his doctorate either, cannot sleep.

And so he speaks to me on the condition that I transcribe his words and email them back to him; he wants to plant what he has said in his own work just like that, raw, off his tongue, without having to bear the pain of writing it down.

'After my injury, in the hospital, it was very difficult for me, Jonny,' he says. 'I made two attempts to commit suicide. It's a dark side of me many people don't know. Life was worthless, Jonny. You find yourself lying in that place. You are helpless. Everybody is doing everything for you. You are lying there. They have told you many times that they will amputate. You have been told that the powder from the bullet will go to your heart and kill you.

'What was happening in Liberia was very bad. The doctors were amputating the legs of the fighters, of the rebels, so they wouldn't go back to the front. My orthopaedic doctor told me that. He said, "Jacob, we don't want them to go back to the battlefield, so when they come with a gunshot wound in the leg we say the gunpowder can go to your heart, we must cut your leg. They say 'Cut! Cut! Cut!' Because they don't want to die."

'I had deep discussions with my doctor, Horatius Brown, once he got to know me. He thought because I was Gio, I was a fighter. Thank goodness he got to know me in time. Jonny, I need you to visit with Brown! Please! Please visit with Brown! The reason it is important to me. In Gio there is a saying: "A liar's witness is across the ocean." Go across the ocean to Monrovia and ask him. These people here in Staten Island who say I was a fighter: go and ask Brown. Ask him why he did not cut off my leg.'

'Is that what caused you to want to commit suicide?' I ask.

'No, I was lonely.'

'Nobody knew who you were there? Nobody understood you?'

'No. I was very aggressive there. I clashed with the doctors, clashed with the nurses. I had several clashes with them.'

'Where were your comrades and friends?'

'That's the part of life you have to understand. My experience has taught me, life is a stage. You play the music, it is finished, put on new music, oh nice party, let's go to the party. It's over. Everyone leaves and goes home. Everyone leaves and goes home. That's what happens. You are like a dead man. People go to the funeral, they cry, but they leave, and you alone are going to be there. You . . . help me with the word . . . you decay, you . . .'

'Decompose.'

'You decompose. What happened, I was dropped there in the clinic. It was rumoured all over the town that they had amputated my leg. People said I was stupid, I was very adventurous, I deserved it.'

'What sort of people are you talking about? Your comrades? Fellow students?'

'Friends. Even some people in my family circle. Some thought I was very risky. Some thought I deserved it. I'm a troublemaker, I'm no good.'

'It taught me something about human beings. It has affected even my romantic life. I have learned to think very hard before I trust 100 per cent.

'I learned three things about human beings. One: whether they are black, white, green or blue, human beings do not associate with failure. We associate with success. Two: human beings are deceitful. I concur with the prophet Jeremiah: "The heart of a man is deceitful above all things, and wicked, and who can know it?" It is so true. Three: be careful how you trust people. You are your best security.'

And yet, there is Azariah Sirleaf. What Jacob does with him, what Jacob does *for* him, speaks of something else.

When I listen to them recount the time they spent together in Brown's clinic, they are really . . . well, they are like a married couple; they are sharing a life together. War is going on all around them; they hear the gunfire booming through the night, every night. In the mornings, they are hungry to gather information, to interpret the meaning of the shooting they have heard the night before. They sit together on the balcony, the closest they will get to the outside world, and they listen to Jacob's radio. They wait, especially, for the voice of Robin White, who hosts BBC "Focus on Africa", for he is the best source of news. And Horatius Brown's head nurse has agreed to bring them a selection of Monrovia's daily papers. They take turns reading aloud to one another. They read, discuss, then rediscuss, every word published that morning.

When Jacob talks about this time, he says that Brown's clinic was his home.

'All my possessions in the world were there: a few changes of clothes, a collection of books, my little radio.'

These he shared with Azariah Sirleaf, save for the clothes, which were far too small for the bigger man. The words in the books he would read to Azariah; the words on the radio they would imbibe together.

They also shared in one another's wounds: not just the ones in their respective legs, but also that invisible wound: the social death

Jacob intimated, the feeling that the world has buried you and left your body to rot.

When I tell Azariah of Jacob's metaphor, the one about the decomposing corpse, he nods his head vigorously.

'Oh, yes,' he replies. 'Where I used to live in Clay-Ashland, although I was the mayor, as a young man I was active: play sports, jog, do things to cement the relationship with my constituents. A friend's house was just below where I lived. When I came home from work, I would stop at his place. I would yell up the hill to my younger brother: bring my boots, my clothes. I would change right there at his place and my brother would take my work clothes back to the house.

'I was in the hospital eight months, and this friend, whom I used to see every weekday afternoon, not once did he visit. So, yes, I know what it means to be forgotten. And Jacob had an extra impediment owing to the fact that he was from the so-called Gio group from Nimba. Gio-shot-rebel. That is the chain of assumptions.'

Azariah was discharged in May 1995, leaving Jacob alone in the clinic. But Azariah would be back; he still had two bouts of surgery to go. Besides, Jacob soon became an honorary member of the Sirleaf family.

'If anything important was happening,' Azariah tells me, 'I would go and fetch Jacob. There was a time I was made father of the year in my church. I went, picked him up, took him to the church. When my sister got married, I came and picked him up.'

Jacob's stay in Brown's clinic would last eighteen months. During that time, he had two major surgical procedures. His right leg was saved, but it was now a good five inches shorter than his left. When he finally began to walk again, it would be on crutches. Later, he would wear an elevated shoe, a heavy, black, Dickensian contraption that looked to me like a manacle.

April 6

In the first week of April 1996, Azariah was readmitted to Horatius Brown's clinic for a third round of surgery, this one to remove plates from his leg. He and Jacob were together once again. Azariah was due to stay for at least two weeks.

Any Liberian reading these lines will have an idea of what is coming next. Liberians speak of the major episodes of the war in shorthand. 'Octopus' refers to the battle for Monrovia that followed Charles Taylor's attempt to take the city in October 1992. 'World War Three' describes the final insurgency to drive Taylor from Monrovia eleven years later. Sandwiched between them is 'April 6'. It refers to an armed conflict that raged not for a day, but for many weeks, beginning in the first week of April 1996. Everyone I have interviewed who sat out the duration of the war in Monrovia describes it as the most destructive explosion of fighting they witnessed in all fourteen years of conflict.

What happened, essentially, is that the uneasy coalition of warlords running Monrovia turned upon itself. The four armies that had been cohabiting, precariously, for the previous two years, went to war, destroying much of the city's remaining infrastructure in the process.

'The Ecomog sergeant in charge of the section of Monrovia in which the clinic stood,' Jacob tells me, 'had become a good friend. On the night of 5 April he came to me and Azariah and he said: "A very big war is going to start in Monrovia tomorrow. Charles Taylor and Alhaji Kromah (who had until then been bitter enemies) are going to try to crush Roosevelt Johnson."

'He guaranteed us that the war would not come to the clinic.

He guaranteed it! He ordered a big, armoured vehicle, full of Ecomog troops, to stand outside.'

At 3 a.m., Jacob and Azariah were woken by gunfire. It seemed to be coming from Sinkor, just to the east of them. They lay awake and listened, waiting for morning, and, when first light came, took themselves to their balcony. They spent the morning watching the battle take shape.

'At about 7 a.m. the refugees came streaming from Sinkor towards the city,' Jacob recalls. 'It was very sad, very, very sad, watching these people with their worldly possessions on their backs. An hour later, we saw Taylor's NPFL forces going at top speed along Tubman Boulevard towards the battlefront. Top speed. They were heavily armed. They were no longer in the government uniforms they had been wearing around Monrovia. They were in rebel gear. They had make-up on their faces, like Zulu warriors. Some were saying they were going to cut Johnson's balls. I watched them and I knew that most would not return. The ambulances were very busy that day.'

And then Jacob and Azariah heard the engine of the Ecomog armoured vehicle start, the same vehicle that had been guarding the clinic since the previous night, the one the sergeant had brought. They watched it edge its way onto Tubman Boulevard, and then drive towards the city, a cowardly old machine, hastening back to its barracks, leaving the clinic to its fate.

'Eleven-thirty,' Jacob continues, 'and Taylor's people are back, fleeing in the other direction: fleeing! Behind them are General Butt-Naked's people. He is fighting on Roosevelt Johnson's side. His people go into battle naked but for shoes and a gun. They are shooting in the air, shooting in the air. They have a container of gasoline in one of their cars. They are just burning houses, one after the other.'

The soldiers torching the neighbourhood were fighting against Alhaji Kromah and Charles Taylor. Kromah was Mandingo. Taylor's father was Americo-Liberian, a Congo. And, at the start of the war, Taylor had, of course, led a largely Gio army. Mandingo, Congo, Gio. These were the three identities one would want to avoid were one to find oneself in Horatius Brown's clinic at eleven-thirty in the morning on April 6, 1996. 'Sirleaf', Azariah's surname, is to Mandingos what Cohen is to Jews or Stewart to Scots. Azariah's mother was Congo. As for Jacob, he was Gio.

Jacob and Azariah were not alone in the clinic at first. A couple of staff members were there, as well as Dr Brown's sister. The head nurse, the one who brought Jacob and Azariah the newspapers every morning, was a Krahn man. Word was going around Monrovia that Krahns were taking refuge at the Barclay Training Center downtown; it was being guarded by scores of soldiers; it was safe. The head nurse offered to take everyone there.

Jacob declined without hesitating.

'I was with Azariah Sirleaf and Sirleaf is a Mandingo name,' he says. 'They would have killed him at BTC.'

He does not seem to deem this information important. He throws it out hurriedly, and only to dispose of one of my questions: I had asked how he and Azariah ended up in the clinic alone. But for me, a person trying to make sense of a life from the stories I am told, it is very important. It is one of two moments that allow me to account for the course Jacob took in the coming years. The first is his imperative never again to become invisible, to ensure that the party he throws never ends. The second cuts against the grain of the first, agitating it, complicating it. It is this spontaneous, unreasoned decision to remain in the clinic with Azariah. Despite his belief that when you go down, everyone forgets you, that in the last instance you are alone, he carries Azariah inside him, implicitly, unreflectively: it is given on this morning that with Azariah he will live or die.

They were alone now in the clinic. The others had gone.

What they saw from the balcony, as Butt-Naked's soldiers moved through the neighbourhood, was grotesque, Jacob tells me, unspeakable.

'They were just burning houses, burning houses, right next to the hospital, allegedly because they were Congo houses. They would set fire to the house, people would run out, and Butt-Naked's soldiers would kill them. We saw that live.

'We saw a human leg, in a military boot, a guy was drinking blood from the boot, sucking the blood.' He tilts his head to the sky and drinks from an imaginary boot, his lips pursed, imitating the noise of a person sucking. It sounds like a hiss. 'They cut the boot off him with the leg still in it. And these guys, Butt-Naked's soldiers, were nude, and some of them were women. We saw nude women. Nude men. They were drinking liquor too, breaking into the liquor store. They drove a Suzuki motorcycle into the store. They broke the store, broke the front of the store and took the liquor.'

He relives some of this as he speaks, something he has studiously avoided until now; his hands are shaking in his lap. When he sees me watching his hands, he shoots me a look of accusation, as if I have caught him out.

'I walked through the valley of darkness that morning,' he says in self-defence.

He and Azariah remember different moments. Jacob, of course, recalls making a plan.

'We knew we were in trouble,' he says. 'We devised a strategy. It was a little clinic. It had about five beds and a surgical room. So, we locked all the doors and went into the surgical room and left the door a little open. It is amazing what you think of in the heat of the moment. Leave the door of our room slightly ajar, and they will assume nobody is there.'

In Azariah's memory, they were already in the surgery, how they got there is unimportant. As they waited for the soldiers to enter the building, Jacob began reciting Psalm 91, the same psalm he had read to Joe, the volatile soldier-boyfriend of his Kissi-speaking protector six years earlier. Among the words Jacob must have spoken to Azariah were these:

> You will not fear the terror of night,
>   nor the arrow that flies by day,
> nor the pestilence that stalks in the darkness,
>   nor the plague that destroys at midday.
>   A thousand may fall at your side,
>   ten thousand at your right hand,
>   but it will not come near you.
>   You will only observe with your eyes
>   and see the punishment of the wicked.

They heard the soldiers break into the clinic. They heard them shooting open the locks on each of the doors. The surgical room, where Jacob and Azariah were sitting dead still, they did not examine;

the open door had fooled them; Jacob's trick had worked. They were leaving the building.

'And then,' Azariah tells me, 'I said: "Jacob, we must go out and show ourselves, because if we don't they are going to burn this house down." He said: "Yes, I agree with that."

'Gentlemen!' Jacob remembers shouting. 'Gentlemen, we are in here.'

'As soon as we opened the door,' Azariah continues, 'a guy we had seen using a GMG gun (a grenade-launching machine gun) burst into the clinic. "What are you doing?" "We are patients." "What happened to your foot?" "Oh, it was a car accident." To Jacob: "What happened to you?" "Oh, it was a motorcycle accident," or something. Because if we had told them the truth, you would not be listening to me now. They would have concluded that we had got shot while fighting them. They would say: "I remember you; you were shooting at me."'

Jacob remembers speaking in Kissi. This had worked before; he felt his confidence growing.

Azariah recalls something else. He told them he was Kpelle. They asked him to prove it.

'One of them,' Azariah recounts, 'had a backpack with a lot of liquor that he'd vandalised from someone's shop. He was boasting: "Oh, see those people lying there in the street; we have killed them."

'It was no joke, if they say they will kill you, they will kill you. So, I said: "You know what, I myself am fed up with this damn thing," excuse my expression. "These damn Congo people come and think they can just take over this town, and those damn Mandingo people. Look, can I take a shot of what you're drinking?"

'He threw me a bottle. I drank. He said: "You can take the whole thing."

So, now, Jacob and Azariah were regarded as friends, or not as enemies, at any rate. They knew that this status could not be relied upon to last, that the drunken ones might change their minds at any minute, that they had to leave. They asked for an ambulance.

'Ambulance busy, my man,' they are told. 'Ambulance damn busy today.'

And so they walked, on their crutches, out into the streets of Monrovia, Azariah having left his passport with his giveaway surname under a carpet at the clinic. They resolved to make their way to Logan Town on Bushrod Island, where Azariah's sister lived.

I have never measured the miles from City Hall to Logan Town, but it is not a distance I would like to walk in Monrovia's heat. Jacob and Azariah were limping on crutches. Jacob had not walked anywhere in eighteen months. Azariah had fresh surgical wounds in the flesh and bone of his foot. They made their way through the bloodiest day of the civil war, through innumerable checkpoints, at each of which they had to dissemble and pose as people they were not. And yet neither seems to remember a single detail of the journey.

Jacob recalls preparing for it.

'What little cash we had, we took,' he says. 'We couldn't hide it in our shoes; our legs were swollen, and we wore slippers. So we made tears in our pants and hid our money there.'

When I press him to remember the journey, he describes it from what seems to me the vantage point of an eyewitness, as if he is watching himself and Azariah from some distance away, perhaps from a height.

'We leaned heavily on our crutches,' he says, 'and we each wore a little backpack on our backs. The rest of our possessions we left behind.'

18

Online

I am at Jacob's apartment on Park Hill Avenue, a week or so after he begins talking to me about April 6. It is a Saturday morning. I am flying to Liberia later that same day, with plans to visit Jacob's village. There is an air of excitement. Jacob's older brother, Ignatius, is there. He gives me $200 with which to buy three bags of rice for the village. He is telling me in carefully chosen words what messages I am to convey, and whom he wishes me to interview with my video camera. He and Jacob want pictures of their father's grave, they tell me, and of their mother's grave; also of the house in which they grew up, the dilapidated old school, the coffee fields, the river on the border with Ivory Coast. And they would like me to bring back to New York a copy of the last extant photograph of their dad.

Jacob is sitting by himself, in a corner, absorbed in a netbook computer he has recently bought. He is debating with himself, aloud, whether to give it me to take to his sister in Monrovia.

'She is studying,' he says. 'She needs it. But does she have the infrastructure for it – online access, electricity? She will just sell it. I know she will sell it.'

Ignatius steps out – he wants, at the last minute, to buy a disposable camera so that his brother in Monrovia can take pictures marking the progress of a special, secret project – leaving Jacob and me alone.

'For the last week,' I say, 'I have been living with the things you have told me. Each time I think about it I am astounded by your persistent exposure to trauma over the years. You are in a small minority of people who have experienced such persistent trauma.'

He nods and smiles to himself, his head buried in the computer. It is a rich, spontaneous smile; he likes what I have said.

I wander through his apartment, stand for a while in the kitchen, and then come and sit next to him on the couch.

'Does your family know what you went through?' I ask.

'No,' he replies. 'I told you: the family was scattered.'

'Yes, but have you never told them?'

'I have never discussed it with anyone.'

'Not even with Jack?' I ask. Jack is a trauma therapist and close friend of Jacob's.

'Not in detail. Not like I spoke into your voice recorder. I do not talk about it.'

He goes back to fiddling with his computer, and we say nothing for a while.

'Everything that happened before that was nothing,' he says finally. 'April 6 was everything. It has shaped me. My family doesn't know because I do not discuss my public life with them.'

I am taken aback. 'Your public life?' I ask. 'This is very much your personal life.'

'My whole public life was shaped by this,' he says, 'by April 6.'

I am left feeling uncomfortable, as if I have just noticed some crossed wires on Jacob's circuit; as if some plugs have been connected to the wrong sockets. Later, sitting on the plane, drifting into sleep, an image of Jacob comes to me: this short brown blur of activity, jabbering, amiable, calculating, never at rest. From the moment '6 April' ends, Jacob is insatiably at work on what he calls his public life: his quest never again to be forgotten.

At first, one cannot see this new trajectory clearly; it is a time of intense warfare, and Jacob is doing what he must to survive. He and Azariah sit out the first period of the April 6 war with a family in Logan Town – they are friends of Azariah's sister's. The two men are receiving no medical attention. They also worry that the hospitality they have been shown will not last. And so they decide to part company and return to their respective families.

'I went to stay with my sister,' Azariah says. 'As for Jacob, he went to stay with his brother on the Old Road.'

Actually, Jacob never got as far as his brother's house. Old Road was many miles from Jacob and Azariah's refuge in Logan Town. And in the wake of 6 April, public transport in the city had ground to a halt. Jacob began the long walk there, but it was not long before he discovered that his injured leg would not take him far. For the first time, he wondered what earthly force had carried him and Azariah from Horatius Brown's clinic.

A little more than a mile into his journey, Jacob crossed paths with an acquaintance, a man called Parker. They fell to talking, and within an hour, Parker had invited Jacob to stay with him.

Encountering Parker would turn out to be a mixed blessing. Parker lived on the fifth floor of a building in Vaitown on the edge of Bushrod Island. His window overlooked one of the two bridges that join Bushrod Island to downtown Monrovia. It was precisely over control of this bridge that the battle for the city was fought. Uncannily, Jacob was once again watching the most brutal episode in the Liberian war at close quarters.

Initially, Parker earned a living pushing marijuana to the people of the inner city on behalf of Nigerian Ecomog soldiers. The soldiers would give him the supplies, and he'd sell them and keep 50 per cent of the profits.

'Parker's Ecomog friend was a lieutenant,' Jacob remembers. 'He came to our place and smoked on the rooftop. He wore his uniform for guys to know not to mess with our place. It was there, from that rooftop, that I saw more horror. Not just once, twice, three times, I saw real cannibalism. Taylor men, Taylor boys, the ones they called the Marines. One afternoon, we heard a commotion. We went up to the roof. They had killed someone and they were taking out his heart. They started sucking it.'

From his vantage point, the war seemed little more than an arena of incessant looting and trading, punctuated by moments of stupendous depravity.

Yet there was something else about the war, something over and above the hunger to loot and the eagerness to maim. It was the visible absence of any sense of self-preservation among the fighters, the sheer carelessness with which they treated their own lives.

'These same boys who would eat the heart,' Jacob says, 'they themselves died like flies. One morning, they would say: "Today, we take Monrovia." They would amass weapons and boys and walk across the bridge, 200, 300 of them, shooting at Johnson's forces. An hour later, they would retreat, and there'd be so many wounded guys in the truck.

'Parker built a business right there, on that bridge, right in the middle of the war. So I was out there selling for him, on my crutches; selling hard liquor, marijuana, right there on the bridge, to survive. What was interesting to me is that these rebels did not disarm. They were willing to fight and die, fight and die. And they were willing to loot so much. They had cars, money, all kinds of valuable things. Parker was providing valuables to them. That was how we lived: a trader and his crippled assistant selling things to these boy soldiers.'

The fighting subsided in yet another stalemate. Charles Taylor had failed once more to take Monrovia. Yet another peace treaty was signed. This one would lead to elections in 1997, and Taylor would win them, overwhelmingly, making him president of Liberia. Some say that Liberians voted for Taylor in large numbers for fear that if he lost the election he would return to war. Yet that is surely not the whole story. On the day he finally returned to Monrovia, having fled Samuel Doe many years earlier, in 1983, Taylor arrived dressed all in white, standing and waving from the back of a jeep, a returning messiah, resurrected. He had a genius for performance, for the display and enactment of power. Many Liberians were, and remain today, seduced.

It was under Charles Taylor's presidency that Jacob began to pay attention to what he calls his public life. He did this ceaselessly, working his way through the filigree of committees, associations, campaigns, fronts and caucuses that comprised Monrovia's notoriously fractious left wing.

'We had several student groups,' he tells me. 'I was Secretary-General of the National Agricultural and Forestry Association. I was the Programme Coordinator of SCOPE. I was . . .'

'What is SCOPE?' I interrupt.

'The Student something for Environmental something. I was on the executive of SIM, the Student Integration Movement. I was very busy.'

He also began a Liberian franchise of Free Teens, the American organisation advocating abstinence among teenagers.

'After a decade of war,' he says, 'if there is anything Liberian kids needed to be taught, it was delayed gratification. Say to boys: "Listen, at age eighty you can still make a woman come. What's the hurry?"'

Yet his Free Teens had neither a budget nor anybody on its board. It was just Jacob and a bunch of volunteers who turned up every day because they were unemployed and had no better way to pass the time. It was an idea in search of a foundation in the real world. Jacob went about building one with whatever material came to hand.

'I had no office,' he recalls. 'One of my friends, a journalist, allowed me to squat in his office. It had an internet connection.'

It was an old dial-up connection; one waited endlessly for a single page to download. But it was one of the only internet connections in the city – much of Monrovia had been left without electricity or telecommunication since the start of the war – and Jacob realised in a flash that he had been given a valuable commodity. He turned up at the homes of some of the most prominent people in Monrovia's left-wing intelligentsia, and lured them to his borrowed office with the promise that they could read whatever they liked online.

One of these people was Dr Nyquor Kargbo, a medical doctor and a veteran political activist.

'The way Jacob got into my home,' Kargbo recalls when I visit him in his adopted New Jersey, 'he came with a young relative of mine, a bit of a dodgy, scheming chap, to be honest. Jacob was tainted by this association, so at first I didn't listen to him. He wrote down the name of his organisation – "Free Teens" – on a piece of paper. To be honest, I think I threw it away.'

Jacob would return to Kargbo's home every morning, without fail, armed always with something to entertain the doctor: sometimes a newspaper article he wanted to discuss, sometimes a thesis on the underpinnings of modern capitalism that he wanted to try out.

'It soon became apparent that he was a very serious young man,' Kargbo says. 'Very astute, full of energy. So many youths at the time were idle or just hustlers. This man was very dedicated, almost obsessive. Here is someone, I thought, who is worth some time and effort.'

And, of course, the availability of Jacob's internet connection in his borrowed office helped a great deal, too. Soon, Kargbo was the chairman of Jacob's board, devoting several hours a week to promoting his work.

Jacob did something else with his internet connection; he joined every electronic mailing list he could and emailed whomever he thought might reply.

'Among the things I joined online,' he says, 'was the global preparations for the Year of the Volunteer. This was 2000. The Year of the Volunteer was to be 2001. Why not? I was involved in numerous organisations and wasn't paid a cent. My staff were all volunteers. If I knew anything, it was about volunteer advocacy.

'All sorts of committees were being formed to prepare for the Year of the Volunteer. I joined many listservs. On one of them I saw an invitation to go to Nigeria: the second regional conference of the International Association of Volunteer Efforts to be held in Abuja. They were advertising grants to go to the conference.

'I applied. I got it. It was a big break for me. $1,000. It was a huge break for me. In advocacy work, I was a peasant. There were many NGOs in Liberia, but most were United Nations organisations. I couldn't get near them. I was a very young man on a pair of crutches.

'I told my brother, Ignatius, that I was going to Nigeria. He didn't believe me. Nor did my sister, Judy. I had put her on the board of Free Teens. The whole board didn't believe me. They said: "You are always going to the board to talk big. You are a big-mouth person. You are not going to Nigeria, or anywhere else."

'It was $1,000: $700 was for the air ticket, $300 was for contingencies. There was big pressure among the volunteers in my organisation to give them all $300. These were very tough times. Nobody had money. People were battling to eat. My office staff came to me, one by one, saying: "This is your time. Let's talk." Somebody offered to sell me a car for $300. I thought I couldn't mortgage my trip for that. I gave my office staff $100, and kept $200 for contingencies.

'It was my first time on a plane. I was sick with flu. Very sick. It was Ghana Airways. It was amazing. I had read about the Wright brothers, about the forces of motion, the theoretical principles governing the laws of motion of an airplane. I had a theoretical education, but no experience. So, it was amazing. We flew from Monrovia to Accra. There was a long, long delay in Accra, then on to Lagos. In Lagos, I met up with other International Volunteer people, and we got on a plane to Abuja. Three planes. It was amazing.'

The conference went very well for Jacob. He presented a two-page paper on the state of volunteer work in Liberia; the field, he said, was wide open; so many people with little to do, so much to be done.

'I was appointed by default as the Liberian representative of the International Association of Volunteer Efforts. They gave me a press kit. One of my duties would be to work with the UN to promote events associated with the International Year of the Volunteer. They gave me a "To Whom it May Concern" letter on their letterhead explaining that I was the Liberian country representative.'

Jacob took the letter, folded it exactly in half, and kept it very, very carefully. It would change his life, ultimately bringing him to America.

'Back from Nigeria with this letter . . . it was a weapon for me. After two days, I went over to the UN Volunteer Programme Office and presented my letter. The whole idea of the International Year of the Volunteer, nobody knew about it in Liberia. The guys at the UN were amazed. I said I am the Liberian representative of this organisation. They thought I must have a lot of people behind me. So they gave me unlimited access to their office. I could use their resources, their computer. That trip to Nigeria was a door opener.

'I was in touch every day with International Volunteers. With some IV members, we started a social entrepreneurial programme in Liberia, started an internet café. I brought my nephews in to learn computers. My friends from Nigeria came over and set up this venture. And they paid the rent for an office on Carey Street in the centre of Monrovia. I had my own office now, my own internet connection. And through IV, I received invitations to go all over the world. I received maybe six invitations to go to America. Every time I applied for a visa, the American embassy said, no, you will stay in America; you'll never come back.'

If Jacob's growing success was bringing him closer and closer to America, it was also nudging him into a zone of grave danger.

By 2000, the year Jacob went to Nigeria, Charles Taylor had been president of Liberia for three years. His time in office had been disappointing. In the decade before coming to power, he had thought of little else but how to wrestle his way to the Executive Mansion in Monrovia. He spent the late 1980s hustling and conniving in one country after the next, had seen the inside of numerous jails, had bargained, betrayed and begged, and finally entered Liberia with 166 fighters and a few weapons. In the 1990s, he had set up a military headquarters in the bush and, attacked Monrovia unsuccessfully three times, financing his endless campaign by dealing with arms smugglers and drugs traffickers and sponsoring a war in neighbouring Sierra Leone.

Now, finally, he had what he wanted. He was in power by virtue of a landslide electoral victory, one that had been endorsed by much of the region and internationally. The world's powers had little interest in Liberia at this moment, and were quite happy to cloak him in respectability. In 1998, he went to France on a state visit. In America, Jimmy Carter was among his most vocal admirers. So was the Reverend Jesse Jackson, President Bill Clinton's special envoy for Africa. Having now connived his way to Monrovia, Taylor had the opportunity to cast off his thuggish past and play the part of national leader and statesman.

And yet, in his years in power, Taylor 'more resembled a street-corner hustler who had become a president than a politician who sometimes uses unscrupulous methods' as the historian, Stephen Ellis, has put it. He dabbled with dodgy black-market traders and entered into the most nefarious of business deals; his allies and friends took pieces of the Liberia's public infrastructure – the corporation responsible for its energy reserves, its ports, its forests – and turned them into personal cash cows. Nor did Taylor make any attempt to accommodate his numerous political and military foes. Instead, he packed the security agencies with his clients and ruthlessly went after any hint of opposition. By 1999, his enemies were in exile, mobilising an army to fight him.

For those in Monrovia's left-wing circles, it was a merciless time. To raise one's voice against Taylor, no matter how meek or reasonable, was to court the prospect of a visit in the night and a stint in a torture chamber. And Monrovia's left wing was hardly reasonable: 'imperialist stooges', 'bloodsucking parasites' and 'neo-colonial lapdogs' were among the names used to describe those who had governed ever since William Tolbert was in power.

During the day, Jacob's International Volunteers office in Carey Street went about its ordinary business. But as night fell, the volunteers would go home, and other people would begin to come: university professors, students, several lawyers and doctors. Anti-Taylor campaign pamphlets were quietly copied; emails to support structures abroad were sent; foreign reporting on the state of Liberia and West Africa would be read and discussed.

'People would meet right at the back of the office, off the street,' Jacob remembers. 'We would all disperse during the day to go about our different business. Aside from running IV, I had to earn money: I was giving extra math lessons to people's kids; I was writing and reading letters on behalf of illiterate people. At night I would come back to the IV office; it had become an epicentre of covert activities against the government.'

A man named Urias Teh Pour was president of the Student Unification Party around the same time. He recalls spending many a night hunched over a computer monitor in Jacob's Carey Street office.

'It was difficult to access the internet at that time,' he tells me when I meet him in Liberia. 'An international panel had just published a report on Taylor's role in the war in Sierra Leone. We read that late at night at Jacob's place, making notes, writing an anonymous pamphlet publicising the findings. Jacob made us laugh. It was a very tense time. He always broke the tension. We were afraid for him, running that office. You yourself, you didn't want to hang out there for long; you got scared.'

Like every other activist from that time, Urias's memories of Jacob are drawn to his ruined leg.

'In Liberia,' Urias tells me, 'people have an obsession with physical condition. Jacob's handicap: most people like that, they would have skulked away somewhere to be alone. Jacob, no: always friendly, always charming, always throwing his sense of humour out there.'

Others saw Jacob's incessant laughter as a joker's mask concealing a man tormented by his deformed body. Alaric Tokpa was a political scientist at the University of Liberia at the time, and one of Jacob's political mentors.

'He and I never really discussed emotional issues,' Topka says when I meet him in Monrovia, 'but I know that his leg was bothering him. He craved normality. He was experiencing deep pain, spiritually, emotionally. He wanted to be a normal man.'

* * *

When I talk to Jacob about this time, he has only one thought on his mind: the inexorable force taking him to America.

'The letter I had been given in Nigeria by the International Volunteers,' Jacob tells me, 'I sent copies to every embassy and consulate in Monrovia, asking for an audience. I think I sent that letter to the American embassy two or three times. I did not receive a reply. Then, one day, a message comes: the ambassador will see you.

'This black car arrives at the office in Carey Street to fetch me. I had prepared my credentials, including a copy of an article from that morning's newspaper that had quoted me talking about the use of children in the military. The ambassador's name was Bismarck Myrick, a black guy, elderly guy. I took some of my staff with me. I said: "Ambassador, I have not come to ask for money." He said: "What can I do for you?" I said: "I have tried to get a visa to go to the States to raise money; my visa has been denied again and again. I want you to reverse that. We need to go to the US to raise support." He said: "Is that all you want?"

'Two days later, I got a letter. Went to my hearing. Boom, boom, boom. They gave me an open visa.

'So, that's how I got to America the first time. It was a speaking trip, primarily in Florida and New Jersey. I was to go from high school to high school, talking to young Americans of the plight of Liberian youth. I brought bush meat with me. Monkey meat. It was confiscated at the airport. They said: "Are you kidding? You think you're going to walk into the United States with *this*?"'

Like most Liberians, Jacob had spent much of his life imagining America. But nothing had prepared him for what he would feel. Coming from the airport, absorbing the world outside the car window: in a flash, he took in the sweep of Liberia's past.

'The roads, the telecommunications infrastructure, the level of human development, the level of political development: it reinforced my belief that the Americo-Liberians had used Liberia as edheir farm, their dumping ground, their pet project. They had their homes here in America. They schooled their children here, went to hospital here when they were sick. I lost all respect for the Americo-Liberians; for all those years, sending their children overseas and leaving us in the dark.'

Of course, these were things he already knew, things he had learned as far back as high school. But it is one thing learning of these matters in the abstract, sitting behind a school desk in Nimba County. It is another *seeing* it, reflected in the mouth-dropping sights of the New York skyline, of Miami.

'I went back home carrying this anger,' Jacob recalls. 'Seeing America diminished my respect for Taylor even more. After all these years of the Congos putting us down, history had handed him an enormous responsibility: to actually develop Liberia and its people, for the first time. Instead, he behaved like a common thief and a thug. I held him in deep contempt.

'And it also made me ask: who are the Congos? It is a philosophy perpetuated by those who believe they are superior to other Liberians, because they have certain names. All the property in central Monrovia is owned by thirty Congo families. The government keeps paying them rent for the buildings it occupies. Some of them don't work; they go around collecting rent. And they have the audacity to call us uncivilised.'

And then the past slams shut. About what happened when he returned to Liberia, he does not speak easily. His memories of this time are vivid flashes, like photographs taken in the night, each disconnected from the next. I turn to others in an attempt to find an ordered narrative.

'Sometime in late 2001,' Urias Teh Pour recalls, 'we had a campaign at the University of Monrovia. A very brave journalist from a publication called *The News* had written a piece that had gotten him into trouble. His article pointed out that civil servants had not been paid in seven months. It also pointed out that the regime had just spent $150,000 on repairing a helicopter being used to fight LURD, the rebels fighting to overthrow Taylor. Why are they spending money on war when they cannot pay their civil servants? he asked. He was arrested for writing that piece. We organised a mass rally on campus to come to his defence.

'On the day of the rally, Taylor's Anti-Terrorist Unit invaded the campus. Scores of students were injured. A warrant was issued for my arrest, as well as for several other student leaders.

'We had to leave Liberia fast. There were sixteen of us. We moved through the bush for six days, making our way to Ivory Coast. We had to go a very circuitous route, avoiding Bong and Nimba, since these were Taylor strongholds. Eventually, we ended up in Accra, where we met with many other Liberian exiles, including the current president, Ellen Johnson-Sirleaf.

'When we arrived in Accra, Jacob was already there. Apparently, he had been warned that government security people were looking for him and he had packed a bag and fled. He was very good to us. We were in a bad way. Taylor had connections in the Ghanaian state. An agency called the National Bureau of Investigation had detained us for twenty-four hours when we arrived. We were scared they would come and get us again and take us back to Taylor. We didn't want to stay in Buduburam, the refugee camp for Liberians, in case Taylor's people found us there. Jacob was staying in a hotel in Accra, through his connections with the International Volunteers, I think.

'I remember, at one time, we were very scared for our safety. We really needed to sleep in Jacob's hotel room. The hotel management said no way. And then Jacob charmed the management. I watched him do it. He said: "I cannot sleep alone. The things that have happened to me, to us, to all of us poor Liberians. We must sleep together." There was no way they could say no to him.

'At some point, a man called Rufus Naufille came looking for Jacob. He was somebody who knew what was going on in Monrovia. He had come to warn Jacob not to go back to Liberia. He knew something.

'And that was the last time I laid eyes on Jacob. Next thing, he was emailing me from America. Then I lost touch with him. We stopped emailing. I only returned to Liberia in 2004. He was long gone by then.'

What Urias did not know – for Jacob would not talk of it at all for several years – is that in the days prior to his arrival in Ghana, he had been detained for three days and serially tortured by Charles Taylor's security personnel. About what happened to him when he was detained he will speak only obliquely, and in the most formal language.

'It became very risky for me to stay,' he explains of his leaving. 'They accused me of espionage against the government. They wanted a copy of speeches I had made. There had been extracts of my speeches in the newspapers. Some of the remarks I made . . . They held me to account.' This is the odd phrase he uses to describe what happened to him when he was taken in.

'A distant uncle of mine was deputy chief of staff for Charles Taylor. After my encounter with the government, I was freed after three days. My uncle came to me and said: "Son, you gotta go. Don't stay here." So even though he was part of the bad regime . . . he took pity. He let me know that I must leave.

'I flew to Ghana. I was there for three months. That is when I met Urias and his comrades. The International Foundation for the Defence of Human Rights Defenders in Ireland paid for my plane ticket out of Liberia and funded me staying in Ghana. I raised money from friends to go to America. I arrived at JFK in February 2002.'

By October, he would be living on Park Hill Avenue in Staten Island, New York, volunteering at a centre established to assist Liberian youths make the transition from warfare to America. The centre's founder and executive director was Rufus Arkoi.

PART THREE

19

Tailor

I remember quite clearly the moment I first listened to an episode from Rufus Arkoi's story. Not the familiar tale that he told to whomever came to see him in New York – of the street corner gangsters he recruited into his sports club, or the child soldiers he turned into soccer players – but *his own* story.

We were sitting together in his centre one winter's evening speaking of nothing in particular. The children were filling in the big square blocks of a puzzle, while the old folk were practising their alphabet.

'Did I tell you that I was a tailor in Liberia?' Rufus asked, apropos of nothing at all. 'I *sew* real well. I sew *real* well.'

He tugged at his sleeve. 'This tracksuit top: I could make one as good as this. Put on a zipper. Finish it off. No different from the one in the store. In Liberia, it was a business. I was *nineteen . . . years . . . old . . .* and I was making kits for the national soccer team, for the national basketball team. I was making *money*. A *lot* of money.'

Tailoring came up once more a few weeks later. We were in the middle of a formal interview. I had put on my voice recorder and asked him to speak of his childhood in Liberia.

He was talking of soccer, of how his youth was soccer, soccer, soccer, and I asked him whether he was a goal scorer.

'No,' he replied. 'Scoring was not one of the things I looked forward to in playing. I made plays. I supported the forwards, the main feeder connecting the goalie and the defenders to the forwards. I made a lot of goals, a lot of goals. I was an entertaining human being.'

He had slid, quite seamlessly, between one's quality as a soccer player and one's quality as a person, and as I noted this to myself, he began telling me of his big injury.

'It was in 1979. I was still in high school. The injury lasted for a year and a half. My knee. I was practising for a game with a rival Catholic school. The field we were practising on was very bad. I was looking for a ball in the air. My leg went into water. My whole knee was twisted. From the erosion in the field.

'That was the end of playing for me. When I eventually went back, I was so scared. I didn't want a collision. I didn't want my knee to be touched. It wasn't properly healed.'

'Is that when you went to tailoring school?' I asked.

'No. Oh no. I went to tailoring school when I was eleven years old. I graduated when I was fourteen. I graduated from designing school at the age of *fourteen*; I could make a *suit*.'

'What took you to tailoring school at that age?' I asked.

He shifted in his seat, throwing his shoulder into the story. He must have been telling it for the umpteenth time, but the satisfaction in his face suggested that it was as fresh as it ever had been.

'My father, you know, he was a funny guy. He didn't know how to handle me: how to handle my *explosion*. I just grew very, you know, *ambitious*. At age ten, eleven, I mean.

'Put it like this. The principal walked in and told my father to keep me at home for a while. I was just too *smart*. They couldn't *deal* with me. I mean, I was not *normal*, I was above normal growing up. Every year, people get one promotion, I had to get double promotion. I didn't go to second grade or fourth grade. Principal said, "No! Stop him! Where is he going?"

'My father was looking around for something to *contain* me, something to *slow me down*. Something is not right with this boy. Let me slow him by challenging him to sew. So, he sent me to an old guy, an old tailor, and bought me a brand new machine, at the age of eleven.

'Old guy said: "What are you bringing . . . ?"

'My father said: "Look, this guy is all over the place; he's doing all kinds of stuff. I want to get him busy."

'At twelve and a half, thirteen, I became the primary helper of this old guy. I increased his production over 200 per cent. I increased his income. This old guy, relying on this thirteen-year-old to hem skirts, to press clothes, to put on buttons.'

'You did all this after school?' I asked.

'All after school hours. I got home at one-thirty, had to be in the shop by two o'clock. Stayed in the shop 'til five, five-thirty. Soccer went on between five and seven. So between two and five I focus on that. Then I'd say to the old man: "I need to go and play soccer."

'He'd say: "Your father don't want you to play too much soccer."

'I say: "I need to go play."

'He say: "Listen, go play, make sure you back by seven, so we can lock up the shop."'

People began walking into Rufus's centre, and it became rude to continue. I switched off the voice recorder, and we started talking of other things. Some time later in the evening, I mentioned Rufus's tailoring in passing. He frowned and grew distracted, and a niggling expression came over his face, as if the way I was speaking of his story demonstrated that I hadn't understood its significance.

'The design for the soccer kit,' he said, 'it came to me in a dream. The old man and I had been thinking, thinking, thinking, for days on end. How do you *do* this? There was no one to *guide* us, no design to *copy*. You know, the neck, the V-line; it is so hard to make it so that it doesn't wrinkle. Some use an iron to hide the crinkle. But you can see that immediately. And then it came to me in my *sleep*, how to do it. The whole thing, the neck, the sleeves. I woke up. I went straight to the workshop. It's working! It's working! The next day, I show the old man a *soccer kit*.

'He says: "Who taught you this?"

'No. It came in a *dream*.'

He sat back in his chair and looked at me, and I nodded and smiled, and now his brow creased in frustration. I still didn't get it.

He stood up, as if the weight of his point required him to throw his entire body into it, and as he spoke, he gesticulated with arms scooped in front of him.

'This was *Liberia*. Nobody had ever made a soccer kit in the whole *country*. Always, since the beginning, our kits had to be *imported*. There was no *precedent*. There was nobody to go to and *ask*. That is why I became *rich*.'

Rufus's childhood began in Bomi Hills, a town some forty miles north of Monrovia. That is where he was living when his father, Joseph Arkoi, sent him to the old man to learn to sew, and where he began playing soccer. Joseph Arkoi was a Loma-speaking indigenous Liberian and a blue-collar man: he was a driver, employed at a hospital, which, along with practically every other institution in the town, was owned by the Liberian Mining Company, the country's first exporter of iron ore. The company paid very well by the standards of Liberian blue-collar labour, its employees constituting something of a privileged guild. Joseph Arkoi's success would show in the size of his family − he would come to have fourteen children, borne by several wives − and in the fact that he would save enough money for one of these children to attend an elite Catholic school.

When Rufus was fourteen, the Liberian Mining Company closed down, and much of Bomi Hills with it. Arkoi senior began the monumental task of relocating his family to Monrovia. Rufus was among the first Arkois to go: he was sent to live with his older brother in a house the family was building, and to attend St Patrick's School, among the best in Monrovia. Why Joseph chose Rufus for this privilege, Rufus says he does not know. The house into which the Arkoi family would move was in area where not a single other child went to a private school: it stood on Twelfth Street in the suburb of Sinkor.

Were two Monrovians to meet on the street and fall to talking some time in the 1970s, and were one to remark that he lived in Sinkor, the other would immediately know, on the basis of his interlocutor's speech and dress, on which side of William V. S. Tubman Boulevard he lived: coastside, or landside. The piece of Sinkor that fell between Tubman Boulevard and the sea was wealthy. Today, decades of war have scrambled the city's social geography, and coastside is no longer universally rich. But you can see from its architecture what it once was: the houses set far back from the road, high walls, the remnants of ornate gardens; one imagines homes full of heirlooms and the portraits of dead patriarchs.

Landside was another world. It was inhabited primarily by country people, rather than by Americo-Liberians, people of modest means. Yet it was also sought after, for in the middle of landside, on Twelfth Street, was William V. S. Tubman High School, among the few public schools in Monrovia reputed to be very good. Tubman High would educate several of the men who went on to topple the country's last Americo-Liberian government. It is also the alma mater of Jacob Massaquoi's older brother, Ignatius, who would have undoubtedly passed Rufus on the street from time to time.

A visitor walking along Twelfth Street, his back to the coast, soon passes the buildings of Tubman High. Whatever the time of year, it is hot, 90 degrees on a mild day, and the sunlight is stark and punishing. A block or so later, the road narrows without warning and becomes a pedestrian passageway. Today it is lined with market stalls at which hawkers sell potato greens, fresh chilli and fish; when Rufus first saw it, it was empty. Some fifty or so paces on, the passageway breaks into several forks, and the visitor suddenly finds that he is in a labyrinth, the houses built close together and on the very verges of the paths. The labyrinth seems to shut behind you as you walk. The rest of Sinkor is gone, the harsh sunlight is muted, and you sense that you are in another place now, with its own damp smells and echoing voices. This is where Rufus lived.

To understand how this labyrinth came to be, you must keep walking. For once you come out the other side you are suddenly in marshland, the mangrove-like reeds chest-high, the squelching of mud underfoot. Sinkor is a very old settlement: the Vai people lived here long before the Americo-Liberians arrived. But in all its history, nobody bothered to build on this particular piece of land close to the marsh.

This was how the Twelfth Street labyrinth came to be. Nobody else wanted it. And so, in the mid-1970s, poor people migrating from the countryside to Monrovia began to put up houses there. The government gave up the land for nothing.

The Arkois seem to have forgotten how Rufus's father came to hear of the Sinkor marshland. They remember only that he sent his wife's younger brother to Monrovia to occupy a piece of ground and begin construction. The brother-in-law's name was Joseph Waifalla Saykor, and I interviewed him eight days before his death, a gaunt, wheezing, visibly ailing man who wore only a pair of shorts, and sat on a bench in the shadow of the house he had built.

'This was a free place,' he told me, 'a government place, not a private place. We never bought it. The thing you had to do is, you had to put something down so that another family would not take the piece of land you had chosen. So we put up a shack, and we slowly built the house around the shack, little by little.'

People from across Liberia built on this marshland, and it became a truly cosmopolitan place, one of many languages and ethnicities. A family from Ghana even came here: the Frederickses. They built a house right in the middle of the marsh, on an island one approaches on a rickety bridge, the sludge not far beneath one's feet. The island became known as Fredericks' Island, and the old matriarch who built the place with her husband still lives there. Rufus was to grow very close to her sons.

When I interviewed the dying Saykor, he had, resting on his lap, two photographs, each in an ancient frame. The first was a portrait of himself as a young man, his face very strong, his eyes boring into the camera lens with a look that bordered on ferocity. The other was a group photograph of the administrators of a soccer team.

A group portrait of Roza's officials taken in Monrovia in June 1983 on the occasion of the club's second anniversary. Rufus is second from left in the back row.

'Can you tell me which is Rufus?' he asked, smiling weakly.

He was instantly recognisable – half his current size, to be sure, his leanness and narrowness something of shock when one considers how much he now invests in his heft – but the eyes, the strong curve in the upper lip, were Rufus through and through.

Saykor took me into the house. A dark corridor bisected it, four rooms on either side. Each, I imagined, had housed a son or a daughter together with an entire nuclear family; the house's architect had squeezed in as many spaces of privacy as its confines would allow. It had about it the air of a place that had once thrived, but had long fallen into disrepair. The ceiling was grey and rotting and missing in places, and the walls had clearly not seen a coat of paint in many years.

At the end of the house, the corridor opened into a room, the only one almost as wide as the building itself.

'This was Rufus's sewing room,' Saykor said, almost with reverence. He paused, looked around, took the place in. 'Rufus sat *here*, his machine on *this* table. Ben Fredericks sat *here*, and his brother sat *here*, and his cousin Frederick Richardson sat *here*. You see, whoever wanted to find Rufus knew he would be here. And the boys came. Rufus was a magnet. People wanted to be around him. By being with him, they learned to sew. And when they learned to sew, their lives changed.'

As I lingered around Twelfth Street over the following days, the meaning of Rufus's sewing slowly came into view. A great deal had changed because of the war; most of the people one met on the street had not lived here for more than a few years, and the name Rufus Arkoi meant nothing to them. But everyone who had been here in the 1970s knew of him. Even people in their early twenties, born at the time Rufus left for the United States: if their parents had come of age on Twelfth Street, then they had heard of Rufus Arkoi. 'Wasn't he a tailor?' a young writer called Aaron Weah asked me. Aaron had just told me that he grew up on Twelfth Street, and I immediately asked if he knew of Rufus. 'Wasn't he a tailor and the owner of a soccer club? I heard his name a lot when I was small.'

The boys in the Twelfth Street labyrinth were poor, the sons of outsiders who had built homes on a marsh in a city whose wealth they could not access. The boys came to Rufus while he sewed, through his friendship they learned to sew, too, and from sewing they began to inhabit improbable futures.

'George Fredericks became a tailor and taught tailoring at Don Bosco Polytechnic,' Saykor told me, counting off his long fingers the ghosts of those who had occupied Rufus's sewing room. 'Kpada went to Nigeria and sewed for a living there. Jesse Cooper prospered as a tailor. They all made a living in this line.'

At his centre in Staten Island, surrounded by his unruly toddlers and his ageing students, Rufus had spoken of his sewing as if he were a conjuror of magic. I had felt a twinge of embarrassment, wondering whether he was making himself foolish. But there are people on Twelfth Street who think of his sewing room as a magical place for a bunch of boys gathered there in the afternoons after school, who each walked out with a career.

20

Roza

The bare bones of Rufus's soccer story are simple in the telling. It was the beginning of 1980, he was seventeen years old, had just finished high school. There were many soccer clubs in his section of Monrovia. One of them approached him to be their president.

'Why they brought me in?' Rufus asks. 'Being a tailor at a young age, I made lots of suits for myself. I dressed *well* as a young boy. I dressed very, very well. That was appealing to people.'

In my mind, I see the young Rufus swaggering out of the labyrinth into the blunt sunlight on Twelfth Street, a bowler hat low on his brow, a good suit tailored close to his lean frame. His nonchalance is studied, but out of the corner of his eye he watches surreptitiously for the heads he has turned. 'Who *is* that man?' he imagines people wondering.

'So this team brought me in,' he continues. 'That was a development I will never be able to measure in my life. What it did for me is immeasurable.'

The team was called the Eleven Eagles. It was a junior team, the players in their mid to late teens.

'There was always a problem with space in Sinkor,' Rufus recalls. 'Many, many teams, not enough fields. As a junior team, we always lost out. When the older guys were playing you couldn't play. And the older guys were *always* playing. You must either play very early, or very late.'

And so a familiarly heroic tale begins. Scratching out time and space in the margins of Sinkor soccer, the Eleven Eagles grew very disciplined and very good. For a year, they nurtured their growing talent, unseen, unnoticed. And then, out of nowhere, they spring:

picking on the very best of the older teams, the Massive Invincible Eleven, and challenging them to a duel.

'The game was set down for a holiday,' Rufus says. 'I haven't got involved in a soccer game like that ever again in my life. On that day, if you were a criminal, you could walk into Sinkor and take what you like. You could walk into anyone's home. The town was empty. Everyone was at the game. There had never been a game so emotional on the Tubman field on Twelfth Street. My side won 2–1; we won 2–1.'

And so Rufus tasted glory twice on Twelfth Street, first as a tailor, then as the president of a soccer club. He had become a young man associated with the audacious, the sort in whose trail others wished to walk. But there was trouble ahead.

'This was 1981,' Rufus continued. 'There was a tendency at the time for people to overthrow government. Everywhere: in school, in the soccer clubs. Because a year earlier, people had seen the government of Liberia overthrown.

'A young man set up a coup against me in Eleven Eagles in May 1981. So, I got the news: "Rufus, you have been overthrown." I was very wounded. I was too wounded to fight back. I said: "Fine, I'm sick and tired of this."

'A group of guys from the club got together. They said: "Rufus, you must fight this coup. Look, you built the team from nothing. We were nowhere before you came."

'I said: "Yeah, but this is a revolution. I have to go."

'So these guys around me said: "Rufus, if you go, we are not staying." They said: "Why don't you form your own team?"

'I said: "Are you serious?"

'They said: "If you don't do it, no one will do it."

'We started throwing out names for our new club. We threw out all sorts of names. One of them was Roza, the initials of my name: Rufus O Zumo Arkoi. Everyone was: "*Yeah*. It sounds like a soccer team. *Roza*."

'On 9 June 1981 we founded Roza. 80 per cent of the guys from the Eleven Eagles came on. I sewed the uniform. We started playing games. We played our first eleven games undefeated.'

Rufus has left out what is surely the most important part of the story. He could have a club named after him because he could pay for its upkeep, and he could pay for its upkeep because of his success as a tailor. Already, from his earliest days, he was turning the magic he sewed in his father's front room into a public legacy, an institution that would bear his name and refigure the world in some way.

Sinkor had only two soccer fields and no system, no co-ordination among the several dozen teams who played there. The president of Roza would meet the president of Executive Eleven on the street, and agree to play at 4 p.m. on Sunday at Tubman High. The two teams would assemble at the venue, only to find that five other matches were scheduled for the same time on the same field.

'Nobody ended up playing,' Rufus recalled, 'because nobody had a right to the field. After the second time this happened to us, I said: "Listen, we can't allow this to go on: we need a broader organisation." This was the beginning of 1982. I said: "We all need to come together to communicate who will play on the field when."

'We formed the Sinkor United Sports Organisation, Susa. It is still in existence today. It covered the area from the border of Congo Town to the German embassy. Within that area, you had more than fifty soccer teams: fifty teams that thousands of young men looked up to. We broke the teams down into divisions, into leagues. The excitement that this new form of competition created throughout Sinkor: you walked down the street, it was the *only* thing people were talking about. "Eagles are a point behind Roza, and playing them at 3 p.m. tomorrow. Wow! Wow!" Sinkor had never known something like this.

'News got around. Other parts of Monrovia wanted the same excitement. The model was the first of its kind in the Liberian Football Association's history. People saw the model. Said: this is gen-i-u-s. The association came to see me. How did he build? How did he? How? They took the model away and implemented it in other areas.'

And there the story might have ended, were it not for the fact that Samuel K. Doe's People's Redemption Council had at this stage been governing Liberia for more than a year. By now, Doe was dimly aware that he could not run Liberia as a united nation. And he was acutely aware that he trusted nobody enough to run it for him. What he could do, though, undeniably and with great accomplishment, was play soccer.

Long before his name became known throughout the rest of the country, Doe was an accomplished soccer player in his home county, Grand Gedeh, a goal maker like Rufus, as skilled with his left boot as with his right. Doe knew that young men across Liberia were mesmerised by soccer, and that the Congo elite had always looked down upon it, encouraging its own young men to play American basketball. The very spectacle of a soccer player governing the country was perhaps the most convincing evidence available that the old regime was dead. And so, improbably, Doe at times fancied that he might govern Liberia through soccer. Under his rule, the boundary between soccer and politics, indeed, between soccer and the world, began to blur.

To be fair, the old regime had dipped a cautious toe into the world of soccer, but in a manner that only pronounced its distaste. In the 1950s, when President William Tubman was accruing clients and allies among indigenous chiefs, there was much talk of building a united Liberian nation. The statues depicting the founding of Liberia no longer showed black American discoverers hoisting a flag over a landscape won by conquest. Instead, a man in a morning coat shakes hands with a man clad in a loin cloth, their meeting taking place under the aegis of a priest. The two parties appear to be equals.

In much the same spirit, Tubman began taking an interest in soccer. He began to invest lavishly in Liberia's only Americo-Liberian team, the Invincible Eleven, or, simply, IE – founded in the 1940s in Monrovia's elite high school, the College of West Africa, where Azariah Sirleaf would study – and charged it with the task of thumping the indigenes soundly. Educated indigenous Liberians involved in radical politics supported Mighty Barolle. The other sides in the national league were little more than fill-ins: Firestone ran a team, and each county mustered together a side. But the significant rivalry was between IE and Barolle. The elite supported the former, those who wanted to overthrow the elite supported the latter, and when the two sides clashed, the stadium was filled with thoughts of treason.

On an afternoon in early November 2008, I met a man who had watched Doe govern Liberia from close quarters. His name is Reverend Emmanuel Bowier. Doe appointed him Deputy Information Minister a few weeks after coming to power. By virtue of serial feats of expedience and wiliness, Bowier managed to remain in Doe's cabinet almost until its end. It was only in 1989 that he fell out of Doe's favour and repaired hastily across the border, an execution warrant following not far behind.

'It is hard to describe the transformation of the meaning of soccer from the day Doe came to power,' Bowier told me. 'Under the old regime, it remained a poor boys' game with nowhere to go, a game of the street. With Doe, soccer is suddenly touched with the magic of state power. The big teams are now transported to their matches in the presidential Cadillac. The Liberian national team, the Lone Stars, get a foreign coach. And when they have a home game, there is a national holiday. Nobody goes to work.

'Before, there was no money in soccer. Now, Doe builds a housing estate for the national team. And the Liberian Football Association, before, it was run on a shoestring. Now, Doe throws a million dollars at it. All of a sudden, to be a soccer administrator is a very big deal. There are several very powerful men in this country who rose because they happened to be in soccer administration in 1980.'

It was more than simply a question of elevating soccer. The sport became personally connected to the president in ways that were almost mystical.

'Say a big game was coming up,' I was told by a man named Barent Karr, who has been playing and coaching neighbourhood soccer in Sinkor since the 1970s, 'a clash, say, between IE and Barolle. And say that on the eve of the game, one of the star players is injured. It is imperative that the president be informed. A presidential car comes to the player's house to take him to Executive Mansion. Doe receives him, and asks to see the injury. Then he puts the player's injured leg on his lap – to give him courage and inspiration, to heal him.

'It was impossible for a big game to kick off if President Doe had not yet arrived at the stadium,' Karr continued. 'If the president was late, the game must wait. It was as if soccer was only made possible by the fact that the president watched it.'

By the end of 1985, after he had brutally put down the Quiwonkpa coup, effectively turning the populations of entire counties into permanent enemies, Doe surely realised that he was incapable of ever running Liberia peaceably. Tubman's political accomplishment was to have centralised power in his office. Doe could only imagine what that must feel like. Inside and outside his government were growing centres of power he could neither control nor trust, and whose workings were increasingly opaque to him. According to Bowier, soccer became his refuge.

'It became a way for him to escape the realities of power,' Bowier told me. 'It allowed him to relax. Until he finally joined the Freemasons in 1988, soccer was really his only contact with Liberians outside his own ethnic group. It was a non-security issue. It was non-threatening.'

Perhaps it was in fact less of a refuge from, than a substitute for, the exercise of power. The things Doe began doing with soccer smack of panic, of unseemly urgency. He genuinely seems to have confused the business of political governance with sport.

'Every cabinet minister and his wife had to support a soccer team,' Bowier said. 'That meant you had to put down what you were doing and attend all of their games. Never mind that you are abroad on government business. You make sure you are back in Liberia when your team is playing. If Doe sees that you are only pretending, that your interest in sport is fake, your political career is finished.

'Go and speak to a man called Peter Jallah,' he continued, warming to the theme. 'He was Doe's Minister of National Security. There came a point when Doe could not watch a football match without Peter being present. Wherever Peter was, Doe's jet would come to fetch him.'

'What about you?' I asked Bowier. 'Did you have to show Doe that you were serious about sport?'

'It was very difficult,' he replied, 'because I really didn't care for it at all. Once, I arrived at my office to find an instruction from Doe that I must go that very day to a sports shop on Carey Street and buy a Mighty Barolle uniform. The instruction said I must put on that uniform, and report for football practice that very evening.'

'What happened?' I asked.

'I was a clown on the football field! I was useless! I was sent home after ten minutes.'

Improbably, Rufus is reluctant to admit any connection between his dream on Twelfth Street and Doe's Liberia. When I asked him what the end of Americo-Liberian rule meant to him, he replied blandly that he had no truck with politics.

'Many of the boys on Twelfth Street attended Tubman High and they were very into politics,' he told me. 'They were *consumed* by politics. But me? Truth of the matter? Coups, political instability: it didn't affect me, as long as it didn't interfere with soccer. I sewed and I played soccer. That is all.'

'But there is surely more to say than that,' I pressed on. 'This was the most significant thing to happen in Liberia in more than a century. What did it mean to you that indigenous Liberians were in power?'

He paused for a long time, reluctant to answer. 'What did it mean to me?' he finally replied. 'Having an indigenous person in the leadership? It gave me hope that I would have a better future in Liberia. Before Doe, I couldn't imagine my generation ever reaching leadership at its highest level. Now, we all felt we had an opportunity. Government was no longer remote. The officials, some came from my neighbourhood. Young guys, almost all of them very interested in soccer. You could call any of them, invite them to come and see your programme. You felt at ease. I thought to myself: "You know what: I can be this, I can be that."'

For a man who likes to paint his world in flamboyant colours, he has presented a strangely muted picture. In truth, Doe's ascent to power appeared to have blasted a corridor between Twelfth Street and national fame.

When I finally visited Monrovia with Rufus, and he walked down the streets of his youth for the first time in years, he could no longer curb his inhibitions, and his memories of the early Doe years spilled out of him.

'This is where Moses Bapi lived,' he said excitedly as we walked away from Twelfth Street one evening. 'He was in charge of Doe's security. The last secret meeting they had before they carried out the coup, it was held *here*. Twelfth Street was a big street, a big political street, Doe himself came here. It was about one in the morning, the dead of night. He drove in here in a white Honda. He was driving himself. He was here to pick up Bapi.'

One day unacknowledged and invisible, the next day Twelfth Street was touched by power; some of the most elevated men in

Liberia were pedestrians on its streets. And this magical rise from nothing was inseparable from soccer. To play on a Sinkor field in 1979 was to be going nowhere. The walls surrounding your world were high, your vantage point utterly closed. By 1982, that wall appeared to have vanished, and you could imagine that you could see forever. The soccer in your neighbourhood was now organised and serious. Important people took Saturday afternoons off to come and watch you play. If you were talented, if you shone, there were scouts watching closely, scouts employed by the famous teams that populated the national league. In a year, in two years, you could become a household name.

This is what happened to some of the boys who played in the leagues Rufus had helped to found. They became wealthy. They became famous. People saw it happen to boys they had known all their lives. And Roza was one of the best teams in Sinkor. To wear one of the jerseys Rufus had sewn was to imagine being inches from glory.

Once a year, all the teams in Sinkor competed against one another in a two-day tournament dubbed the 'Olympics'. For the duration of the tournament, teams could field guest players from other parts of Monrovia. In 1982, a Sinkor club called the Green Eagles fielded a sixteen-year-old guest player from Claretown, a poor neighbourhood at the other end of Monrovia. The boy was dazzling. When he returned the following year, much of Sinkor turned out to watch him play. His name was George Weah. Before his career was through, there would not be a soccer fan on the planet who had not heard his name.

A decade and a half later, when Weah ran for president, he stood up on platforms and told his young supporters of soccer in Monrovia before the war. 'I will bring those days back,' he said. 'They will return.'

Across Sinkor, people were dreaming and Rufus was part of this new dream. In the narrow world of Twelfth Street, the name Rufus O Zumo Arkoi became associated with breadth. To spend the afternoons in the front room of his father's house was to learn to sew one's way to riches. To take the field in a jersey he had sewed was to take a step towards greatness.

* * *

And yet, if Twelfth Street was widening, by the mid-1980s Liberia itself was narrowing, the meanness and paranoia of its post-coup politics increasingly evident. I put this to Rufus. 'You are a Loma,' I said. 'By the mid-1980s, Doe was giving positions to Krahn people and no one else. Is that why you left for America?'

'That's not really true,' he replied with a hint of irritation. 'No, that's not true. Yes, Doe was a Krahn man, and Krahn people saw Doe as an opportunity to come into government. And they came. But, Doe . . .' He was palpably annoyed now. My comment had offended him. 'If I had been in Doe's shoes, I would have done the same. Obviously! Obviously knowing the history of Liberia, I would feel very comfortable surrounding myself with my own. Immediately. That's easy. I wouldn't do different from what Doe did. No, I wouldn't do different. Knowing what I know about Liberians. I wouldn't do different.'

'Knowing what about Liberians?'

'That they are hypocrites. They would deceive you so quickly. They come close to you, but secretly they are bringing in their own, until they have critical mass, until they can move you out of the way. So, if I were Doe, I would bring in my own.'

'There is little trust in Liberia,' I comment uselessly.

'Very little.'

'Why?'

'That's how we are as Liberians. Put it like this. Here, a simple place.' He gestures to the room around him, his centre, Roza's space. 'People will see it, and see me being successful. They start building jealousy. That's all.'

'They want to throw you out?'

'Exactly, exactly. So I need to have friends I trust. When I leave, they will protect these computers for me. Even inside Roza. I come to meetings every day with others, they come out of the meeting and they say many negative things about what we're doing here, and stop others from joining the club. Yet they come back and have more meetings with me.'

'What is it about Liberia that produces the suspicion and the jealousy?'

'I always say it is because of how our families are structured: one man, four wives, four sets of children, four sets of goals, not one set of family goals. Jealousy among the four sets of children. This mother is only looking at the interests of her children and is wishing that those children from the other mothers do badly in life. That's the family structure. That's the society.'

When he told the story of how his club came to bear his name, he had spoken with uncharacteristic bashfulness, as if it had happened in spite of him, as if it were almost an accident. It was in fact the essence of the matter. He branded the club with his name to caution others from stealing it. Whether you run the government of Liberia or a soccer club on a dirt road, you build a shield of clients and kin and acolytes as hastily as you can. And you must not turn your back on them for long. Whatever is yours is yours to lose.

21

Half a Chicken

And then Rufus left Liberia. Just twenty-four years old, a successful tailor, soccer club owner, guardian of a legacy others would destroy. One Saturday afternoon in September 1986, hours after his team had finished playing a game, he boarded a flight at Robertsfield Airport. He arrived the following morning in New York. He had told almost no one of his plans. In his passport he had just a visitor's visa; in his pocket enough cash to last a few months. He had no work prospects, no papers admitting him to a university. All he had was the phone number of a Liberian in Newark, New Jersey; a former Roza player called Dave Jackley, who had beckoned him to come.

It seemed to me an extravagant gamble. The fate of Rufus's beloved Roza now rested upon two uncertain legs: on the competence and trustworthiness of those he had left behind to manage it; and on his earning enough money in America to maintain his team's existence and to keep supporting his family.

Yet for Rufus this was an obvious choice. Through soccer, he had rubbed shoulders with the new elite of Doe's Monrovia. Now he wanted to become one of them. To do that, he had to go to America and come home with a graduate degree. That is how it had always been in Liberia.

I have asked dozens of Liberians what struck them most powerfully on their first day in New York. For some it was a glimpse of the World Trade Center on the bus from JFK; 'It is simply too *tall*,' an elderly woman called Esther Cooper remembered thinking to herself, with a prescience she could not have known. For others it was the notion of a subway system that worked ceaselessly beneath their feet, carrying people across the city all day and night.

For Rufus, it was a piece of chicken.

'I had to wait at JFK a long time before I could get a ride to Newark,' Rufus recalls. 'About six hours, I think. By the time I got to my friend Dave Jackley's place, I was very, very hungry.

'Dave goes to a Chinese store, he comes back with rice and half a chicken, and he puts it down in front of me.

'I stare at it. "That's for me alone?"

'He says: "Yeah, eat."

'I say: "Wow! Now I am in America."

'I was happy. I was happy. Not that I was suffering in Monrovia. I was okay compared to my peers. I was fine, well respected. But to have a half-chicken in front of you, so casually, just like that.

'Dave Jackley worked as a security guard in Elizabeth. Took me to his company, said this is my friend, he wants work. Next thing, I am working. I am *undocumented* at this point. And the job: you just show up. You don't do anything. Day or night. Just show up, sit down, and watch: $290 a week. A lot of free money. You want more money, you work more hours.

'The warehouse I was guarding was on Grafton Avenue, North Newark, right next to the airport. I would time the planes on my watch. Every three minutes a plane landed. Never mind that it's *midnight*. Every three minutes. I just looked at the belly of the plane. It came right over me. Man, this place is *busy*. The *movement*. It never *stops*.'

That $290 a week, he told me when I pressed him on it, was earned largely through overtime: he worked eighty, sometimes ninety hours from Monday through Sunday at $3.30 an hour. And a good quarter of his earnings went straight home to Monrovia, to support his family, and to fuel Roza.

When he wasn't at work, he told me, he was at Dave Jackley's place, watching soccer on TV.

'The commercials made me laugh,' he remembers. 'Old guys being so stupid, dancing and playing the clown, in the name of selling a product. I loved commercials.'

It seems a bleak existence to me: twelve hours of every day idling at an empty warehouse, then going to one's rented room, watching television, sleeping, going back to the warehouse.

And yet for every dozen or so planes that flew over his head on Grafton Avenue, another dollar of hard currency torpedoed in the other direction, across the ocean, to Roza. All he needed to do was sit. And, although, for now, he was doing nothing but watching planes, there were more than a dozen universities in New Jersey alone, compared to just two back home in Liberia, and scattered across the cities on the eastern seaboard were scores and scores of Liberians who had all done it before, and who would show a newcomer without documents how to make it.

'In the history of Liberian people coming here,' Rufus told me, 'the number of people failing was little, too little. Just coming here meant I'd almost made it.'

But made what? I asked him. What would it mean to come home clothed in American success?

'Look,' he replied. 'Living in America, you are on a training basis. Those trained here have a different behaviour, have got a different approach to things, have different moral standards, very different. You put an American-trained person in an office, you get way less corruption. I can't sell my office to you for $100. I have played with much higher value money. You know, things you used to get with $50 you do not get from me; I value myself more than $50. You put people in office who have not been in America, have never played around with US notes, for a little thing, you can just get their office.'

Dave Jackley, the man with whom Rufus shared living quarters, played soccer in a Haitian league. It was a novelty for Rufus, this expatriate soccer geography: a Haitian team from Newark, another from Elizabeth, another from Brooklyn, all in a single league.

Dave took him to a game. He climbed up into the stands, settled down, and watched.

'I don't think I'd ever done that before, you know, just watched from the stands. I had always been involved. I looked around. I was more interested in the crowds than the game. It was the first time I'd watched a football game, really. First time I could sit back and watch the *spectacle* of it.'

But it was not long before he was involved.

'In this league,' Rufus recalled, 'there were Africans playing in all the Haitian teams. I sat there thinking: why must they play in the Haitian teams, why not their own teams? There weren't enough players from each individual country to survive in a competitive league. But all together . . .'

It so happened that, around this time, a team called Club Afrique was assembled, an all-African side that played in the Haitian league. Rufus soon became involved in its management.

'We selected players from all over Africa to make a strong team: Guinean, Liberian, Nigerian. Some were from Maryland. Some were from as far away as Chicago. I was adviser to that team in the late 1980s, manager in the early 1990s, for three years. It was very good soccer, that league. We fielded a competitive team.'

In one another's lives, the players of Club Afrique, all them young African men in America, found mutual recognition.

'There was big pride to being an African,' Rufus recounted. 'We accomplished a lot. We had big, big focus. The connection between here and there. The responsibility to spend on people at home. We had no time to fool around. There was a statistic I heard when I went to college: more African immigrants in this country end up getting degrees than any other immigrants. I was shocked when I heard that.

'Many employers in those days wanted to beat the colour barrier, say, look, I got a black in my firm. Actually, they would have an African. Good on the job, hardworking, submissive. African-American: you gonna be slow on the job, don't care, talk back. We didn't use the phone to call people from work. African-American: you sick, you take two more days' sick leave. We Africans didn't have time to be sick.'

'And now?' I asked. 'Your daughter was born here, and she is black. If she were to marry an African-American, how would you feel?'

He picked up a toothpick lying on the table in front of him, put it in his mouth, rolled it across his lips to the side, then chewed on it thoughtfully.

'Our girls are not attracted to Americans,' he said finally. '98 per cent marry Liberians. Some Ghanaians. A high number marry Jamaicans. But not Americans.'

'Why?'

'Culture.'

'What do you mean?'

'There is a high divorce rate with Americans, very high. Tolerance is not built into the culture. Instead of resolving issues, they walk out of the relationship. The husbands spend too much time hanging out with friends, take the motorcycle, hang out, sit down and just drink.'

Later, Rufus's relation to black Americans would become more complicated. He would feel himself to be among them and apart from them in equal measure. But here, in the story of Rufus's early American days, black people of all hues and nations do not come off well. There are the corrupt ones who run Liberia, and the wounded American ones here, who slouch around the margins of their country. Rufus's task was to leapfrog them all and grab a piece of heartland America. He would learn to deal in its hard currency, to exude something of its values; he would return, finally, to Monrovia, a man of far greater consequence than a Twelfth Street tailor ever could hope to be.

In the end, it was an African-American who provided Rufus with his ticket to legality. Shortly after arriving, he married a black American woman. He will not talk about her much. She was from Pennsylvania, he met her when she visited Newark. They fell in and out of love quickly.

'Green-card love?' I asked.

'No, real love. Or what I thought was real love.'

'What went wrong?'

'Incompatibility. Cultural.'

That is all he will say.

Perhaps it was not green-card love, as he says. But when he met his American bride there was already a woman in his life, a Liberian named Cecilia Kasay Johnson, who lived on Park Hill Avenue, Staten Island. Rufus and Cecilia would later marry and raise four children together. The first of their children, Tricia, was born in 1987. By the end of 1989, the couple and their child were living in an apartment on Park Hill Avenue.

The eight project buildings of the Park Hill and Fox Hill developments together swallow a long, narrow block of Vanderbilt

Street and Park Hill Avenue in Staten Island. This is where Rufus would raise his children, plan his future, and meet Jacob Massaquoi.

The development was built in the 1960s, some time before anyone imagined that America's urban housing projects would incubate black poverty. Its first tenants were white: Irish and Italian Americans ushering their children into the ranks of the middle class.

By the early 1980s, every last resident of the Park Hill Avenue project was black, and its kids were at war with those from the project in neighbouring Stapleton. The crack-cocaine era was in full swing, and the geography of Park Hill Avenue seemed designed to foster open-air drug markets: a sealed enclave with just one access point, its merchants could see the police coming from miles away.

By the time Rufus set up house there in 1989, about 200 Liberians were living among the African-Americans of Park Hill Avenue. Why Liberians ended up there, rather than in another New York housing project, is perhaps unknowable by now, but why they chose to gather in a project is not mysterious at all. Like Rufus, most were indigenous Liberians of modest means who had come to New York for education, or for high-wage work; they sent most of their wage home, and they never imagined dying anywhere but on Liberian soil. Self-consciously itinerant, living as cheaply as they could, they wanted, above all, to preserve their Liberianness.

'There isn't a better place in America for Liberians to live,' Rufus told me. 'When I go back home, people say: "Wow! Your accent is the same as if you never left!" And then, after I've spent a bit of time there, they say: "Wow! You can solve Liberian problems as if you'd never left!"'

On Park Hill Avenue, one can cheat geography. One can take a short bus ride from a slice of Liberia to the heart of New York. One can drench oneself in America without fear of drifting from home.

'What about the crime, the drugs?' I ask Rufus. 'It's hardly the best place in America to raise your kids.'

He shrugs. 'Either you raise your kids right, or you don't,' he replies. 'Wherever you live, there is opportunity for them to go astray.'

A few days after finishing a draft of this book, I give a copy of the manuscript to Rufus and ask for his comments. Replying via email, he points out a handful of mistakes. Among them is this. '"There isn't a better place [than Park Hill] for Liberians to live." I know that I did not say that. It must have been mistaken or misunderstood.'

He did say it, and reading what he has said makes him uncomfortable because it speaks to later troubles, to accusations that will be levelled against him. It is not just the awkwardness of implying that the best place for Liberians is alongside an open-air crack market policed by armed youths. It is the sorts of lives Liberians were living when Rufus arrived on Park Hill Avenue.

By the standards of those around him, Rufus was doing very well. He had a green card, and thus the right to work. He had a high-school certificate from a good school, and could register, free of charge, to study at a state or city university. Many others around him were struggling. They had arrived in America on visitor's visas, like Rufus, and then melted into New York's underground. They seldom ventured too far into the city because the illegality of their presence there made them cautious. They did not seek medical attention when they were ill for fear of being found out. They earned very low wages; just enough to live on Park Hill Avenue, and to send a little home. Above all, they were shamed. Like Rufus, they had gone to America to triumph, but they had failed. In the letters they wrote home, they pretended to live the American lives they had once dreamed of.

'Wow! You can solve Liberian problems as if you'd never left!' Rufus exclaimed of Park Hill. Later, he would be accused of enjoying Liberian problems, because it was from them that he built his legacy.

On Park Hill Avenue, Rufus began working astoundingly hard, living two, perhaps three lives, all at once.

When he moved there in 1989, he found a job in New York's health care system, as a home health aide, as so many other Park Hill Liberians did. It was unskilled, poorly paid and hard, and it was women's work.

'Some of it was in people's homes,' he recalled. 'Sick people. Homebound. You shave them, you clean them, you feed them. You keep them company for four or eight hours. The rest of the work was in group homes. People with special needs: eight or ten of them in one house. They need grooming, they need help taking a shower, eating, going to bed. They are all disabled. Some of them are retarded. You help them do the stuff they can't do.'

Not long after he started work as a home health aide, Rufus enrolled at the College of Staten Island for a degree in engineering.

'My first week in school,' Rufus told me, 'something happened that I still talk about. The professor asked us to read a section of a book. There was a girl on my right, another on my left. When I'm one or two paragraphs in, they are both staring into space, waiting. I say: "No. Finish reading." They say: "We are." I say: "No!" They say: "Yes, the professor said to read from here to there." I say: "Never!" They say: "The professor asked us to read from *here* to *there*."

'It was the most amazing thing I noticed about American education: the speed at which they read; the girls, not the boys. Read, read, read: whole book finished. Look at me, the schools I went to, I went to a very good Catholic school. I could never read that fast. The *foundation* those girls had. It's about *foundation*. You can never catch up.'

It was not lost on Rufus that this American foundation would be his children's too. No matter where they spent their adult years, that they had started life in America would be a blessing. Already, just by being here, Rufus had reset Arkoi family history on a new track.

It was also on Staten Island, though, that Rufus first experienced blunt American racism.

'Maybe it was there in Newark,' he said. 'But if it was, I didn't really notice. We were just a bunch of black guys. Every now and then, we'd interact with white guys. The boss was white, yeah, but so what? If she was mean to me, I'd think, she's a mean person. But you come to Staten Island. Racism. Yeaaaah.

'You go shopping for a carpet for your living room at Fox Carpet Store at the Staten Island Mall. You want it delivered. Guys says: "No, no, no. We're not going down there. Park Hill area? Too much crime and violence."

'In the same mall, I ordered a pizza. I waited: ten minutes, fifteen minutes. Four whites order after I order. They get their food. Mine still isn't done.

'I say: "I ordered before all these people."

'"Look man, you just have to wait."

'"Oh, no. You welcome me. You take my money. You don't serve *anybody* else before you serve me."

'He: "I'll call the cops."

'Me: "I don't care who you call."

'I start getting loud. People are watching now. Seeing how this thing is going to end. It ends with him trying to overcharge me for my food. I had to fight all over again. Staten Island. Oh, yeah. Staten Island.'

But this is something Rufus speaks of only when I press him. He was too busy for American racism. It never came close to stopping him from lapping up the country's bounty. He was in a decent university, paid for by the state. He was living in a federally subsidised apartment. Life was inexpensive enough for him to send enough money home each month for both his family and for Roza. And he was working every waking moment of the day: his home-aide job from 8 a.m. to 4 p.m., then over to the college for classes, then home to study. And on Wednesday and Friday nights and on Saturday afternoons: soccer. He was managing Club Afrique. The Haitian league was a very serious business. He was also starting a team on his street: the Park Hill Rangers. He was never still.

And yet this was an odd time for him, for everything was in the future now, very little in the present. As for the past, it would not survive much longer. He was still sending money back to Roza, it remained alive, but it was not in capable hands. He suspected that the manager was pocketing the money he wired, that the coach was distracted. Roza was *his*, and for every passing month he was not there, it died a little. As for Club Afrique and Staten Island soccer, they were surely little more than the thin shadows Twelfth Street cast, reminders of what once happened on the field at Tubman High. These were not his teams, after all, and whatever they might accomplish, they would never hold the weight of his being.

And so he was waiting, training, for the future. He would return to Liberia with an engineering degree from a New York university. But that was years and years away. For a long time, he would be idling through the present, the future an ornate creature of his mind, growing heavier every day with the burden of his expectations.

22

War Far and Near

And then the Liberian war began, and by early August of 1990, the conflict had picked Twelfth Street off the ground like a toy, and shaken the people from their homes.

I spoke to a man named Johnson Davies who was living on Twelfth Street at that time.

'Charles Taylor had Robertsfield Airport,' Davies told me, 'and was preparing to march on Monrovia. Doe's forces had the University of Liberia. They were firing rockets at each other. Sinkor is right between the university and Robertsfield. The rockets from both sides were landing on Sinkor every morning, every afternoon. It was not safe there. I had to leave.'

But leaving was also dangerous. Beyond Sinkor, the city was strewn with checkpoints. Doe's soldiers were butchering everyone they suspected of being Gio, and many others besides. This was some two weeks after the massacre at St Peter's Lutheran Church, when Jacob had run for his life. As the endgame grew closer, the line between soldier and civilian was no longer clear. One could die arbitrarily at any of those checkpoints. Some Twelfth Street residents took their chances and fled. Others took their chances and stayed. The choice was between risking death by a bullet or by a rocket.

Aaron Weah was eleven years old at the time, living with his family on Twelfth Street, just a few doors from the Arkoi homestead.

'We hung in there,' he recalled, 'until it became clear that Taylor's forces were actually going to come into Sinkor itself and take the place over. My father decided it was something not to wait for. The family would walk out of Sinkor together.'

'At the time, there was a young man staying with the family, a brilliant young lawyer whom everybody said had a bright future. He was a Krahn. My family had a long discussion about him. In the end, my father approached him and said he could not come with us. Being a Krahn, he was at risk, and since he would be with us, he would be putting us all at risk. And some of us were young children, and my father didn't want to take a chance with our lives. The young lawyer understood. We left him on Twelfth Street.

'We walked all the way across Monrovia to Paynesville, and there we moved into a house a family had abandoned when Johnson moved through there. And we knew that, just like we were moving into strangers' houses here, strangers would soon move into our abandoned house on Twelfth Street. That's how it was during the war: the populations of streets changing over and over. We would move from Twelfth Street when the fighting was there, move back when it ended, back and forth, back and forth.'

As for the young Krahn lawyer: 'Between Paynesville and Sinkor there was little communication. What news came was rumour; you could not trust it. So it wasn't until much later we found out that he was shot on Twelfth Street by Taylor soldiers two or three days after we left. Apparently somebody on the street told the NPFL soldiers that he was a Krahn. The body lay there a long time.'

If news didn't travel easily between Monrovia's eastern and northern districts, it certainly didn't travel much better to New York. Day upon day, Rufus did not know whether his family was safe. Over the next six years, the war would take two of his brothers, one of them in the most ghastly fashion.

As much as he worried about his relatives at home, Rufus surely worried a great deal about himself. He was a man heavily invested in his own dream life, a man prepared to play a long waiting game. And the foundation of everything he dreamed was Samuel Doe's Liberia, a Liberia in which soccer was a sacred national institution, a Liberia in which a man of Rufus's pedigree and values might flourish. And it was this Liberia that was now under attack.

From early on, Rufus took a robust and vehement position on who was responsible for the war. First and foremost, it was the Americo-Liberians. They had been chased from power in 1980, and now they wanted it back. Having regrouped here in America, they sent their man, Charles Taylor, with American complicity, to steal Liberia from Samuel Doe. To succeed, they would of course need pawns to do the actual dirty work, people who could be duped into killing and dying. For this, they chose Liberia's most vengeful and power-hungry people, the Gios and Manos of Nimba County.

That is how Rufus saw it. The war was an assault on Doe's Liberia, and thus on Rufus's Liberia too. There were surely times during 1990 when he imagined Twelfth Street devoid of familiar faces, the people who bore witness to him and his accomplishments now dispersed across Monrovia. He must have wondered, too, whether the war would end, or, if it did, whether it would not leave his world permanently disfigured, the very idea of Twelfth Street just a symbol of a lost time.

What would he do then? What if there was no country to which to return? He was a good student. There was little question that he would graduate as an engineer. A place in America's suburbs awaited him. What he had invested in his Liberian future he could surely now transfer to his children's American futures. He could give them the best of this country: that was surely an Arkoi story fit to sustain the hungriest appetite.

Yet it was a prospect that scared him enormously. To take his place in the American suburbs was to disintegrate into them, to vanish.

During the time we discussed things he had a mantra he repeated over and again: everything he did, he said, he did for his kids. When I had heard him say it for the umpteenth time, I ventured to disagree. 'Your career would surely have advanced much, much further than it has if you'd forgotten Liberia.' I said. 'You knock off work at 4 p.m. sharp every day and drive as fast as you can to Liberia. If you were doing everything for your kids, you'd be getting ahead at work.'

He demurred at first, and began to say something in disagreement. But then he stopped and checked himself. 'You're right, you know,' he replied. 'I could have lived the life you described. I've done that: just work and make money. It's boring. I would die early. Make money. No contact with people. No. I would die early. My position is on the street, on the sidewalk, talking to the kids, redirecting their minds. But to just focus on make money, make money: I wouldn't cope with that.'

Perhaps if he had never met Cecilia, his wife, and moved to Park Hill Avenue, perhaps if he'd stayed in New Jersey he would have found a way to point himself in some other direction. But as it happened, the more the war ate into the flesh of his country, so its refugees began arriving, slowly at first, on his doorstep.

'One of the professors at the College of Staten Island was principal of PS 57,' Rufus told me, 'the elementary school here at the end of Park Hill Avenue. One day she is on campus looking for someone who knows how to speak the Gola dialect in Liberia. Says there is a little boy at her school, fresh from Liberia. It is difficult for his teachers to communicate with him. We are looking for a para-professional to help. Is there anyone on this campus who speaks Gola?'

Liberia is home to sixteen languages. If the boy had been Kru or Krahn, or Kissi, or Manu, or Vai, Rufus would not have been able to help. As it happened, Rufus's mother was Gola, and he spoke it reasonably well.

'I said: "Yes, I can understand Gola."

'"Can you come and help?"

'I said: "Yes."

I went. We communicated. First thing, we brought laughter to the boy. Relaxed him.

'They said: "You got the job."

Rufus would work at PS 57 for the following nine years, first as a teaching assistant, then as a fully-fledged teacher. His job was to construct a bridge between Liberian kids, their schooling aborted during the course of the war, and New York's public school system.

But he would never regard this work as his vocation. He did not even bother to tell me about it until we had been speaking for many months. It was not for teaching that Rufus abandoned a career in engineering. It was for something far closer to home.

The young Gola boy appeared in October 1993. At that stage, Liberian refugees were arriving on Staten Island in no more than a trickle. The deluge would come early the following year. A gigantic camp of displaced Liberians, its numbers swelling by the week, had been established by the United Nations Commissioner for Refugees in Ghana. The camp was called Buduburam. Soon, everyone on Park Hill Avenue knew the name Buduburam. Everyone received letters from near and distant relatives, from neighbours and friends, from people who went missing when the war began, people who had not been heard from in two or three years. They were writing from Buduburam, and they were asking, begging, to come to America. Camp life, the refugees wrote, was indescribably awful. Rations were inadequate. Schooling for the children was worse than rudimentary. They were not permitted to work in Ghana. People were idle and frustrated.

In their droves, Liberian Staten Islanders contacted the Lutheran Immigration and Refugee Service, which was facilitating bringing Liberians from Buduburam to the United States.

The first large batch of refugees, more than a hundred strong, arrived on Park Hill Avenue in early 1994. For Rufus and others who had sat out the first four years of the conflict in Staten Island, the newcomers were the first live, human evidence of what the war had done.

Laurenzo Stevens, a Pentecostal priest, established one of the first Liberian congregations on Staten Island in the late 1980s.

'Before the war,' Stevens said, 'Park Hill Avenue was a refuge for Liberians. New York out there was wild, wild, wild. You could go out into it, knowing you'd be returning home in the evenings. You would come back after work, and on your way home, you would stop and sit under the tree. Come on, don't go straight home; you *must* come and sit under the tree. Any food from Liberia, you would find it there. It was a place of sharing. It was just very good, sitting together.

'But after the war began, the refugees who started coming here, they had not been living lives that we knew. They had come from foreign countries – Ivory Coast, Ghana – where they had been living without support. They came here with prostitution, with violence, with crime. And, of course, some them fought in the war. Now they are suddenly here without any education. And Park Hill Avenue is a place with many temptations.'

If Stevens's memory of pre-war Park Hill is a little nostalgic, his recollections nonetheless capture the discomfort Liberians felt in the presence of their newly arrived compatriots. The refugees were seldom in nuclear families: a mom and dad and kids rescued from the war. Everyone who came had been torn from family, was alone, or in awkward, newly cobbled-together groups.

Resettlement was meant to be ordered, the adults shepherded into work, the children into school. But by the late 1990s, there were more than a hundred children on Park Hill Avenue living without adult supervision. Some had settled in a couple of apartments on a block at the end of Bowen Street, just off Park Hill Avenue, where they hung around in groups late into the evening. Various attempts were made to get them into forums where they might talk of their experiences and get help, but most had slipped through the cracks of the immigration process, and worried that if identified they would be deported. So they remained slippery, guarded, aloof.

A sense of great unease descended on Park Hill Avenue. Everyone, by now, had lost someone in the war. Everyone knew that the streets on which they had grown up were deserted or filled with strangers. Until the refugees arrived, the devastation had resided only in their imaginations. Now the destruction took human form, embodied in these apparently feral beings. They were evidence of war's power to mangle the familiar into something strange.

Soon, rumours abounded about whom among them might have been child soldiers. Did this one fight for Charles Taylor? Did that one perhaps fight for Johnson? These kids are already forming a street gang to take on the African-Americans; surely they learned to fight back home. That one is from Buchanan. My brother was murdered in Buchanan. Could this boy on the street corner have pulled the trigger? The refugees, especially the young men among them, were not a welcome sight.

But they did play soccer. And Rufus Arkoi watched them gather on the Stapleton Fields. What he saw nobody else on the planet could possibly have seen, his vision so thoroughly soaked in the memories of two sewing machines and a soccer field.

By September 1994, the Park Hill Rangers had been rechristened. Their name was now Roza Rangers. Rufus had resigned from his job as a home health aide and abandoned a prospective career as an engineer. To earn a living, he taught at the school. The rest of the time, he was on the soccer field. As Rufus completed more and more forms applying for funding, New York philanthropists asked him what 'Roza' meant. It was an African word for 'survivor', Rufus replied.

Advance

With a staff of more than a dozen reporters covering every district in the borough, the *Staten Island Advance* is a scrupulous chronicler of neighbourhood life.

'When I got the job,' an *Advance* reporter named Tevah Platt told me, 'I moved to Staten Island. Sometimes, I think that may have been a mistake. There is no escaping work. Even when I buy vegetables for dinner, the *price* is a story.'

It did not take the *Advance* long to catch up with Rufus Arkoi. At first, he appears in its pages as a folksy fellow, coach of an under-ten girls soccer team called the Roza Angels. The reporter finds the team on a bad day. They have been thumped 4–1:

'I was just trying to help out,' explained Jimetta Brown, referring to the time she left her defensive position to help her mates try to score a goal. Soon after, the St Clare's Bumble Bees made one of their many scoring moves and, with Arkoi yelling to her, Brown realized she was in the wrong spot and had to sprint back the entire length of the field.

'Yes, I do want you to be aggressive, but you still have to remember your positions,' Arkoi told his team as they sipped orange drinks on this unseasonably warm, sunny day . . .

'Hey, let's go back and practise right now at PS 57,' said an eager Loretta Stevens, who played goalie as her brother, Laurenzo, served as volunteer linesman for the game.

'No, I have a better idea,' smiled Arkoi. 'Who wants to go to McDonald's?'

The kids screamed in unison, 'Me!'

With that they took off for the parking lot at Miller Field. Usually Arkoi borrows a friend's van to transport his players. But, when that is not available, he packs the kids into his own car and sometimes that of a parent.

The reporter mentions in passing that the Roza Angels represent just a slice of the time this generous man gives to children, for he also 'helps coach' Roza Rangers, an under-nineteens team, Roza Lions, the under-fourteens, and Roza Tigers, the under-tens boys team.

It is in this last paragraph that we glimpse Rufus. He is a veritable Pied Piper. Liberia's war children are arriving in their hundreds, and they are all following him down Park Hill Avenue, assembled by age and by sex, each wearing Roza's yellow and blue.

Rufus on the day he graduated in 1997 with a bachelor's degree in psychology from Staten Island College. He gave up engineering for psychology after he founded the New York branch of Roza.

In October 1997, the *Advance* reports a fundraising dinner Roza has convened to raise money for its work. The guest of honour is Democratic Councilman Jerome X. O'Donovan, who, in his speech, commits the borough to find substantial funding for Roza in the near future. The executive director of Roza is described as 'Rufus Zumo Arkoi, a former executive with the Liberian national soccer organisation.

'In soccer circles,' the *Advance* reporter writes, 'he is a legend for having trained AC Milan's George Weah, the world's best soccer player.'

'My wife is my witness to how many [refugee] children we have personally kept in our home in Park Hill,' Rufus is reported as saying. 'We are facing very serious problems with our children.'

The following year, the outgoing principal of PS 57 announced that his legacy would be to ensure that the Liberian refugee children in his school were cared for after he had gone; to achieve his aim, he has secured the appointment of Liberian community leader Rufus Zumo as a full-time teacher helping to bridge the gap between Liberians and their school.

A delegation of Liberian priests was taken on a tour of the school to meet Liberian children and to witness Rufus's work. In front of a class, Rufus took a clergyman by the hand and held up his sleeve. The story was taken up by the *Advance*:

'Do you think these men just picked up these clothes in America?' Rufus Zumo asked. 'People in Liberia dress like you, they live in houses like you. Before the war, the millionaires in Liberia were living better than the millionaires in America. The schools were very good.'

Zumo said the educational system was so competitive in Liberia that when he came to America in the mid-1980s to attend college he had an easy time of it.

'However, now, after a long civil war which turned Liberian against Liberian, the children have in many cases been displaced into refugee camps and have missed years of school. When they move to America, they find themselves years behind their peers here.'

On 22 March 1999 the largest single event in the history of Staten Island's Liberian community won a lengthy piece in the *Advance*. More than 300 new refugees had arrived on Staten Island, and Roza had thrown a party to welcome them. The Roza Dance Troupe performed to music from home, the restaurant hosting the reception was covered in balloons, and over a hundred Staten Island Liberians were there to greet the newcomers.

This time, Rufus had wheeled out a phalanx of support. According to the *Advance*:

> There was Timmi Pierce of Lutheran Immigration Services [sic], an organization largely responsible for the mass resettlement. There was Ernie Duff of Victim Services 'Solace' program, offering counseling to those who find themselves struggling with post-traumatic stress disorder and other war-related conditions. Two Liberian priests, Laurenzo Stevens of the New Life Church, and Philip Saywrayne, pastor of Christ Assembly Church, address the refugees.
>
> 'You've been asking God during the war to preserve your lives,' Saywrayne toldells them. 'And now you are here.'

An unidentified young Liberian man addressed the gathering. He praised Roza, declaring that his life in America had been saved by soccer, and by the educational opportunities it had brought; he was determined to leave Park Hill Avenue for university soon; he swore before these hundreds of witnesses that he would do so, and that his ticket would be a soccer scholarship. The audience rose to give him a standing ovation. Here was living testimony. Here was *everyone's* possible future, in flesh and blood. Here was what Roza could do.

Finally, five years after its launch, real money began to flow. On 5 November 1999, a story appeared in the *Advance* declaring that a 'small miracle had happened in Stapleton': Rufus has received a grant of $300,000 from the federal government. And once that grant came through, New York's philanthropists lined up to fund him. By the end of 1999, he had hired a building in Staten Island and was about to take on a dozen full-time staff. Turning war children into American immigrants had become a veritable business.

In February 2003, four years after the big $300,000 grant turned Rufus's brainchild into a real organisation, the director of a large New York not-for-profit organisation walked into Roza's headquarters on Canal Street for the first time. She had come for a meeting to address the problem of homeless children in the Liberian community.

'I was a little late,' she recalled six years later. 'I walked into a meeting that had already begun. I sat down, took out pen and paper, and listened to whoever was speaking. Being late, I was a little disoriented. My mind drifted. I began looking around the room.

'On the wall opposite me I saw the strangest sight. My first thought was that it was a shrine, that the man in the photograph was dead. There were flags and rosettes and scarves of all different colours. And they all centred around a portrait of a man. He was dressed in flowing African robes and smiled into the camera. It was a very formal portrait, very stiff; it seemed that the photograph had been taken in a studio. I thought to myself: this man must have died in the war. He must have been a very special person, a priest, perhaps, or a community elder, who was killed by rebel soldiers in the war.

'Then I looked again at the man who was speaking, glanced back at the shrine, looked at the man speaking again . . . They were the same man. Only, the one in the meeting was wearing jeans and a sweatshirt instead of robes. I thought, okay, this must be *his* organisation.'

The director was meeting Rufus at the height of his success. The $300,000 was just the beginning. An organisation dedicated to turning child soldiers into American college students: it was an attractive cause. By now, anybody who wanted to work with African immigrants in the Park Hill projects came to Roza. Roza *was* Park Hill Avenue. Rufus was soaring.

Yet behind the man whose portrait hung on the wall was a world of growing darkness. In April 1996, just as the dreamscape in Rufus's head was becoming real, Arkoi family history took a new turn. It happened during one of the terrible battles of 'April 6', the ones Jacob Massaquoi witnessed and survived. Rufus's oldest brother, Richard, and his sister, Margaret, walked through an NPFL checkpoint on their way across town. One of the young soldiers there stopped them and ordered them back. He recognised Richard's face.

He stood there, his gun pointed at the two Arkois, wracking his brain. Now he remembered: Richard had worked for the Interim Government, he said, for Liberia's former interim president, Amos Sawyer. The Interim Government was no friend of Charles Taylor's NPFL; it was regarded as a puppet of the Nigerians, and the Nigerians had chased Taylor out of Monrovia.

Richard said no, the young soldier said yes; he was adamant. Richard was a mechanic. He had, in fact, worked on the cars of several Interim Government politicians. He told the soldier this. In reply, the soldier shot him in the head.

Later in the day, two of Richard's brothers set out to retrieve his corpse from the checkpoint. There was too much gunfire. They could not come close without risking their own lives. The body lay in the street, through the night, and into the next day.

Three days passed before the Arkois could get to their brother. By now, his corpse was decomposing. They gathered his remains, wrapped them, and burned them in a ceremony attended by his four young children.

Roza Across the World

On an evening in July 2008, nearly nine years after his offices opened on Canal Street, and some three years since he was forced to leave them, I join Rufus in his makeshift headquarters at Foxhill Apartments. Tonight he has around him a group of exceptional young women. They are here because they have several things in common. They are in their late teens or early twenties. They grew up on Park Hill Avenue. They have Liberian parents. Most pertinently, they have made it to college, and so they are halfway out of here. It is summertime, and they have come from around the country to be with family: from Howard University in Washington DC, from the University of Florida at Tampa, from several colleges in upstate New York. They will soon be teachers and psychologists, librarians and nurses. They will marry middle-class men and live in middle-class places. They will not live on Park Hill Avenue again.

Rufus regards them as his prodigies. They were all members of Roza Angels, the under-ten girls soccer team on whose 4–1 defeat the *Advance* reported eleven years earlier. He points out to them that only one member of the team did not make it to college, an unlikely feat in a neighbourhood such as this. They are living testimony of his work.

Now, Rufus has persuaded them to form an organisation of their own, one that will inspire young Liberian girls to travel the same road they have, from Park Hill Avenue to college.

Tonight, they are meant to be discussing modalities: the writing of a constitution, the election of office holders. But Rufus is in an expansive mood. He is painting their future, and he is doing so with the colours of his own past.

'Think twice before you look for a salaried job with a boss and a clock-in time,' Rufus tells them. 'Black people from the projects, when they get educated, they go into legal slavery. They work all day for just enough money to pay the rent. Me, I did not work for others. I'm talking when I was *your* age. I was self-reliant, from the start, from the age of *nineteen*. Already then, I had income from being a tailor. I worked for *nobody*. When I was older, I had income from Roza. I was self-employed, always.'

The young women listen attentively, respectfully. When they address him, they call him 'Mr Rufus', a very Liberian custom for these women, many of whom have never set foot in Liberia.

'Form yourselves into a not-for-profit,' Rufus continues. 'Get a little office. Not on Wall Street, just a little office close to here, in Tottenville, say. Be self-reliant. To break poverty, you have to be self-reliant.'

His way is to speak in wider and wider circles, to make the same point again and again, each time with more flesh on it.

'When I was twenty,' he continued, 'my uncle offered me a job at the electricity company. He said: "Take any job you want." I said: "What's available?" He said: "Reading the electricity meter. You'll make at least $85 a month."

'That was a lot of money for a twenty-year-old. It was a lot of money for reading electricity meters. In fact, it was for taking bribes to not switch off the electricity.'

The women laugh appreciatively.

'But, no, I did not take his job, because already at the age of twenty, I was buying plane tickets to watch a soccer match. I was a *tailor*, I had a *business*. I was self-reliant.

'You must form an organisation that travels the world, looking at what girls want, at what girls need. You do that, money will come to you. There are millions of dollars waiting around. Seven years ago I went to Ghana to start Roza in the refugee camp there, everything paid for. Ticket, hotel, everything. By the time I left, they were playing soccer in the refugee camp. I have started ten organisations with the name of Roza. Each has flourished. These hands of mine are blessed. Who would have thought that a Liberian soccer league would have been established here on the east coast of the United States? These hands of mine are blessed.'

I look into the faces of these young women in a vain attempt to borrow their ears. I want to know what it is they have heard. For it seems that a great many things, things that are usually separated from one another by time and space and logic – a young Liberian tailor, an African immigrant soliciting American grants, a group of young black women, more American than African – have been swept together into a vortex, a Rufus-vortex formed by the blast of his biography. In here they are all connected.

The tailor and the not-for-profit director are the same, for both are alchemists: both have conjured something from nothing. The tailor lived on a no-hope street where boys became wage labourers if they were lucky. On a sewing machine in his father's house, he made careers for his friends and a shrine of soccer around which his street could dream. The dream was Twelfth Street's, everyone could partake, but it was branded with *his* name, it was Rufus O Zumo Arkoi, Roza.

The not-for-profit director was simply an older incarnation of the tailor, the same stitcher of dreams. Only this time, the fabric on which he worked spanned continents. He had been set to disappear into the American suburbs, a grey man in a workaday job, but that was not a cloth he could wear, so he sewed his own. Once again, what he made was a shrine on a poverty-stricken street. He would turn its girls into college graduates; he would take its boys out of street gangs and onto soccer fields across the country, where they would be watched by crowds of thousands.

The *Advance* got only the beginning of the story. Once the $300,000 federal grant was spent, more came in, then more still. According to the tax returns it filed with the IRS, Roza's annual revenues for 2003 totalled $291,304. Rufus was drawing grants from a wide selection of borough and city philanthropies. The New York Foundation, the Robin Hood Foundation, the Staten Island Bank Trust, the JM Kaplan Fund, the Pinkerton Foundation, the Open Society Institute and the New York Community Trust's Fund for New Citizens were all among its donors. Child soldiers on college scholarships; refugee camp children in afternoon tutorials; former street gangsters on the soccer field: Rufus had touched every chord among New York's grant givers. They were singing now, and it appeared that the song might go on for ever.

Nine years earlier, all of this was a mere fantasy in Rufus's mind;

a feeling of lightheadedness that came over him as he watched a group of refugee children kicking a football around on Stapleton Fields. From his imagination to the world.

Things went so well that in 2002 Rufus resigned from his teaching job at PS 57. From now on, he would draw a salary from Roza. In truth, the school post had been shackling him. It was somebody else's show. Now he could be free; and there was so much to do.

During this period, Rufus made a famous return to Twelfth Street in Monrovia. In the Arkoi family homestead, his visit was preceded by a great deal of polishing and dusting and sweeping; there was much speculation about where Rufus would sleep. In the end, he did not spend a single night under the roof of his father's house.

When I visited Sinkor and members of Rufus's family described his return, each had his own explanation for why Rufus chose to sleep where he did. Some said that in America he had grown accustomed to flushing toilets, and that Twelfth Street was beneath him. Others said that the demands on him would simply be too great. 'Everybody would want a favour,' I was told. 'Everybody would be desperate and would need something *now*. The man needed space to breathe.'

Rufus installed himself in a room at the Royal Hotel on Tubman Boulevard, just a ten-minute walk from the Twelfth Street labyrinth, but worlds above it in stature.

'A line would start outside Rufus's hotel room at seven in the morning,' his niece, Sonie, told me. 'Some came to pay their respects, some to ask for support, some to catch Rufus up with what was happening in their lives. The whole of Twelfth Street came to see him.'

When he said goodbye to Monrovia after that trip, he left behind him several new institutions. There was Roza International Academy, a fledgling elementary school for young Twelfth Street children whom the war was depriving of an education. The school was set up in a building near Sinkor, and had a couple of full-time teachers. Their salaries and the rent came from Rufus.

The original Roza, the soccer club on Twelfth Street, had slept through the years of war. Now, with American money in his pocket, Rufus woke it from its slumber. It took to the field once again. Its players received monthly stipends now, courtesy of Rufus. They wore the finest uniforms in Liberia, sewn on Rufus's machine in Staten Island. They spent the night before big games together in a motel, and they arrived for the match in a hired bus. They were envied. Talented young men lined up to play for the club. They began to excel. The name Roza was again on the lips of Monrovia's soccer lovers.

And the boys who took the field in Roza jerseys would be saved, they would go to school. In 2000, a college opened its doors in Sinkor, run by Bacchus Matthews, one of the famous and distinguished Monrovians who rose against the Americo-Liberian regime in the 1970s. Five of Roza's players enrolled at that college, each of them sponsored by Rufus.

Rufus also visited the Buduburam refugee camp in Ghana, full of young Liberian men, and by the time he left, Buduburam Roza had a president, a secretary, a coach, and a squad of fifty.

Rufus with the branch of Roza he founded at Buduburam refugee camp in Ghana in August 2002. This was at the height of Rufus's success when he imagined establishing Roza branches across Liberia, the United States and wherever else Liberians had settled.

Back in the States, he visited Minneapolis, home to the largest Liberian population in the United States, and there too, a branch of Roza was established.

What sort of accounts his office kept on the money it received, I do not know. Whether these ventures were reflected in Roza's budget, or whether they came from Rufus's salary, I am not sure. But, certainly, Rufus was dispensing money freely at this time.

A neighbour of Rufus's from Twelfth Street, a man who asked that his name not be written here, for the story he shared is about his fall, told of a chance encounter with Rufus on the streets of Staten Island some time in 2002. The neighbour had sunk a long way. In his prime, he had been a ranking member of Liberia's diplomatic corps, an undersecretary in an important embassy. Now, he was down and out, and such was his humiliation that he was avoiding Park Hill Avenue and its familiar faces. Rufus sighted his old neighbour on Bay Street and crossed the road to greet him; when the two men fell to talking, the neighbour spilled out the story of his poverty and his shame, and Rufus took him immediately to a nearby hotel and checked him in.

'I stayed for two weeks,' the neighbour told me, 'while Rufus helped me to find work. And when I checked out, the bill was already paid, and Rufus wanted nothing from me, he wanted me never to pay him back.'

I asked Rufus to confirm the story.

'In those days, I had money,' he said.

Here, tonight, in July 2008, the meeting has adjourned, and Rufus's young prodigies are talking idly. The opening ceremony of the Beijing Olympic Games had been held two nights before, and some of the women had watched.

'Did you see the Liberian delegation?' a girl called HD asks. 'There were only five of them. And none were athletes. They were all officials!'

'Kenya had athletes,' says a girl called Laureta. 'Ethiopia had *plenty* of athletes. Liberia: no athletes.'

There is a long silence, for what more can one say?

It is Rufus who breaks the quiet. 'Reminds of me of the Moscow Olympics,' he says. 'I think it was in 1980. In the whole tournament, there was just one Liberian athlete competing. One lonely Liberian among all these athletes.

'The Games finish, there's the closing ceremony, and he refuses to go home.

'People say: "What are you going to *do* here?"

'He says: "No way I'm going home."

'The translator leaves, the Liberian officials leave. Everyone leaves. He stays. They're talking to him in Russian and he's *freaking* out, man. But still, he stays: this is his *opportunity*.

'A month later, he's seen on the streets of Monrovia.

'"What happening, my man? Thought you in Russia."

'"Aw, man. I couldn' unnerstan' the *language*. Couldn' unnerstan' what they were *saying*."'

Rufus's audience is laughing freely now, these lean young girls gathered around their large mentor. Their enthusiasm provokes another story.

'You hear about the Haitian team that came here to play soccer?' Rufus asks. 'Big game. The national Haitian team. Came to play the United States. Game was to be televised on cable. Every Haitian in America found his way to cable. Game was set down to be played in Florida. *Seven players* turn up for the game. Even the *coach* didn't turn up.'

'Where were they?' a woman called Tylah asks.

'Brooklyn, Queens, New Jersey. They *all* wanted to stay in America. *Nobody* wanted to go home. What I can't figure: you'd think they could have waited 'til *after* the game.'

Rufus alone is silent now, for one does not laugh at one's own stories. As the others giggle at the Haitians, he sits there looking pleased. He, of course, recognises himself in the people at whose expense he jokes. He too came at the first frail glimmer of opportunity, vanishing undocumented into the cracks of immigrant America; he too could have ended up going home a month later, complaining that he just didn't understand what they were *saying*. Between farce and glory the line is very thin.

But tonight he feels a world apart from the chancers and the losers. Tonight he feels that in essence he is an artist. He works neither on canvas nor with pen and paper. He works on the world around him: on Twelfth Street, Sinkor; on Park Hill Avenue Staten Island; on their youth; on the girls who are now throwing back their heads and laughing. They are here because they were Roza Angels once, and Roza Angels began life as a vision in his mind.

Roza Boys

It is long past 2 p.m., the hour at which Rufus was meant to come. They are sitting in a line on a waist-high wall, waiting. In front of them is Bowen Street and its Saturday afternoon crowds of children and teenagers and ice-cream vendors and old men walking in pairs.

Most of them wear vests, for it is mid-June and hot, their boots strung around their necks by their laces or in small canvas bags at their feet. Some wear do-rags, and some have in their ears fake diamonds the size of marbles. They are the players of Roza 11. They have an away game somewhere in Pennsylvania. It is a long drive from here.

A two-door Ford pulls up, and you can hear from the music that it is the car of a West African: a silky, sexy, lazy voice is singing in French over throbbing percussion. As the car approaches, the line on the wall breaks up, and everyone is on the street, surrounding the car, and now they are guiding it into the narrowest of spaces on the side of the road. It will not fit; but everyone is patient; it will just take time; and it takes six, seven, eight tries, and still the car is not parked, but nobody is perturbed. Each joins the campaign at leisure, then tires and pulls away and goes back to sitting on the wall, then joins the campaign again.

The man in the car is Laurenzo Stevens, the seventeen-year-old son of the Pentecostal priest. He is among the team's finest players, bound for a soccer scholarship at whichever college he chooses. In the passenger seat beside him is a pretty girl.

The car is parked, finally, and Laurenzo has opened both doors and the trunk, his vehicle yawning to breathe in the world, and he has turned the music up very loud. A Roza boy takes to the sidewalk and begins to dance, his head bowed, his eyes watching his feet. He is joined by another, then another, and then another still. The sidewalk is now full of dancing boys. Each takes no notice of the next. Each is on his own stage. The old men are still walking in pairs, and the children have now formed a line, taking turns to close their eyes and run through a fount of water spurting up from beneath Bowen Street.

Among those who remain sitting on the wall is Teah Jackson, the young man who stole into Rufus's centre to use a computer on my second evening there. His accent is thickly Liberian, but in fact he has not set foot in the country of his birth since he was a small child. His memories of it are dim; he is not quite sure of dates. He and his family lived in a house on Bushrod Island, he tells me, near Monrovia's Free Port, just across the water from downtown.

When Prince Johnson's forces swept into Bushrod Island in July 1990, en route to the Executive Mansion, they took control of Teah's neighbourhood. He was five years old at the time. His mother was a radio operator in Samuel Doe's army, and worked in the Executive Mansion. With Johnson in control of the neighbourhood, the family knew that Teah's mother was in danger, for it would take just a stray whisper for the rebels to learn that she worked for Doe's army. And so she did not come home.

'I don't remember how long my mom stayed away,' Teah says. 'Maybe a month. Then, one day, she arrives, suddenly, and we're packing for the ship. She says the ship is leaving, it's leaving *now*. Me, my brother, my sister, my cousins, my mom. That was the last time I saw Liberia.'

Mother and children spent the next five years at Buduburam refugee camp in Ghana, where Teah's education came to a standstill, a vast, five-year hiatus that Rufus would later try to fill. Teah had an aunt in Queens – she had moved there long before the war – and the money she wired across the ocean saved the family from the scant rations of the UNHCR. And it was thanks to his aunt, too, and the fact that she found the Lutheran Immigration and Refugee Services in New York, that mother and children were registered as refugees and put on a plane bound for JFK.

'I was twelve when we arrived in Queens. There were no Liberians at school. The Jamaicans, first time I opened my mouth, knew I was

African, and they after me. And my aunt's house was too small. It was her whole family, plus my mom, my brother, my sister, my cousins.'

So he escaped as soon as he could and found himself at high school in Newark, New Jersey, not far from where Rufus had first experienced America a decade earlier. In New Jersey he was in and out of school, in and out of jail; the first time because of a fist fight, the second for something about which he will not speak. There were more Liberians in New Jersey than in Queens, and more Africans of so many different hues, but the first time he felt truly comfortable, he told me, the first time he felt he might have a home in this country, was when his soccer team went to Park Hill Avenue, Staten Island, to play a Liberian team called Roza. There was something beckoningly *Liberian* about them, Teah told me, Liberian in the sense of the refugee camp in Ghana, in the sense of people being exiled together, for what it might mean to be a Liberian in Liberia was now just a shrinking sequence of disparate memories.

He went to Staten Island whenever he could, and he soon got close to Roza's founder Rufus Arkoi.

'It is thanks to Rufus that I finished high school,' Teah tells me. 'When I was visiting Staten Island at weekends, I said to Rufus: "I'm going to give up school. It's so hard. And my family is not working; I must work." He put his hand in his pocket and it came out with $100, and he said: "Go home. Go back to school. Come here every weekend and play for Roza. I will stand with you."

I later learn that Teah is leaving out what is perhaps the most important part of this story. When he came to Staten Island at weekends, it was not just for soccer. He would go to Rufus's house and take out his textbooks, and Rufus would tutor him, hour after hour, through Saturday and Sunday. It would be fair to say that Teah climbed on the big man's shoulders and was piggybacked into America; for, without Rufus, he would have been a black immigrant boy without a high-school education in a big city.

With Rufus's help, Teah did finish high school, and moved to Park Hill Avenue as soon as he graduated to play for Roza, to be among Liberians, to be close to Rufus. A year later, he moved his mother to Staten Island too.

'He loves us all like sons,' Teah says. 'Everything in my life Rufus knows about. I am studying now at a college in downtown Manhattan, studying accounting, because Rufus got me a soccer scholarship. I study because I must, but I don't enjoy it, and I play soccer for the college because I must. But I prefer playing for Roza. Because that is about being Liberian.'

It is past 3.30 p.m., Laurenzo's car still belting its music across Bowen Street, when Rufus finally arrives.

'Women, man,' he says as he gets of out his car. 'Wife needs the car. It doesn't matter there are a dozen of us need to get to Pennsylvania: she needs the car, she *gets* the car.'

The boys are unimpressed. It is disrespectful to leave them waiting so long. Some of them cluck audibly. Rufus winces momentarily, almost undetectably; he pretends he has not heard.

Besides, now that he is here, there is another problem to deal with: there are not enough cars. Eddie Taylor, Roza's captain, is here with a friend in a two-door Audi cabriolet which has no back seat and can take no passengers. The friend wears impenetrably dark glasses and sits motionless behind the wheel. The only other two cars are Rufus's and Laurenzo's, and there are two guests today: me, and a Pentecostal priest visiting Rufus from Monrovia, a youngish man who leans sullenly against Rufus's car and perpetually dusts off his jacket.

And so we stand for a long time, not quite knowing what to do; I suggest that I stay behind, but Rufus will not countenance that, and eventually the cousin of a player is dragooned into coming along with his car. We are on the road at 4.30 p.m.; it is a two and a half hour drive to the venue, and the game is scheduled to kick off at 7.00 p.m. The rules of the league state that if a team is not there one minute after the appointed kick-off time, it forfeits the game. We ought to get there in the nick of time.

Out on Interstate 78, Rufus recovers his good spirits and is soon bantering melodiously with the priest; he is telling a story about a player from Sinkor in the early 1980s who refused to play wearing boots.

'You go' get your fee' broke,' my man,' he says, his American English left behind in Staten Island. 'You go' be a cripple, my man.'

At the first toll gate, he lowers the window, opens his arms wide, and breaks into song, a long operatic note that hangs in the air between the cashier and his open window.

'Remember this tune,' he says to the cashier, a sweet smile on his face. 'You going to hear it on "American Idol", I swear to you, God be my witness.'

With three minutes to go, the eastern skies to our left a swollen mauve, we exit the freeway into a southern Pennsylvanian village of modest clapboard houses. Roza will be playing a local team in a league game, an exclusively Liberian league that takes in Liberian settlements from Pennsylvania through New Jersey up to Staten Island. Rufus himself has founded the league, he is its president, and he is immensely proud of it.

Several months earlier, I had been with him on the morning he was to drive to New Jersey to open the first meeting to establish the league.

'I am going to speak *eloquently*,' he had said. 'In twenty years, Liberians have done nothing in this country. It is time to inspire people.'

'What does it mean,' I asked him, 'for Liberians to form a league here on the eastern seaboard? Why is it so significant an accomplishment?'

'To show outsiders that Liberians are capable of organising something,' he replied.

'To what end? What will happen if people see Liberians organising something?'

'In the long run, that is the only way Africa will get out of its immense poverty,' he said. 'If outsiders witness for themselves that we have the ability. You know Africans here have a link in Africa. They are desperate to show something of themselves at home, desperate to impress, to open a business there. In the end, they are very selfish. They take so much money home that they cannot do anything here. It is like a farmer who spends $20,000 when he knows his crop is worth ten. He thinks he'll make up the rest by magic. This Liberian league: it is about an investment in *here*.'

It was one of those comments of his that emerges from time to time, unheralded, from the great swirl of thoughts that clatter around the inside of his head. I remembered an earlier discussion, when he had said that Liberians come to America to work the corruption from their bones, and thus to return home immensely powerful. Now, he was saying not only that one comes to America to learn self-sufficiency, but to show America, and by this he surely means white America, that one is self-sufficient. Where the mask ends and the face begins is not certain. One is always performing, even in the most private corridors of one's soul.

We find parking on a street at the edge of the village's municipal sports grounds, and somebody rushes ahead to tell the referee that the team is on its way. There on the side of the road, the boys strip off their street clothes and put on their yellow and blue Roza uniforms, and then sit on the sidewalk to lace up their boots.

Within minutes, they are on the field, and it is good football, the twenty outplayers a single body of thick liquid, its outline forming and reforming around the movement of the ball like a wide, shifting glob of oil.

The local Liberians have decided to make a day of it. A good seventy or eighty people stand on the touchlines, and several barbecues have been freshly lit. A long concrete pavilion with a tin roof stands back some distance from the field; it is ready with a table full of salads and rolls and paper plates.

The game is but seven or eight minutes old when the heavens open, suddenly and ferociously, the rain so thick one can barely see the ball. The spectators move in hasty clumps to the cover of the pavilion, leaving just Rufus and me on the touchline. Even the linesmen have gone. Within minutes we are both drenched, our coats so heavy with water that holding our backs up straight has become a task of its own, and we abandon the game and take cover with the rest.

The match is destined not to last. A deep pool has formed just outside Roza's penalty area, another in the centre circle. The rhythmic drift of movement has been broken now by the unpredictable bounce of the ball, and the shape of the game is cracked and confused. The referee calls off the match, the players join us, and the pavilion is far too crowded now. The rain thumps against the roof and everyone shouts to make himself heard.

Rufus is a special guest, and I am his guest, and we are fed as soon as the first round of meat is ready. We sit on a bench in a corner, our paper plates on our laps.

Some of the Roza team has gathered a few paces from us. They have discarded their wet uniforms. Some have wrapped towels around their shoulders, others are back in their street clothes. Rufus watches them as he chews his food.

'What are you thinking?' I ask him.

'What am I thinking?'

'You're staring at your soccer team. What are you thinking about them?'

He picks up a lamb chop, takes it to his mouth, then changes his mind and puts it back on his plate.

'Put it this way,' he says finally. 'One year, it was 2004, I managed to get eight boys into various colleges. The college coaches all know me. They call and they say: "Rufus, we're looking for talent. Have you got talent for us?" If I recommend somebody, he is taken very seriously. I don't suggest a boy for a soccer scholarship lightly.

'So, there were eight of them that year. Each one, I put him in my car and drove him to college. Some, I dropped off at the gate. Others, I escorted them right to their rooms and settled them in. Each of them I tutored, every spare moment, to pass his exams. The following semester, four of the eight left school and came back. The following year, *all* came back except for two. The following year, those last two are also back. What's going on? They didn't have the foundation to maintain college requirement.'

'Because they started school in Liberia, not here?'

'Yeah. Most of them came as teenagers. The schools took these kids free because of their talent. But the discipline is not there.'

'Just for academic work, or for soccer, too?'

'For both. To be a professional soccer player you need a foundation just like you do for college. These kids have no foundation.'

'Where are those eight boys now?'

'All are on the soccer team. Three are back in college, and I'm tutoring them. The rest, I'm pushing them into trades because they will not make it at school. Last Friday night, the team was together, I spent three hours talking about trades. Two of them called me the next day to say, yes, they are interested in plumbing. On the internet I found a plumbing school in Staten Island. I will try to link them to it.'

'How are they supporting themselves in the meantime?' I ask.

'Some are security guards. Some work in stores. Many work with E-ZPass.'

The opposing team's goalkeeper comes up to Rufus. He is an enormous man, well over six feet tall, and meaty. He begins to shout, leaning into Rufus as he does so, bursts of spray coming from his mouth. I can hear nothing of what he says, there is just the deafening tin roof, and the image before me appears to come from a dream: this uniformed colossus, shouting silently for all his worth. For a moment I think he is angry, and I search Rufus's face, but it is steady and calm; the big man is merely bellowing above the noise of the rain.

I am left with my thoughts. What comes is a picture of Rufus and his boys. He disperses them into the world, and they keep coming back to him, one after the other, like boomerangs. Park Hill Avenue is their fate.

When the goalkeeper is gone I ask Rufus what it was he was shouting. I am shouting myself now, my mouth close to Rufus's ear.

'He played for Roza at Buduburam refugee camp,' Rufus replies. 'He was telling me what happened to some of the other players on the team. One is in Philadelphia. I did not know that. And three are back in Monrovia.'

He pauses, looks around. His gaze settles on a group of players from the opposing team.

'Most of these boys have been touched by Roza in some way,' he says. 'There was a Roza in Minneapolis. Two of the boys who played today used to live there and played for Roza. Some played for Roza in the refugee camp. Others in Monrovia. Wherever I go in this country, wherever there are Liberians, boys come to me to say they have worn my uniforms, they have played somewhere for Roza.'

He pauses again, draws back and looks away, then leans in and speaks.

'I am going to go home one day and become the president of Liberia,' he says. 'Because in that country, the one problem they have no clue how to deal with is youth. And it is their biggest problem. Nine out of ten youths in Liberia have no work. They do not know what to do with them. I know what to do with them. I know them. That is my life.'

We sit and watch the rain together. I take a bite out of a lamb chop and chew it carefully.

He has shared this thought with me because it is raining so hard. The words were swallowed by the noise the moment they left his mouth.

PART FOUR

26

Liberia on Park Hill Avenue

Jacob Massaquoi arrived in the United States in February 2002. This time, he knew, his stay must last a long time. He could not go back to Monrovia, not while Charles Taylor was in power. He had a few friends in the United States, a sprinkling of family, some colleagues. In his passport he had a visitor's visa that would last him a few months.

For some time, his existence was itinerant, unsettled. He spent the late winter and early spring with relatives in Maryland. Then he moved to Florida where he boarded at the home of an official from one of the not-for-profit organisations that had supported his work in Liberia. By the summer, he had located his dear friend Azariah Sirleaf in a small town in Kentucky.

'He was studying there at a prestigious seminary,' Jacob recalls. 'Azariah, I can tell you, is a very pious man.'

'Actually,' Azariah tells me when I relay Jacob's words, 'I enrolled for the music, the choral church music. Unfortunately, there was too much theology, not enough music.'

When Jacob called, Azariah implored his friend to come to Kentucky. 'My home is open to you for ever and always, my brother,' Azariah recalls telling Jacob, 'no matter how modest my circumstances.'

'I didn't want to live in Kentucky,' Jacob remembers. 'What can you do from Kentucky? I said: "Azariah, I'm sorry, that won't work for me." He said: "Jake, what can I do for you? Anything. Anything."'

'So, he called his sister who lived in Staten Island, New York. Asked her to let me stay as long as I liked. She was married to a man called Billy Curtis.'

Azariah's sister and her husband lived at 55 Bowen Street, a project block a few steps from Park Hill Avenue. They were warm and hospitable, and their place was nice, but they had only an old, dial-up internet connection, and it was far, far too slow. It was like being in Kentucky, Jacob thought. Within days, he had reunited with an old childhood friend from Sanniquellie. In the friend's apartment on Park Hill Avenue was a faster broadband connection. Jacob spent the next eleven months sleeping on his friend's couch. To avoid monopolising a facility that was not his, he would wait until his hosts were asleep and get online after midnight, often working until breakfast. Among the first words he googled were 'asylum' and 'United States'. He found instructions, downloadable application forms, links to tract upon tract of congressional law.

As fall became winter, the business of getting asylum grew increasingly urgent. Jacob could not work on his visitor's visa. He was living off the largesse of the man on whose couch he was sleeping. Nor, without permanent residence, could he get treatment for his leg. Indeed, it would not be long before his visa expired, driving him underground.

'I was introduced to a man at 55 Bowen Street to help me with my asylum application,' Jacob recalls. 'I was told that he had processed many asylum applications here. He was a Liberian who had been in the US for many years. He interviewed me for five minutes, and I interviewed him to know his strength, his knowledge, skills and abilities. I found out he was weak when it came to computers. I told him I was going to write my story and bring it to him to connect the dots. He said no. He gave me all sorts of information that I found out later was not true. He tried to present the asylum process as very difficult. He tried to convince me that only he could do it.

'I went home, downloaded the asylum application form, brought it to him the next day and said what do I do next? It's pretty simple and straightforward. He didn't like that. He went on and on about complications. I did not go with him. I did not allow him to work on my paper.'

The encounter troubled Jacob. Liberians had been living on Park Hill Avenue for a long time. Practically everyone who came to settle here had some sort of immigration trouble. Could it be that between them and America's legal edifice stood one dubious man?

The more he watched, the more disturbed he became. 'I saw lots of flyers about activities in the community,' he recalls. 'There were so many meetings and events. But what were these events about? Why were they not about the basic things? There were people who had been living in the community eleven years, but who still were lost. They didn't know where to . . . just basic information, about health care, about benefits. They knew nothing, nothing, nothing.'

He arrived in Park Hill in early October. By the end of the month, a faint, flickering notion would pass briefly through his thoughts, never solid enough to grab hold of and nail down. Here were his fellow Liberians in New York City. And yet between them and this great metropolis stood a few men behaving as if they and they alone could provide access to the city. Could it be that wherever Liberians settled, some among them would become Congos, the rest helpless indigenes?

Jacob scanned Park Hill for signs of organisation. He wanted to work among Liberians. He found two bodies, Roza Promotions, run by a veteran Staten Islander called Rufus Arkoi, and another, newer organisation. Roza was larger, richer, busier: around Arkoi there was a buzz. He approached the big man and asked whether there might be work for him at Roza. Not before you sort out your immigration status, Arkoi told him. Not even as a volunteer. But when you've got that sorted, come back. My door will be open.

By then, Jacob had strong ideas about what he wanted to do. The man who had almost taken his money in exchange for bogus expertise; the lonely, late-night slog to acquire the right to stay in America: it was neither right nor necessary that Liberians go through this alone.

'I did not like the way Liberians were treating one another,' he recalls. 'People within the community who had connections out there presented themselves as elitists, the bureaucrats, the people you had to deal with in order to deal with America. I didn't like this middleman business. There had to be a way to create many more middlemen, let me put it that way, lots and lots of middlemen. There must not be one man who says: "without me, you can't do x, without me, you can't do y."

As his knowledge of the neighbourhood grew, he found its condition increasingly disturbing.

'People I met here,' he tells me, 'I had seen some of them in Monrovia when they returned to visit. They would be received as heroes, and they would claim to drive flashy cars. They would present themselves as if they are living in a mansion, living in heaven. Yet most of these people . . . I met someone who told me he was a doctor. He wore a white suit to work. He showed it to people. He said: "I'm a surgeon. This is what I must wear to theatre." After a few weeks here, I found out he was a home health aide with two weeks' training.

'What I saw was so depressing. Not just the lying to people back home. The futility. People who had been here many years couldn't return home because they had lived above their income, they had never saved, they didn't educate themselves to get a better job. They were stuck in their little cycle. Occasionally they get credit, go to Liberia with dreams of starting up a business. But they can't because they don't have the skills to function in the Liberian economy. So they come back to Staten Island and their jobs as home health aides.'

Jacob soldiered on alone with his asylum application. He downloaded the form once more and answered the questions one by one. He explained why returning to Charles Taylor's Liberia would be very dangerous for him. He got a friend to edit the story he had told.

He soon realised his application would require full-time work. Each instalment of the story he narrated had to be backed up with evidence. Evidence took the form of affidavits. Affidavits had to be credible. He contacted many organisations: the ones in Ireland and Florida that had helped him, the ones in Monrovia with whom he had worked, the US embassy, the UN mission in Liberia. He began in mid-October 2002. By mid-December, his application was complete, his affidavits signed and authenticated, his asylum hearing set for the day before Christmas. And then, at the very last minute, he learned something crushing.

'You needed a lawyer. For the hearing. It was a legal hearing. You needed representation. Where was I going to find a lawyer?'

He got online at 2.30 a.m. By the time the rest of the house was waking, he had found a New York organisation specialising in this type of pro-bono work.

'I waited until exactly 9 a.m. and called their offices. They said they could not help me because they did not know my case. Either they must go through my case with me from the beginning or they could not accompany me to the hearing. It was barely two weeks to go. I looked frantically for other assistance. I met someone from another agency who said he'd help. He gave me guidance as to what to do, what not to do. He was a social worker. He encouraged me. Pep talk. Encouragement. He took me through the paces. With that encouragement, I felt confident, and I knew I had a solid case. I went to my hearing, and represented myself. And I made it. My hearing was on 24 December, just before Christmas. A few days later I got a letter in the post. When I went back I was given a little white paper saying I was granted asylum and a document listing my rights and privileges. That is what opened the door for me.'

In the new year, Jacob went back to Rufus and showed him his asylum papers. They agreed that Jacob would begin on a trial basis, as a volunteer. In the evenings, Jacob found paying work, at a homeless shelter on Atlantic Avenue in Brooklyn, a ninety-minute commute from Park Hill.

He dreaded going to work each evening. The clients at the shelter were volatile people, always ready to fight. Jacob felt that the work required physical strength, agility. One needed to show that one was physically strong. His ruined leg made him feel vulnerable. He would hobble into work and think: 'Any one of these men could push me over if they wanted to.' He compensated with his demeanour: he was sprightly, upbeat, with a constant smile on his face.

To Roza Promotions he gave his services for free for some months, and then Rufus Arkoi put him on staff and on a salary. His position was 'Co-ordinator, Youth Programmes'.

'Young man was clearly bright,' Rufus remembers. 'Clearly dedicated. Clearly had something to contribute. My organisation was at its height. I opened my door to him. Said: "Jacob, I put you on salary, I open the resources and good will of this organisation to your disposal: use your energy to make something."'

Within a month, Jacob had resigned.

'Rufus was not into having innovative people around him,' Jacob tells me. 'In the month that I worked for him as a programme co-ordinator, we never once met to discuss any programme. There was no programme. There was Rufus. I wanted to grow. I wanted to exercise the abilities I had begun to develop.'

What Jacob did next he now regrets. At times, he calls it a mistake. At others, a misunderstanding. With the American education he has now acquired, he says, he has learned new things about relations between people. 'I wish I knew then what I know now,' he tells me. 'That there are many ways to skin a cat.'

Sitting in Roza's offices day in and day out, a number of questions emerged in his mind. Rufus was so busy with all things Liberian – why had he not been in a position to help Jacob, or anyone else, it appeared, with his application for asylum? With all the not-for-profits and advice centres and pro-bono lawyers in this city, why had Rufus, with all his resources, never established a decent immigration service for Liberians? And if he was not doing this for Liberians, what on earth was he doing?

His thoughts wandered further. Rufus was *the* Liberian on Park Hill Avenue. Those who wanted to work with the Liberian community came through him. He was thus Liberians' de facto representative. But he was *not* a representative. Nobody had elected him. He ran an organisation that provided services. In fact, strictly speaking, his services were not intended for Liberians in particular: Roza's literature claimed that the organisation provided services for *immigrants*.

By the time he resigned from Roza, Jacob's imagination had formed something solid and defined. He believed that he had seen Rufus's kind all too often before. Here was a man who took American money in the name of his fellow Liberians, but used it to make a personal fiefdom. Was this smudging of public representation and private empire not the story of successive Liberian presidents? Never mind that the benefactor now was the Robin Hood Foundation rather than the Firestone Rubber Company: the principle was the same. Arkoi was the middleman standing between Liberians and America, keeping his countrypeople dependent and useless. It amazed him that he had travelled all the way to America, only to find Liberia writ small.

'I began to see Park Hill Avenue as a country,' Jacob tells me. 'A country should have a leadership with a mandate to represent its people. A strong government. If someone goes out in the name of the community and speaks on its behalf, they must have a mandate from the community and be accountable to it.'

In mid-2003, Jacob and others formed a political party with the intention of contesting that year's bi-annual election for the executive of the Staten Island Liberian Community Associaton (SILCA). Jacob himself had no desire to stand for office; he wanted to start an organisation that provided people with services, real services. He convinced another to stand for the position of president.

Rufus immediately saw this new campaign for the threat that it was. He could not have a SILCA executive filled with loud voices questioning his authority to represent Liberians.

Jacob says: 'Rufus saw this new party and shook his head. He said: "I can't support this. You people are nobodies. You have not been in this community five minutes. Nobody knows you here. Nor do you have a Congo to stand for you. I will form another party to contest you, and I will win."'

Rufus's party took the name Liberian Action Party (LAP).

Right at the beginning, the battle between Rufus and Jacob exhibited signs over which an outsider might puzzle. The most widely known Americo-Liberian in Staten Island's Liberian community was Billy Curtis, the brother-in-law of Azariah Sirleaf, with whom Jacob had stayed when he came to New York. He was an ample man who worked in a city government job through the night and slept until very late in the mornings. When I arrived at his home at midday for an interview, he greeted me in a pair of boxer shorts, rubbing the sleep from his eyes.

'These Liberians in Staten Island,' he told me with one eye on the giant television screen that dominated his living room, 'they have brought terrible values with them from wartime Liberia. I have spent a lot of my time wishing for the Liberia that existed before the war when we were still a civilised and respected people. Is it gone for ever? I want to go back and see. I want to go home and start a business. Problem is my wife. Like a rock. She won't move.'

Jacob and Rufus began to compete for Curtis's allegiance. Both badly needed him to lead their respective parties. Eventually, after countless toing and froing, and wooing and counter-wooing, Curtis announced that he would be standing for president of the Staten Island Liberian Community Association on Rufus Arkoi's ticket, the Liberian Action Party. To this day, many of the Liberians I speak to say that Curtis went the way he did because he was offered money.

I have asked Rufus and Jacob and several other people why both parties needed an Americo-Liberian as president. Both Jacob and Rufus, after all, are thoroughly and proudly indigene, both outspoken opponents of Congo influence.

'You don't understand,' one of the people I interviewed told me. 'The people of Park Hill Avenue are not politically educated. All their lives, power has come with an Americo-Liberian name. That is how power has come.'

In the end, the person Jacob got to lead *his* ticket, although not a Congo by birth, had married into a family with one of oldest and most famous Americo-Liberian names. Her name was Jennifer Gray Brumskine.

The need for an Americo-Liberian as president, the insistence that he would have to be bought: it was clear from the start that much of Liberian history would be played out on the stage that Jacob and Rufus had erected.

Among the first things Jacob did when he received the pamphlet listing his rights as a person granted asylum in the United States was to examine the medical treatment to which he was entitled. By mid-2004, he had enrolled for experimental reconstructive surgery at a university hospital. The surgeons he was consulting told him that there was little precedent to go by, that by their best guess, and it was only a guess, his chances of recovery were 50/50. The first time Jacob told me about it, he did so with bravado.

'The decision was easy,' he told me. 'If the surgery failed, I'd stay handicapped, as I would have been without the surgery. It would not have been the end of the world. I would have adjusted.'

Perhaps, but the fact that he was handicapped was tormenting him, and the adjustment had already cost him a great deal – in emotional pain, in the exhaustion he suffered through constantly compensating for his short leg.

Today, in an album on his coffee table, there are photographs of him in his hospital bed, a cellphone stuck to his left ear, his right leg hoisted in front of him in a great black cage, like a portable enclosure for a ferret or a cat. Staring at one of those photographs one Wednesday afternoon, his bravado suddenly vanished. For some time, he could not talk.

'It was a terrible two years, Jonny,' he said finally. 'In 2004, just a few days before my surgery, I already knew it would be a long and protracted recovery. Jonny, when I think about my recovery it would make several volumes of a book.'

'Give me a taste,' I said.

'It was excruciating pain. Always. Without a break. Night, day. Walking, sitting. To be followed by this pain, everywhere, always . . .'

When I asked him about physio, he shook his head.

'That is one of the volumes, a long, long story. Suffice it to say, I had two sessions with a physiotherapist. And then I was on my own. I got the regimen and I did it myself, every day. It was sheer agony. Each morning, I woke up: "God help me, I have to do those exercises."'

Throughout the two years of his recuperation, he lived alone. He had an aunt on Park Hill Avenue, a woman who has subsequently died. She would come every day to help him wash, and to clean his dishes and his apartment. He had friends who would come to assist. His first few visits to the doctor were enormous ordeals. He could not use New York's subways. For each trip, he was ferried by ambulance. The journey from his fourth-floor apartment to the ambulance's open door today comes to him in nightmares, distorted, fragmented, mixed up with things that happened in Liberia during the war.

Holed up day in and day out, he studied, burning his way through online degrees in rapid time: first he did a bachelors, then he registered for a masters. He did not choose to study his beloved physics. The PhD for which he finally enrolled was in Leadership Studies. The circumstances in which he might have become a scientist seem to have passed. The war had swept them away. There was now other business at hand.

When he was not doing his exercises or his studies, he was working on African Refuge, his new organisation providing services for immigrants. He had no salary, just the support and guidance of a trauma studies programme at Columbia University. Sometimes he would see clients in his apartment. Sometimes he would gather his crutches and walk the 500 or so yards to the African Refuge office. And when he wasn't doing that, he was fighting Rufus Arkoi.

Over the following three years, Jacob's and Rufus's respective parties would go head to head in two elections for the Staten Island Liberian Community Association (SILCA). Rufus's Liberia Action Party would win them both. But everything about both elections would be the subject of fierce dispute.

In the run-up to one of the two elections, Jacob's party claimed that Billy Curtis had contrived to appoint a partisan election commission, and that the elections could not go ahead. They appealed to the one body in the community sufficiently authoritative to mediate: a triumvirate of priests who headed the three largest Liberian congregations in Staten Island: the Ministerial Alliance. And yet no sooner had the Alliance convened to adjudicate than it split into opposing factions. The community was rudderless now. There was nobody left to stand outside of the fray and administer the rules. There was nothing left to do but fight.

Jacob and his comrades lost the 2003 poll and immediately claimed that the opposing side had bribed the election commissioner and stolen the election. They threatened court action, but did not go through with it. That would come next time around.

Jacob's party settled into the searching, scrupulous role of opposition. They questioned every cent of money raised by or in the Liberian community. Their first target was $300,000 of federal money Roza had been awarded. Where was it now? Could Rufus account for it? How had he spent it? Reverend Stevens had been Roza's bookkeeper at the time. Why was some of the money used to rebuild his church? How could he be both bookkeeper and beneficiary?

Next, the new party turned to SILCA's charitable works. One was a food pantry for needy Liberians on Park Hill Avenue. SILCA officials were accused of selling food at a profit on the side.

In 2004, SILCA went door to door on Park Hill Avenue collecting clothes for Liberians back home. Billy Curtis was about to visit Monrovia; it was thought that his trip should be used to take something of value to those suffering. SILCA accumulated several thousands of dollars worth of goods, it was said, which

Curtis duly took with him. When he returned, members of Jacob's party accused him of having sold them, and perhaps sharing his proceeds with other executive members.

Jacob's party demanded that SILCA reveal each of its banking transactions of the previous few years. SILCA finally complied, and when Jacob's party found no hard evidence of fraud, they accused SILCA executive members of operating a secret parallel bank account.

The time soon came when no transaction involving a SILCA member could take place without controversy. At a soccer tournament to celebrate Liberian Independence Day, Billy Curtis set up a stall selling cold bottled water. Jennifer Gray Brumskine confronted him and demanded to know why he was using a public event to run a private business. She said that if he were to charge for water, she would charge an entrance fee to members of the crowd. She picked a couple of prominent Americo-Liberian visitors, an incendiary gesture, and demanded $20 from them. Curtis called the police.

The following year, a New York bank offered to donate money to help the Liberians celebrate Independence Day. Curtis, as SILCA president, formed a committee to administer the funds. He appointed Rufus to chair the committee, and Stevens as vice chair. The opposition party objected strenuously; how can three men so mired in controversy administer such a large fund together, they asked. They appealed to the Ministerial Alliance once again. But Stevens, of course, was one of the triumvirate that constituted the Alliance, and the meeting quickly ended in acrimony. The bank withdrew its offer of a donation.

Public confrontation Liberian-style is bodily and visceral. You come up close to your opponent, nose to nose, and shout your words from the pit of your stomach, as if the sound of your voice alone might fell him. You punctuate your argument with your limbs, bending your knees and pumping your arms with each accusation, as if your anger has taken hold of your very body. And your rhetoric must leave no room for doubt. Attacks are brutal, ad hominem: the aim is to scorch, to flatten. For an outsider, the pumping limbs and thrusting chests, the rudeness, the sheer volume of noise, is an affront. The police were called on several occasions during the Park Hill conflict; more often than not, it was non-Liberian bystanders who did so, either because they mistook the performance for real violence, or because they felt that the spectacle was polluting their neighbourhood.

In 2006, when time came for the two sides to contest another election, Jacob's party, now called LUTA (Liberians United for Transparency and Accountability) convened late at night behind closed doors and tried its hand at political cartooning. In the early hours of the morning of the election, they paid a group of boys to slip copies of their handiwork under each of the 1,074 doors of the housing projects on Park Hill Avenue. The figures in the cartoons had names: Pastor Snake-Eyes Stevens was one; Rufus My-Money Arkoi was another. Another cartoon had Billy Curtis climbing up Rufus's back. The bubble coming from his mouth said: 'Rufus, where is the $300,000?'

Nearly two-thirds of the votes cast that day were in support of Rufus's party. Jacob and his comrades cried foul once more, refused to accept the outcome, and filed a motion in the state Supreme Court. Four months later, the judge denied their petition, saying that LUTA had not only failed to substantiate their claims, but could not produce a copy of SILCA's constitution to show that there were any electoral rules to break.

New Yorkers who witnessed the spectacle were aghast. In 2007, an officer in the New York Police Department's Immigrant Outreach Unit was assigned to liaise with Liberian community leaders about their relationship with the police. He was reported to have come back with the news that the community was too fractured to meet with: 'They need protection from each other, not New York,' he apparently said. 'Can't somebody go in and mediate so that they can agree on who it is I should be talking to?'

The borough did indeed appoint a mediator, and the rival factions agreed to sit down with her, and yet one wonders what chance she had, for the sources of this bitterness lay deep in the wells of a country's unhappiness.

In the midst of the Staten Island conflict, Rufus would gather his soccer team together to talk of the fight in which he was embroiled. His organisation was in rapid decline. More and more, the club was preoccupied with how it would raise funds, and with the question of who was responsible for its unhappy situation.

'My son came home from soccer practice one day with a story,' a middle-aged Liberian parent who didn't want to be identified told me. 'He said the Roza players had been discussing what was happening inside the community.

'"Jacob is from Nimba," one of the boys had said. "Which border did Taylor cross when he invaded Liberia? The border between Ivory Coast and Nimba County. You know why Jacob limps? Why do you think he limps? Have you asked yourself that question?"

'My son knew Jacob well and was troubled by this. "Do you know Jacob from Liberia?" my son asked.

'"No," the boy replied. "But ask Rufus. He has credible sources. Very credible sources."'

The rumours about Jacob spread. One of the market women who sells food in a street market just off Park Hill Avenue told me that she had heard that Jacob had killed more than 300 Krahn soldiers on the battlefield before one of his foes shot his leg to pieces.

'Who knows whether it's true?' she said. 'Jacob is such a helpful young man, so warm. But the past is hidden from us here in America. Everyone you greet on the street, who knows what they were up to in their other life?'

Jacob would become much loved in the Liberian community. He was to build an organisation that brought an array of valuable services to Park Hill, and many would be grateful to him. And yet, for all that his authority and his likeability grew, the story of Jacob the rebel soldier proved strangely, almost magically, resilient. It would disappear for long periods. And then, whenever Jacob found himself in a fresh conflict, it would arise again, fresh from its hibernation.

A woman visiting from Monrovia, for instance, soon skirmished with Jacob. In retaliation, she told both me and a reporter from the *New York Times* that she had hard, documentary evidence that Jacob had been a child soldier in the early days of the war. Her mission in Staten Island, she said, would be to get him to tell the truth in public. When I pushed her about her evidence, she soon retreated, saying that she knew in her heart that Jacob had been a rebel.

And then there was SILCA's 2008 election. Everybody thought that it would turn out fine. The two sides had made peace, and were backing the same candidate. Jacob and Rufus were often seen in public together, working amicably. Yet, once again, the elections broke down: there were threats, accusations and finger waving, and somebody called the police, who closed the election centre down. Jacob's old allies had backed a new contender, and they were now accusing Jacob of having rigged the voters' roll. As Jacob walked down Park Hill Avenue that afternoon, his old allies approached him one by one, pointing long, accusing fingers at his chest.

'Where did you get your limp, Jacob?' one of them asked. 'Today's events prove where you got your limp. There are a quarter of a million Liberians dead, Jacob, because of people like you.'

Jacob stood up on his toes and laughed with an imperious sneer, his chest puffed and confident. Walking away with him, though, his back now turned to his accusers, it was just he and I and an awkward silence.

He turned to look at me; his eyes were far bigger than I had ever seen them, round as moons, the pupils little pinpricks.

'How much of your book did we say was going to be about me?' he asked. 'A chapter? Half a chapter?'

In August 2003, just a few months after Rufus and Jacob went to war, peace returned to Liberia. Park Hill residents gathered around websites, phoned home every day, and discussed the new settlement incessantly. It was only two years later, though, on a Wednesday evening in the late summer of 2005, that Staten Island Liberians got a taste of that peace for themselves.

Many Liberians called in sick on the day, or swapped shifts with colleagues, or knocked off at lunchtime. On Sobel Court, the market women packed up their salted fish and peppers in the mid-afternoon lest they miss out on good seats.

'Walking up Park Hill Avenue towards the venue,' a man called James Davies remembers today, 'I saw the strangest sight. The Liberians were lined up outside like a row of ducks, waiting for the doors to open. Single file, one Liberian after the other, all the way down the sidewalk, like ducks.'

The occasion was a visit to Park Hill Avenue by Ellen Johnson-Sirleaf, a presidential candidate in the first elections to be held in Liberia since the fighting ceased two years earlier.

It was a time of great uncertainty. The Liberian civil war had been over for precisely twenty-four months. The armed factions had disbanded, for now. An interim government was running Liberia. But was the war truly over? Nobody could say for sure.

At the negotiations in Accra, Ghana, that ended of the war, Liberia's warlords had called the shots. Quite openly, they bargained with one another for positions in the ministries and state departments, and for control over the government petroleum company and Monrovia's lucrative port. At one point, when a member of an armed faction with the improbable name of Liberians United for Reconciliation and Development (LURD) was not getting his way at the negotiating table, he made a cellphone call to his commander on Bushrod Island, ordering that downtown Monrovia be shelled. The negotiators watched the ensuing bombardment live on CNN, and the LURD leader got his ministry.

Charles Taylor was out of the picture for the moment: he had been indicted by the International Criminal Court for war crimes committed in Sierra Leone, Liberia's neighbour, and had taken refuge in Nigeria. But Liberia's other warlords were all very much present – men like Alhaji Kromah and Prince Johnson. Their aim had always been to gather wealth and power, whether by war or through politics, and such men littered Liberia's postwar scene, speaking a language of peace that no one believed. The young soldiers they had commanded were sitting idle, some of them disarmed, others not. Nobody could say for sure that the peace would last.

Was Ellen Johnson-Sirleaf the answer? She had been in exile in the United States for a long time, chased from Liberia first by Doe and then by Taylor. She was the West's darling, clearly America's candidate. She spoke America's language so well. If she came to office, she would surely bring a lot of Western money and support. Perhaps, if she were in charge, the West would really want to keep the peace; perhaps United Nations soldiers might even be prepared to stop a coup, should one occur.

Yet there were questions about Johnson-Sirleaf, too. She had been the Finance Minister in the last Americo-Liberian cabinet before Doe's coup, and thus a member of the old elite. Was she a Trojan horse bringing Congo rule back to Monrovia? She had been a strong supporter of Charles Taylor when he invaded Liberia. 'Let him level the Executive Mansion,' she had famously declared in a BBC interview.

'We will rebuild it.' Wasn't it an open secret that the exiled Congos backed Taylor in early 1990 in an attempt to get back to power?

The venue for her visit was a recreation centre in the basement of one of the Park Hill buildings.

'Liberians are notoriously late,' the Reverend Laurenzo Stevens, founder of the first Liberian Pentecostal church in Staten Island, tells me. 'You want to get a bunch of Liberians together at 4 p.m., you must call a meeting for 2 p.m. Maybe you will start on time. But that evening, forty-five minutes before Madame Sirleaf was due to speak, you could not get a seat.'

From the very beginning, the mood in the room was not right. Everybody entering was handed a pamphlet, and once they were seated and began to read, they looked around nervously. There was going to be trouble; that much was clear.

'On the front page of the pamphlet,' Reverend Stevens recalls, 'was a question: "Who is the real Ellen Johnson-Sirleaf?" You turned the page, and there was a very familiar picture of Madame Sirleaf from her election campaign, dressed in beautiful West African traditional dress. "Is this her?" the pamphlet asked. And then you turned to another picture, an old one of Sirleaf from the late 1970s, dressed in a smart Western suit, as the Congo politicians of that time dressed. "Or is this the real Madame Sirleaf?" the pamphlet asked. Clearly, the implication was that she was the old elite coming back in disguise.'

The moment Sirleaf got up to speak, the people who had handed out the pamphlets rose to heckle her.

'Why did you tell Taylor to burn down the Executive Mansion? Why did you not lift a finger when the Americo-Liberian regime was oppressing us? Was it not you who brought war? Look at your hands? Do you see blood? We do.'

'They would not let her speak except to answer their allegations,' an elderly woman called Evelyn Cooper recalls. 'Every time she started her speech they shouted louder and louder and louder. I watched her face. I did not know whether she was more frightened than angry, or more angry than frightened. Eventually, she wagged her finger and told these people to stop besmirching her name.'

As people left the venue, they eyed one another nervously. 'You never know what is in a Liberian's heart,' Evelyn Cooper told me.

'If I learned anything that night, it is that I should think twice before sharing with anybody on Park Hill Avenue what is in mine.'

Over the following days, many wondered to themselves what the connection might be between the ill-feeling Sirleaf's presence had fostered and the fight taking place between Rufus's and Jacob's respective parties; between the peace at home and the war on Staten Island. I, for one, came to think that the connection was intimate. Liberians, after all, have for a long time played out big, national dramas on small, local stages. In the years before and after 1980, for instance, students at high schools across Liberia established student bodies and overthrew them, as if an entire generation of the country's youth was practising and foreshadowing the great coup that was to come.

What had happened on Park Hill Avenue was not dissimilar. The fight began as the Liberian civil war was ending. The new peace back home was very uncertain. Many of those who began filling the ranks of Liberia's postwar elite had been deeply compromised by the fighting. Notorious warlords were about to stand for public office. Famous wartime profiteers were looking for new ways to make money. All of these people began speaking a new language: of human rights, of democracy, of atoning for the past and maintaining peace. Public discourse was rife with insincerity. Secret agendas hid behind stated intentions. Public office was assumed to be a disguise for the pursuit of wealth. Could peace last under these circumstances? And, if so, what sort of peace would it be?

On Staten Island, it seems to me, the conflict had two faces, one looking towards America, the other towards home. The anxiety about what was happening in both places erected the stage on which Rufus and Jacob fought. With regard to home, Rufus and Jacob were stand-in figures: people who could not be trusted to spend public money; people incapable of running for power without cheating; people with terrible acts buried in their pasts. The uncertain future everyone feared for Liberia was condensed into the figures of Rufus and Jacob.

Both men had played these stand-in roles before. Rufus had been overthrown in a soccer club coup in 1981. Jacob had organised a high-school coup in the late 1980s. In a sense, what had happened on Park Hill Avenue grew naturally from both of their biographies.

27

Refuge

Late one night in 2007, a Staten Island nurse called Cheryl Nadeau found the African Refuge website while browsing the internet. She called Jacob the following day and made an appointment to see him. Nadeau had not practised nursing in many years, having quit her job in frustration. Now, she was working three days a week in a Manhattan law firm and hated every minute of it. She was looking for a way back into public health.

Jacob was hardly one to say no to a skilled professional who knocked on his door offering her services for free. Much of Park Hill Avenue had little access to health care, either because they couldn't afford insurance, or because their fragile immigration status made them fear contact with officialdom, or, in the case of many of the elderly, because they simply did not have the wherewithal to negotiate New York beyond the block in which they lived. The question was what the presence of one volunteer nurse might do to address this situation.

At much the same time, a member of Jacob's board put him in touch with a research professor at NYU Medical School interested in studying the epidemiology of high blood pressure among the city's immigrants. The professor designed a survey and gave it to Cheryl to implement. Jacob went onto the street and began coaxing elderly Liberians to come to African Refuge on Wednesdays to get their blood pressure tested. At first, they came slowly and cautiously. Three or four people on the first Wednesday, five or six on the second. Jacob served coffee and doughnuts. Many of those who arrived were lonely people who on most mornings had only their television sets to entertain them; they came for the company.

The results of their blood pressure tests were troubling.

'You have no idea just how much hypertension there is in this community,' Cheryl told me. 'Of the first thirty people we tested, 75 per cent had significantly elevated blood pressure. The old, the young: even people in their twenties and thirties.'

'What's the explanation?' I asked.

'I truly don't know. I can only guess. One reason is that black people are genetically predisposed to high blood pressure. Another, perhaps, is the stress of war and relocation. A third is that people test in emergency rooms, the only place you can go for health care if you have no insurance. Managing chronic illness requires a relationship with a health care worker. Going to an emergency room every few years doesn't provide you with one.'

Through his connection to Wagner College, just a stone's throw from Park Hill, Jacob arranged for a battery of nursing students to join Cheryl at African Refuge every Wednesday to assist with her client-load. The students were Italian-American women, in the main, and they arrived with varnished nails and an aromatic trail of hair products. They sat in a wide circle drinking coffee, and would tell me that for all of their nineteen and twenty-year-old lives on Staten Island, they had not heard of this street, or of Liberia, or of Liberians; that it was wonderful to be here, and that the incidence of high blood pressure in this community truly shocked them.

Jacob also sat on the board of the Richmond Community Health Care Center, the only primary health care site within a reasonable distance from Park Hill, and arranged for the clinic to shuttle patients between African Refuge and the clinic every Wednesday. In early 2008 he discovered Staten Island's only free medical insurance service, available to all, even the undocumented, only to discover that it was about to close down. He signed up every Liberian he could lay his hands on, and began lobbying that its members be provided with an alternative.

It was humbling to watch this incurably entrepreneurial man at work. Within months, he had brought first-rate primary health care to Park Hill Avenue for the first time in its history, and had coaxed most of the street's elderly residents to visit his centre by June 2008.

Each Wednesday morning, African Refuge would appear to sink

a few inches deeper into the earth under the weight of the Liberians assembled there. The middle-aged and the elderly would congregate early on plastic chairs in staggering numbers, and they would stay until long after their blood pressure had been read. There was much else to do besides seeing Cheryl and the Wagner nursing students. Jacob had arranged for a weekly food pantry run by an organisation called Project Hospitality, so there was plenty to eat. He was also working with a paralegal immigration caseworker, Michael Kavanagh, and had found an organisation to pay him a salary for his work at African Refuge. He was immediately deluged with cases.

'People come to my office,' Michael told me, 'who quite literally have no idea of their immigration status. I make an appointment to see them at their apartments and ask that in the meantime they gather all the documentation and correspondence they can find.

'I arrive the next morning, and the client gives me a shoebox stuffed with a decade's worth of correspondence with the INS. I spread all the documentation on the floor and begin to work through it. I feel like a forensic scientist reconstructing a life through paperwork. Eventually, it will start making sense, sometimes after an hour, sometimes not until late afternoon. Often you look at the papers and you see that someone in the family was dealing with it very competently. Then, suddenly, after a certain date, everything stops. The INS keeps sending letters, but the family is not replying. And then the INS letters stop, too. Silence.

'I say to the client: "Did someone in this household leave or pass away in August or September 1999?"

'She'll say: "Yes, my husband died on 24 August nine years ago."

'After his death, the family fell out of status and became undocumented without knowing it.'

On a Wednesday afternoon in the late summer of 2008, I sat in African Refuge's offices waiting for Jacob. Cheryl and Michael had both gone for the day, and just half a dozen or so clients remained. From the hallway, we heard raised voices. They were interspersed with banging sounds, and they grew louder, and their tone became shriller and more menacing. The conversation among the Liberians ceased.

I walked out into the corridor. At the elevator, two women had rounded on a man. Each had picked up a shopping bag and was using it to bash his head and torso. He had backed into a corner and was shielding his face and neck with raised arms.

'You wanna fight me?' one of the women was saying in an American accent. 'You wanna fight me? I'll fucking fight you til you're fucking dead! I'll fight you til your head is fucking pulp!'

From the elevator, a tall, bespectacled man emerged, moving smartly. He wedged himself between the man and his attackers, faced them full on, and opened his arms wide.

'Easy,' he said. 'Back off. I'll take him away. It's over. I'll take him away. Easy.'

I had seen him before. He was a Sierra Leonean who occasionally did volunteer work in Jacob's office.

The battered man, his attackers now distracted, edged away slowly, a strained nonchalance in his gait, as if he was about to start whistling; hands in pockets now, he made his way down the corridor.

'You still want to fight?' one of the women called after him. 'Anytime, motherfucker. I will take you to fucking pieces.'

When I returned to African Refuge, a brittle and unpleasant pallor had fallen over the place. The Wednesday blood pressure clients were now in huddles and whispering, as if the women outside were about to invade. The tall Sierra Leonean came in, his eyes wide with fear.

'They would have killed him if I hadn't been passing,' he said. 'I swear, they would have killed him.'

'Why they hit him?' someone asked.

'He was asking for it. She wanted to get into the elevator with him, and he didn't want her to. So he kicked her shopping bags. Just kicked them.'

'Just kick her bag, for no reason? He wanna die?'

'That man is my African brother,' the Sierra Leonean continued, 'but I cannot defend what he did. Those people will kill you if you do bad by them. One foot out of line and they will kill you, even the women.'

There were murmurings of fear and disapproval. An elderly woman began to weep.

'My son musn' come here,' she said. 'He must stay in Monrovia.

Never min' I haven' seen him i'seventeen year. If he come here they will kill him.'

Jacob walked in at that very moment. His clients gathered around him and threw their story at him in serial bursts. As he listened, he seemed to absorb not just their words, but their fear too. By the time they were finished telling the tale their voices were even and steady. Jacob went to his desk and made himself busy, checking his emails and making a few calls; the fact that he was there soothed and placated. People made coffee and went to the bathroom, and soon began talking of other things.

If Jacob calmed them, they calmed him. In my experience, he was at his most tranquil on Wednesdays. He would stand in the doorway in his office and watch the dozens of faces and know that he was seeing the fruit of his hard work. His brood of elderly, ill or lonely Liberians, on whose behalf he took on this illegible and uncertain city, stilled him.

Jacob's youth centre was housed in a long, windowless room on the ground floor of 140 Park Hill Avenue, less than a block from the walk-in centre where his elderly clients assembled on Wednesdays. A line of workspaces ran across the length of one of the walls, a computer terminal in each space, a child in every chair. They came after school and stayed until their parents returned from work.

An apparition appeared in the doorway of the youth centre one afternoon. At first it seemed to be one being with two heads. But they were two quite separate beings, young men, each extravagantly thin and very tall, 6 foot 4, perhaps, or 6 foot 5. Both wore brown suits, not quite identical, and white collared shirts, their respective ties slung low on their chests, their tie-knots tight, tiny and round, like bulls'-eyes, their shirt tails dangling from underneath their jackets. They ducked their heads under the door frame and sloped across the room on impossibly long legs, one a couple of paces behind the other, their gaits all kneecap and swagger.

'Yo, Jacob,' one of them greeted. 'Whatup.'

'Give me a few minutes,' Jacob replied. 'And then I will get on the phone and do this thing.'

The man nodded and turned and went up to the kids on the computer terminals, displaying, as he walked away from us, two thin, bony buttocks under white cotton underwear, his suit pants slung over the top of his thighs like gangbanger jeans.

'What brings you here?' I asked the one who had remained behind.

'We sales executives,' he replied. 'This man Jacob our customer.'

'What you selling?'

'A whole package. You can have just phone line for $19.99 a month, first month free. You can have phone and cable; or you can have phone, cable and wireless. We have multiple packages, tailored to your specific requirements. We sit down and talk rates. You find better rates on this island, we beat them. But you won't find better rates because there is no better rates on this island: a fact.'

'Who you working for?' I asked.

'Verizon.'

'Since when?'

'This our second week.'

'They are Liberians,' Jacob told me without looking up from his desk. 'This is the first time they have employment. It is an experiment. You put a Park Hill address on your résumé, people don't want to employ you. They tried to work it the other way around. They said there is so much business in Park Hill and you cable companies are too scared to come and get it. They have to show that they can get 100 customers on this street.'

'We'll do it easy,' the sales executive replied. 'All the folks here wants cable.'

'So you're changing to Verizon?' I asked Jacob.

'No. I'm going to sign up with Verizon now and cancel next week, before they do the installation. Their trial period will be over by then.'

Jacob got on his phone and was put on hold for a long time, while the salesmen wandered around the room and bantered with the kids.

One of the kids danced around and pretended to spar.

The sales executive stood dead still and peered down disdainfully from his great height. 'You expect me to flinch? I'm from the 'hood.'

When Jacob finally got through, there was a problem, and one of the sales executives asked to borrow my phone to call his supervisor. He waited a long, long time, far longer than Jacob had waited, and just as he got through he was put on hold, indefinitely this time, it seemed. After thirty-five further minutes, when it had become clear that he was going to be on hold for ever, I asked for my phone back. At first he ignored me and turned his back. I moved around him and asked again. He hung up sulkily and turned his face from me as he passed the phone back, as if I were the cause of this missed sale.

The sales executives did not want to leave like this. They went back to the boys at the computer terminals and bantered some more, but a sourness followed them now, and a shortness, as if something unpleasant was about to burst through a thin crust.

'We be back tomorrow, Jacob,' one of them said. 'You here tomorrow?'

They slunk out of the door side by side, their half-clad asses moving in perfect time, and although their faces were turned from us, and we could not witness their humiliation, their double-gait dragged and their shoes scraped as they left.

The following day, I walked with Jacob down Park Hill Avenue towards his youth centre. We were accompanied by a young boy whom Jacob had introduced to me as Craig. He was twelve or thirteen years old, I thought.

Craig said something to Jacob I could not hear. Jacob stopped in his tracks.

'How much you get paid? You want to know how much you get paid! You do not get paid. You are doing community *service*. Service. Do you know what that word means? When you run your own business, you make a profit. Community service is about helping others. And do you know why you are doing community service? Because the alternative was *incarceration*. The judge was doing you a favour. *We* are doing you a favour.'

We were inside 140 Park Hill Avenue now, and Jacob was fumbling for his keys. Craig had hung back and was out of earshot.

'What does he need to do at the youth centre?' I asked Jacob.

'Nothing. He needs to sit there every afternoon for a few months, and then he can go. This keeps him out of the detention centre. And he wants to know how much he will be paid.'

'What did he do wrong?'

'He did something terrible. He is here as restitution for something terrible he did.'

Jacob unlocked the door to the centre and invited us in. He walked briskly across the room towards his desk. I was putting down my coat and rummaging in my bag; it took some time before I noticed that he had stopped in his tracks and was staring at the workstations along the wall. At first I did not see what he saw. On every desk, where a monitor had stood yesterday there was now just a coil of naked wires, standing up straight and reaching out to nothing. Jacob went to his storeroom and looked inside, then turned and put his hands on his hips and bowed his head low. He stood like that, perfectly still, for a long time.

A large meeting of youth service providers was to assemble at African Refuge that afternoon, and within an hour of discovering the theft of his computers, Jacob's centre was full of kind and supportive people.

'This is what our work is about, right?' said a woman called Lisa from a not-for-profit organisation named Citizens Committee for New York City. 'If there were no problems, there'd be no work for us to do, right?'

Jacob sat slumped on a chair, staring at his hands. 'I am peeling from the inside,' he said. 'Do you understand? This community is the *worst*.'

'No, they are not,' Lisa continued. 'No they are not. You think we don't have this in Crown Heights? This is why you do what you do, Jacob. This is why you are here. The point is how you handle it once it's happened. You do not let it slide. You confront and engage. I'll talk to the kids individually. On the street, they talk. I have my ways. We'll soon know which of your kids did it, and that is when the challenge begins.'

Jacob was no longer listening. Two uniformed police had just arrived and already he had latched on to them and begun to unburden himself.

'Have you had previous thefts?' one of them asked.

'Previous thefts? Have I had previous thefts? *Sure* I've had previous thefts. Where do you want me to begin? One of the boys from this centre came up with me to my apartment on a Sunday morning. I was about to go to church, to *church*. When I went to the bathroom, he took my front door key and pressed it into a piece of putty. While I was out at church, he made a copy of my key, came back and robbed me blind.'

'You want other examples?' He turned to me now. 'Remember the Verizon guys in the suits? A few months ago, they stole the doorbell off the door of this youth centre. They did it in front of the kids. They said: "You tell, we will beat you up." One of the kids told me anyway. I confronted them. They said: "How did you know? Who told you?" I said: "That doesn't matter. Where is it? Give it back." And they said: "We tore it off in frustration when we kept knocking and there was nobody inside. Then we threw it away."'

'And now they are salesmen! In suits!'

I went to see Jacob late that night to commiserate. When I arrived, he silenced his television. He sat on his sofa, his body uncharacteristically still, and stared at the flickering screen.

'A part of me,' he said, 'has learned from the conservatives in this country, the Republicans. I am talking about self-reliance. Look at this place. Look at Park Hill. And every other black neighbourhood in this country. The security cameras in this neighbourhood have all been broken. The place is rife with crime. I do not use the elevator because it stinks of urine. My neighbour upstairs, his music is going to come on in an hour or so, and he will play it right through the night, loud. What sort of person does that? He must be sick. There must be something wrong with him.

'People say the whites are keeping them down. They say you have opportunities they don't have. It's not true. This neighbourhood is perfectly positioned. You hop on a bus, get on the ferry, and you are in Manhattan in under an hour.

'I am an immigrant. I come from a civil war. I was disabled in that war. I went through two years of reconstructive surgery when I arrived here. And yet I got my bachelors and my masters in business administration, and soon I am going to get a PhD. If I can do it, they can do it. Sometimes I wish that I'd wake up in the morning, and the whole neighbourhood would be gone.'

'Why do you stay?' I asked.

'Because I am doing good work here. I have built something here. And, in any case, I will not be here for ever.'

'Where will you go next?' I asked. 'What are your plans?'

He did not reply, not for the record, at any rate. To discuss his future would be to paint himself as a man with plans, with personal ambitions. Between an ambitious Liberian and a greedy Liberian the line had grown awfully thin. Discussing his future, he believed, was as dangerous as discussing his fight with Rufus. In both, he might appear to be too hungry.

Over the summer and fall of 2008, African Refuge flourished as it never had before. Each time I visited Jacob I found him in increasingly good spirits. The pain triggered by the theft of his computers appeared to be stored away for now.

'Jonny Steinberg!' he would shout as I walked through the door of African Refuge. 'I am so *pleased*, no, so *excited* to see you. We have so *much* to talk about.'

At around that time, the newscasters on Jacob's television screen had begun to report the planet's decline into deep recession. Yet, the fortunes of Jacob's organisation, African Refuge, were turning in the opposite direction. The years of incessant labour – sitting on a dozen boards, schmoozing with New York City Democrats and charities and public health experts, attending the executive meetings of a score of immigrant coalitions – was finally paying off. After a long drought, African Refuge was bringing in money. Jacob had a modest monthly salary, and was beginning to pay off his debts. The office was filling with hired staffers: young American women, primarily, who moved about in a spirit of cheerful professionalism. As the services on offer grew, so Liberians began coming to the centre in even greater numbers. On some mornings, there was nowhere left to sit or stand.

Jacob believed he had cracked America. And as his confidence swelled, so did his involvement in its politics.

In early November, I found him driving a borrowed car, a star-spangled banner attached with copper wire to the radio aerial. We sat in the car, parked in the lot outside his apartment building, and spoke.

'What's with the flag?' I asked.

'Been campaigning for Obama in the Bible Belt,' he said. 'I was in southern Virginia yesterday.'

'Going to the rednecks door to door?' I asked. '*You?*'

'They take me seriously, Jonny. I had a Baptist education in Liberia. I know the Gospels as well as anybody in this country. So when they start to talk pro-life and the sanctity of marriage I can talk back in their language. We can *engage*.'

'In this country, you need a story,' Jacob said to me about a month later. I had just arrived at his apartment. It was late afternoon and almost dark outside. 'It's how the place works. Look at Obama. Man has a story. He came to office on the force of the story he told about himself. And it is not just Obama, it's everyone. It is the nature of this place. Look at Caroline Kennedy.'

Kennedy had just announced that she was interested in the New York Senate seat Hillary Clinton was vacating to take up the position of Secretary of State in the Obama administration. Kennedy's announcement was received sourly by some. America was on the cusp of a long recession. Murmurs of populist resentment were growing louder. The idea that an heir to a dynasty should walk into office by virtue of her name seemed to come from an ethos that was fast growing rotten.

'Obviously, she's qualified,' Jacob continued. 'This is America. You need a brand to walk though doors. *Kennedy*. A lot of work has gone into that name.'

'So what's *your* brand?' I asked.

He laughed and said nothing.

It had been some time since I had been inside his apartment. During the course of the afternoon, I noticed that much had changed. On the walls, which a month or two earlier had been bare, were framed pictures: one of Jacob shaking hands with New York mayor Michael Bloomberg; another with Staten Island congressman Michael McMahon. New furniture had appeared: a small dining-room table, for instance, so that one need not watch the television over one's meal. There was also a new coffee table, its surface unoccupied but for a large photo album.

'Open it,' Jacob urged.

The pages were double-sided. Each sported a variation of the same picture on one side: Jacob in his hospital bed, recuperating from reconstructive surgery, his right leg elevated in front of him. On the other side of each page was a document congratulating Jacob: a copy of his masters degree, a letter of thanks from New York City's immigrant liaison officer, an invitation to attend a ceremony to be presided over by the mayor.

'My story,' Jacob said, 'is that I arrived here badly disabled from warfare and will go home with a PhD. That is my brand. It is a hell of a brand. It will get me places. I am testimony to the power of resilience.'

'You are indeed,' I said.

He frowned. Perhaps he had detected some sarcasm in my voice, or a hint of amusement.

'God saved me on April 6,' he said in a chastising voice. 'I could have died a thousand times on that day. A thousand times. But instead, God saved me. What do I do with *that*? I must do something, Jonny, something very big. Otherwise, what's the point? What's the point of having survived?'

28

Roza

From the airport building Rufus Arkoi emerges hatless and weary, stooping with the weight of his luggage. It is a Monday afternoon in July 2009. This is his first visit to Monrovia in six years. In the intervening time, his fortunes have declined. He has never returned to Liberia like this, with neither money nor plans. He is anxious about what the following days hold in store.

Rufus scans the crowd waiting outside the airport terminal. His expression is not only tired, but a little vulnerable. Every face, it seems, is that of a stranger. And then a deep smile chases the uncertainty from his countenance, and he makes his way through the people and puts his arms around Pastor Arthur David, one-time Roza goalkeeper and Rufus's dearest friend.

Rufus takes a step back, smiles mischievously at the pastor, puts his palms together, and then weaves his shoulders and hips as if he is swimming like a fish.

'Water will always . . .'

' . . . find a way!' Pastor David interjects. 'Water will always find a way! You are here! You are here!'

Our driver is a young man called Ignatius.

'God bless you for coming to fetch me,' Rufus says by way of introduction. 'There is a place reserved for you in heaven.'

In the car, I ask about Pastor David's career as Roza's goalkeeper.

'The thing about Junior,' Rufus says, for that is Pastor David's nickname, 'he didn't rely on jumping around so much. He could tell where you would kick the ball *before* you kicked it. You take a penalty, he knows from watching you which corner you will aim for. He knows before *you* know.'

It is a classic Rufus story. Out of a goalkeeper's skills he creates something mystical, as he does when he describes his tailoring. He has a weakness for fairy dust; he sprinkles it on everything that pleases him.

It strikes me that this is the first time Rufus has seen Monrovia in peacetime since the day he packed up in 1986. When he was last here, in 2003, the war was not quite over. I ask him if things look improved.

'The ride from the airport is much smoother, man, much *smoother*. Last time I was here I hired a car. Car hire guy see how I drive: "My shock absorbers, oh! My shocks, oh! My . . . !" Also, the drivers here too slow, man. I had to learn to slow down. Car hire guy: "Rufus, slow *doooooown*!"'

He stares out of the window.

'Yeah, man. Monrovia.

'Junior,' he says. 'It's too late for business as usual, man. We are getting old. There is no time.'

'No time?' Pastor David asks carefully.

'I'm done with America, man,' Rufus replies. 'There are things to do *here*.'

Our first stop is Pastor David's house, where his wife has prepared a meal. For the duration of Rufus's stay, all our food will be cooked in her kitchen; 'Rufus must never eat a meal prepared by anyone he does not know or trust,' Pastor David tells me gravely. 'Everything he eats must be prepared in my wife's kitchen.'

I look out of the pastor's window onto the rooftops of Monrovia, and I wonder who among the strangers living there would want to see Rufus, who has not been home in so long, get sick and die.

Around the dinner table, it is me and Rufus and Pastor David and his wife and daughter. But for Rufus, we are merely a silent audience, for he is on stage now. He cannot help it; whenever there is a crowd of people he has no choice but to entertain.

'Two years,' he announces to the pastor's wife, 'two whole years in Staten Island I was unemployed. And my life had been at a high level. Kids in private school; wife used to me getting her a new car every two or three years. And I had a mortgage to keep: not rent, but a mortgage.

'I was self-employed, you see. Used to work as a teacher, then gave that up for self-employment.

'I did not run. I stayed in my house. Man knocks on the door, I answer it. He says: "Where is my money?" I say, "You will get your money."'

Rufus turns to me and touches me on the back.

'Your Jacob,' he says.

He need not finish the thought. It is a private exchange between us, and it is the first criticism he has levelled at the book I am writing. Your Jacob ruined me, and yet you see fit to give him half your book.

Why Rufus lost his organisation during the course of his feud with Jacob is, like everything else on Park Hill Avenue, contested. His sympathisers say that his enemies secretly contacted his funders to spread nasty stories about him. For a long time, a rumour circulated that Jacob had hacked into the files on Roza's hard drive and used the information he found to divert some of Roza's funding to his own organisation. That the story was not credible didn't matter; it was told and retold for years.

Rufus's detractors insist that even if he had had no enemies, his poor accounting practices had doomed him; the foundations would have pulled the plug sooner or later. Perhaps, in this case, the truth does in fact lie in between. Perhaps the warfare on Park Hill Avenue drew special scrutiny to Roza: to its bookkeeping, to its programmes. Once the air around Rufus had grown fetid with ill feeling, continued investment in his organisation's future perhaps did not seem such a great idea. Indeed, it is possible that the task of keeping the Liberian and Ghanaian branches of Roza flourishing required vague accounting; perhaps the very nature of the organisation he had built made his relationships with American foundations precarious.

In any event, Roza's decline was rapid. In 2003, the organisation had raised almost $300,000. By 2006, the offices on Canal Street were closed, the coffers dry, the programmes shut down. Rufus was unemployed and would remain so for two years, stubbornly refusing to look for a job, insisting that he remained blessed, that if he hung in there, money would come to him. He waited until his family was on the brink of catastrophe before applying for a job as a caseworker at the Staten Island Mental Health Association. When he knocked off from his new job at 4 p.m., he repaired to Foxhill Apartments, which allowed him to use their premises in exchange for running an after-school programme. He thus had a space in which his soccer team could meet and talk. As for financing the club, the boys now paid $50 a year for membership.

As Rufus's fortunes declined, so did the transatlantic creature Roza had become. Rufus had spent much of his adult life preserving the man he had been at the age of nineteen: the tailor and soccer club manager through whom Twelfth Street had dreamed. He had done so with money, pouring all he could into keeping the original Monrovian Roza, and thus the meaning of his own name, alive. Doing so by remote control, from New York, was no mean feat. Now, with his ruin in America, the African hinterland of Rufus's organisation began to feel his pain. Roza in Buduburum refugee camp in Ghana had died. So had the Roza in Minneapolis. Monrovia Roza was still alive, but only just.

The speech Rufus has delivered for the pastor's wife about his two jobless years, is, I think, a rehearsal for what lies ahead. The last time he was in Monrovia he came as a patron, the dollars spilling from his pockets. It is said that Twelfth Street people lined up outside his suite at the Royal Hotel from dawn each morning, in the hope of getting an audience. By the time he returned to New York, several Roza Monrovia players had scholarships to study. He had also opened a school.

He does not know what it means to walk onto Twelfth Street without a penny in his pocket.

He will be staying at the Royal Hotel again, but on my buck this time. I invited him to meet me in Monrovia, air ticket and hotel bills paid. And so he will have to recalibrate his relationship with Twelfth Street; he will have to find a way of explaining that although he is once more staying at the Royal, it does not mean what it meant before.

On the pastor's wife, I believe, he was trying out something new: how to spin from his misfortune a tale of fortitude, of the extraordinary. He must convince Twelfth Street that although he is no longer a patron, he can still be a leader. He will have to make magic with his tongue.

Earlier, in the car, I had asked him whether he would visit Twelfth Street that night or the next morning.

He had sighed heavily. 'I must be at my resting place before I decide,' he replied. 'I must put my bags down and sit alone for some time.'

In the end, he does not go to his resting place first; between the pastor's house and the hotel we stop in the landside section of Twelfth Street, the car idling in the dark outside the house in which Rufus's sister, Margaret, and her daughter, Sonie, live.

Sonie is the secretary of Rufus's soccer team. We met in preparation for Rufus's arrival, and his name appeared in every sentence she uttered. 'When Rufus walks down Twelfth Street,' she had told me, 'hundreds and hundreds of people will come out and greet him. You wait and see.'

Sonie was born a year after Rufus left for America, and they have met only on his brief visits home. Yet he believes that she is the person he can best trust with the money he sends for Roza, and around her job as the keeper of his funds she has erected a high wall.

Now, Sonie comes out to meet him, and together they walk into her mother's home.

Rufus moves slowly, silently, hands in pockets. About him there is an aura of studied coolness. Aside from Sonie, he has told nobody that he is coming.

A teenage boy stands in the doorway of the house. He looks at Rufus quizzically. They are eyeball to eyeball now, and in the boy's eyes there is wariness.

'Rufus,' Rufus murmurs, barely audibly.

At the sound of the name, the boy's eyes bulge wide and round, and he throws his arms around Rufus. Then he scurries inside to announce the news, leaving me with this image of a boy who has expressed joy, not because of the presence of a man, but because of the idea of him.

Margaret's house is just two tiny rooms, and we are squeezed in, sitting on plastic chairs. Rufus is leaning back, relaxed, patriarchal, murmuring and nodding and summoning the children to stand before him so that he can get a good look at who they have become.

It is a very modest room, with only plastic chairs for furniture. No sooner has Rufus settled than we are off again, Sonie in tow, to Rufus's family home, the one Joseph Wayfather came to Monrovia to build, the one in which the neighbourhood boys came to watch Rufus sew. It is very dark, the older people are out visiting, there are only young people about, and they gather around Rufus quietly, curiously, laying circumspect eyes upon this man they do not know, but whose name they have heard a great deal. Even in the dark, we can see that the house is in poor repair: what remains of the ceiling is rotten and smelly; in the room where Rufus sewed, the walls are discoloured, the plaster gouged and full of holes.

'This is not a proper visit,' Rufus says to those who have assembled, 'just a courtesy call. I am just off the plane. My bed is waiting at the hotel. I did not want word to get around that I had slept a night in this city without coming to see you.'

Throughout the evening, Rufus has been telling members of his immediate family to come to his hotel room the next night for a family meeting.

'I need to explain to them why I stopped supporting them,' he tells me on the way from Twelfth Street to the hotel. 'Also, I need to help them make a plan; they are still living in poverty.'

'It is hard to make a plan in this country,' I say, 'where most people are unemployed.'

'It is hard because of dishonesty,' he replies. 'For instance, I come to Monrovia, we discuss ways to generate money for Roza. I buy two buses to use as taxis. From the income, Roza can be supported. The then president of Roza, whom I taught to sew, he steals the buses and opens his own taxi business.

'Another time, the idea was to open a video shop. I bought the TV, the VCR; it never happened. Another time, we rent a building and sublet. Roza's next president pockets the money himself.

'They can't move from poverty without staying together.'

By 10.30 the next morning we are on Twelfth Street again, the road lined with stalls selling spices and vegetables and salted fish. It is very crowded, people brushing up against us whenever we move, and for Rufus it is like walking through a place he knows very well and yet hardly at all.

'In the old days,' he says, 'there was no market, and the street was almost empty. Those people you come across, you had seen them a thousand, no, ten thousand times before. These people, they have all moved here in the last decade.'

We walk, and we are strangers among strangers in the crowd. By eleven o'clock, just two people have recognised Rufus, greeted him warmly, moved on. There is a film of sweat on his brow.

'The heat, oh!' he says. And he buys a handkerchief from a stall and mops his brow.

We are in the grounds of Tubman High now, and Rufus is awash with memories: 'The battles fought on this ground, oh! Man, they are swimming in my head! Each and every minute of each and every high-stakes game we played. I can still tell you what happened *each* minute of the game.'

And now we are on an embankment overlooking the soccer field. It is a very poor field, not a blade of grass, just hard, baked soil and fine, red dust. Two teams are playing.

'Is one of them Roza?' I ask.

'I don't know.'

Of course he doesn't. It may be his team, but it has been six years since he was last here, and he has not met a single one of Roza's current players.

Sonie comes, and she leads us to a group of young men sitting under the shade of a tree, and when they see the big man with Sonie, they know it is Rufus, and they stand up and gather around him.

He says that he will speak to them just briefly now, that there will be a full team meeting tomorrow evening where everyone will speak for a long time, as long as they like, until everything in their hearts is shared. For now, just a few words: Roza was founded in 1981, he says, and none of the other teams founded in that era still exist today. Why Roza? he asks. Is it coincidence that Roza is the only one left standing? No, it is God's will.

'Roza is something bigger than you and me,' he says, and then he walks away, and the faces of the young men are blank. Rufus is silent for a long time as we walk back onto Twelfth Street. When he eventually begins to speak, it is not about Roza.

We spend the rest of the day on Twelfth Street. By early evening, something undetectable has changed, something in the shifting patterns of those who inhabit the street; now, every second person we encounter knows Rufus. Our progress slows, and then stops entirely. I walk off a few paces, sit on a low wall, and watch the scene. Rufus is at the centre of a throng of people trying to greet him. He is beaming and he is magnificently gracious; every new person he greets occupies the whole of his attention as if he has thought of nobody else all day.

Finally, we are off Twelfth Street, and it is dark now.

'All these memories of me,' Rufus says, the excitement in his voice quiet but palpable. 'It is an opportunity that should not be wasted. We can use it for a political campaign.'

We walk in silence for some time.

'You know,' he continues, 'in all my time in America, I never got a US passport. I kept my Liberian one. Just in case. Just for that chance that the day would come when I'd be politically involved here.'

Antoinette Tubman Stadium

Back in New York, Rufus had shared with me his understanding of what transpired between him and Jacob. In his mind it was quite clear: the Liberian war had chased him to America and grabbed him by the throat.

The first time we spoke of it, we had been discussing African culture. Rufus had said that polygamy was the primary cause of African conflict, for it wove jealousy into the fabric of family life; every woman wanted the children of the other wives to fail.

'Is that what caused the civil war?' I asked. 'Samuel Doe was now the big husband, and one of the wives and her children, Nimba County and the Gios and the Manos, were excluded?'

'No,' he said, his voice immediately filled with indignation. 'It's not true. Doe never excluded the Nimba people. They were very well represented at the beginning. They had more key positions in government *than any other ethnic group*. But they were never *satisfied*. And the trouble you are seeing here in Staten Island, it is led by Nimba citizens. It's really just their *nature*. I mean it. It is just their nature that they must rule. They refuse to be led. They must lead.'

'The Gios caused the war?' I asked.

'No, that would give them too much credit. The Americo-Liberians caused the war because they wanted to come back to power. They needed proxies. They looked around for the most destructive people. They found the Gios.'

He did not mention Jacob by name. I am not sure why not. Perhaps because the obvious should remain unspoken. Or perhaps because he was following the letter, if not the spirit, of a truce that a medley of mediators had negotiated between them. Among the rules was that they would not badmouth one another.

During another discussion, I asked Rufus whether he believed that Liberia's war was finally over, whether the democratic system that came to the country in 2006 would stick.

'It will,' he answered. 'A lot of lessons have been learned. Here in Staten Island we have a government, SILCA, and the same crazy elements from Liberia came with the same crazy mentality. Their way or no way. To them, everyone is suspicious, everyone has done something wrong. They don't trust any soul. It's the mentality they brought from home. And they polluted this neighbourhood so badly. From 2002 to 2008 this community was *horr-i-ble*. But it's over now. We've fixed it. And it will be fixed in Liberia too.

'Was the craziness that came here caused by the war,' I asked, 'or was it the cause of the war?'

'You can't blame it all on the war,' he replied. 'You've got to narrow it down. Look at particular people and what they were doing before the war. Adults in their forties. Go back. Ask which high schools they graduated from.'

'I'm not following you.'

'Before the war, seasoned politicians came and recruited young, bright high-school students, and made them feel they were revolutionary. Put a lot of ideas in their head. Took them to the University of Liberia. They felt they were the top of the world. They got used to challenging authority. They were just like gangs, political gangs. Whoever was in government, they attacked. Before Doe, it was Tolbert. Then they kicked Doe. They wanted government to fall so they could get into government.

'That's what we faced here in SILCA. Rufus has power. Crush him. Human beings behaving like animals. Call a leader corrupt, a criminal, with no evidence. Say things about his family. Scandalise a person's name until he is useless. This is the training they got from Liberia. Frankly, I say no.'

'But what were they fighting for?' I asked. 'You can understand it in Liberia, they were fighting to be in government . . .'

'The same. SILCA. It's power. You are president. It doesn't matter you operate out of your house. You are the one known to be president. A member of that group should be known to be president. It's power.'

Improbably, Rufus claimed to have won the war. And by the narrow logic of his argument, he had. The usurpers had come to capture power, in the form of SILCA, and they had failed.

'But Roza was so badly damaged,' I protested. 'How can that possibly be a victory?'

'You know,' he replied, 'there are people in this community who are very, very surprised that I am still standing. They are very, very surprised that Roza still takes the field every weekend, that I am still here running literacy classes and after-school programmes. They are shocked by my resilience.

'They do not understand that there is no other life for me. My place is on the sidewalk, in the street, with the kids. Anywhere else, I would die.'

The Monrovia branch of Roza, wearing kit sewn on Rufus's machine, July 2008.

On the evening of his second full day in Monrovia, on the narrow sidewalk between Margaret's house and the street, Rufus meets the Roza players. It makes for a curious sight: a row of lean, fit young men sitting side by side on a low wall; opposite them an ample, middle-aged man on a plastic chair, his back to the traffic. What might this gathering suggest to a passer-by? A male choir, perhaps? The remains of a battalion of soldiers and their erstwhile commander? The cars and trucks moving west to east pass within inches of the back of Rufus's head.

The first to speak is Roza's captain. His name is Wallace Morgan. He is short and very lean, and when he speaks he brushes skinny dreadlocks from the sides of his mouth.

'I will get straight to the point,' Wallace says. 'There are many problems. The main one, we have no contract with the club, even though the Football Federation stipulates that you cannot play without a contract. The contract must stipulate salary, health care benefits. There is no contract. Second, we have no transport to games, and yet we do not have money to come to games.

'We have been praying, Mr Rufus, that you would come. Now you are here, we must express our differences honestly. We have no shin guards. Can you imagine that? At practices, there is no money for water. We go through a three-hour practice without drinking. Can you imagine? There is nobody to appeal to. We appeal to Sonie; she says we must make our own way to the game. You arrive at the game with one side of your boot split open. You make a joke of it. Mr Rufus, it is no joke.'

Earlier in the day, I met with Wallace, together with another Roza player named Emmanuel Arizieh. They had travelled half-way across Monrovia to see me in the hope that I would name them in my book, that some soccer scout somewhere in the world would pick up the book, read their names, come to Liberia to see them play, take them off somewhere to play professional soccer.

Emmanuel is from Nigeria. I asked him why he was playing soccer in Liberia.

'To strengthen my CV,' he replied. 'In Lagos, the football is so competitive. Here, you come, you immediately play semi-professional in the top leagues, on salary, with health care provisions; you put that on your CV and go home, maybe it will give you an opportunity to turn professional back home.'

'But there are no salaries or health care for Liberian teams,' I say.

'No,' he replies. 'The Football Federation stipulated that there must be a contract, and the contract must stipulate salary and health care, but nobody has money for either.'

'How old are you?' I asked.

'Real age twenty-nine. Football age twenty-one.'

I looked at him quizzically.

'When opportunity comes,' Wallace offered, 'they need a lesser age, not a higher age. I myself, I am twenty-eight real age, twenty football age.

I smiled at them both.

'I have played all over Liberia,' Wallace explained plaintively. 'I have played for both Mighty Barolle and IE, the two most famous teams. Neither could afford to pay me. I live in a small room I rent from my family. I do not have money to pay my mother rent. In a few years, I will be hanging up my boots. What then? I cannot finish with football until it has given something back to me. I need help. I need a sponsor. I need somebody to lift me higher.'

As Rufus gets up from his chair to speak, he knows that the young men in the audience are gamblers. They have seen living proof that the odds against them are not quite zero. There is George Weah, of course; and there is also Alexander Chookee, who started at Roza and went on to play professional football overseas. They know that there is a chance – a thousand to one, perhaps, or ten thousand to one? – that on a Saturday afternoon at a stadium in Monrovia, one of them will effect a dummy, or land a visionary cross-field pass, or score from thirty-five yards, and in the stands that day will be a scout from somewhere in the world where there is money. Nobody from Roza has laid eyes upon such a scout in years, but every weekend there is rumour; a scout from America was seen with the national coach; the director of football at Barolle has brought somebody out from Italy. There is always talk.

'My presence here will not resolve all the problems this club has had over the last few years,' Rufus tells them. 'My circumstances have changed. I have to adjust. As I am adjusting, I let down a lot of people who have been depending on me. As I cope with the changes in my own life, it has affected you here. From the bottom of my heart I thank all of you for finding a reason for playing in my team.'

He pauses a long time, and there is the sound of the traffic and the growing darkness. The players can barely see his face now.

'You may build the best boat,' he continues, 'but the sea may be rough. You may be in a very good boat, but you do not feel the beauty of the boat. You concentrate on the roughness of the sea. Roza is a beautiful boat built to sail in rocky sea. It takes courageous men to stay around this boat long enough to feel the sea calming. Some hold on for a shorter time. Some have the patience to hold on longer. Things get tough; it can be dangerous to your health. You keep holding on, and you are hurting yourself physically. You feel you must let go.

'We have to take real men, a few good men, to stand when times are tough. One thing I know, when a soccer ball is placed anywhere, you will have young people attracted to it. Let the ball keep rolling.'

Rufus carries on speaking for a long time, although the meaning of his talk is already clear. The big man has come from America, but he is broke. Will he always be broke, or is there something waiting in the future? He has told them that if they are brave, they will stay, and if they stay, they will be rewarded.

Rufus is talking now of his glory days, of the early 1980s; he sprinkles his story with famous men, and he reminds his audience that each of the men played for Roza under his tutelage.

'I refused to tolerate players that mumbled,' he says. 'I wanted all warriors around me. We had a practice round one day, there was lots of mumbling because there were no sponsors, and things were tough. I said I only need men around me. I want nobody who mumbles. I will sign your clearance papers today. A lot of players walked that day, a lot of very good players.

'Those who stayed were ready to be trained in the warfare of soccer. Every one of the guys I coached in Sinkor Defenders are now successful men, including your administrator Ben, who you see advancing in this country's football ranks. *Every one* of the players who worked under me is a very successful man today.

'Hear me, and hear me clearly. I had an invitation to come to Liberia on urgent notice. I put aside everything. I came. Two things I knew I would benefit from: to associate with you, and with my family members with whom I have disconnected myself over a good period of time. They say similar things like you are saying. We do not get the support we used to get. We do not receive what we used to receive. The barrels, four, five barrels: you get whatever you ask for. I can't do that now.

'Let me conclude with this. I like the game. I have invested thousands and thousands. Last time I checked I had invested nearly a million in sport. Something went wrong. God is above. You went through last season bad. You are almost ending this season. It may not get better. I will make one promise I stand by. After seeing you and hearing you, I will not see this team in old boots.'

He stops speaking for he is crying. Now he has covered his face with his hands, now he has taken his hands away and lifted his head, and the dampness on his cheeks is quite visible in what is left of the light. Beside him is a bag full of new soccer boots that he has brought with him from America. How he acquired them I do not know, for he is truly broke.

The Monrovia branch of Roza up against a team from Bushrod Island at the other end of the city, July 2008.

Rufus's fifth day in Liberia is a Saturday, and Roza are scheduled to play at the Antoinette Tubman Stadium in downtown Monrovia. We arrive as the game is starting and settle in the gated, VIP section of the stands.

The field below is covered in well-kept AstroTurf, and the stadium itself is built of sturdy concrete, the walls in the passageways behind the stands thick and solid and reassuring. High up in the VIP section, one looks over the edge of the arena directly into the shabbiness of central Monrovia; the newest coat of paint is many years old, the plaster is peeling off the buildings, and the tin shacks stand precariously on the steep slopes of the downtown hills. That so solid and permanent a stadium stands among such raggedness reflects the values of the man by my side; the dignity of soccer, the weight of the burden invested in it: the game must be played in a venue that exudes both endurance and grace.

There is a scattering of people in the stadium. Roza has slumped to the Second Division in recent years, and today's game is the curtain raiser to a match between two big Premier League teams. The stands will begin to fill later.

Rufus says nothing at all for the first ten minutes of the game. His chin is cupped in his hand and he is frowning, whether in concentration or anxiety I am not sure.

'A penny for your thoughts,' I say.

He turns and speaks with great seriousness. 'The defence is playing too flat, oh. The opposition is putting through penetrative passes and number four is following the ball, not number nine. He is dragging number five out of position too. The whole defence, they are not *reading* this game. Nobody has taught them how to *read* a game of soccer. The coaching of this team is very poor, very poor.'

As the game edges towards half-time, the score is still 0–0, but Rufus's anxiety has by now turned to despair.

'It hurts me to see a team called Roza like this,' he says. 'They are in a condition of *neglect*. I need to spend three months with the team, coach them every day for three months. The raw talent is good. But it is entirely raw, utterly and entirely raw.

'Do you think I can go and speak to them at half-time?' he asks. His tone is that of a man in a stranger's house, uncertain of the rules of etiquette. 'Is it my place? I tell you, this is very hard to watch. If I speak to them at half-time I will talk tough, talk honest. I will tell them they are lucky still to be in this game.'

He does talk to the players at half-time, but he soon loses heart, and what he says is not especially tough. The speech he was to give smouldered hot in his imagination, but once he is with them in the flesh, it is clear that he cannot teach them to read a game of soccer between the two halves of a match. He speaks briefly and ends by wishing them luck.

In any event, by the time the second half is under way, another rhythm has begun to form around us, and it has nothing to do with the game on the field below. In the prelude to the big match that will begin once this one is over, the VIP section is beginning to fill. Most of the people climbing the stairs are Rufus's age or older, and each and every one of them comes to greet Rufus, and wants to talk with him, to ask him of his life in New York. By the time the referee has blown the final whistle Rufus is in deep discussion with a woman who, I am told, is the president of the Liberian Football Association. Before that he had been locked in conversation with an elderly man with thick dreadlocks. I had tried to follow their discussion, but it was spoken in the codes that develop between people who share an intimate history.

Rufus had seen that I was eavesdropping and called me over.

'This man before you is a great man,' he said. 'The Liberian national coach in the early days of George Weah. This man has been to the *heights*, to the very *heights*.'

Now, as I watch Rufus murmuring with the president of the association, I am struck by the fact that his history is stored here, in this scene, in the collective memories of the people gathered in this stand. They all witnessed the 1980 coup, and they experienced it as a triumph of soccer. For them, Liberia's best days were undoubtedly in the 1980s; everything since has been a process of fading.

I think back to a scene that I witnessed just a couple of hours before. Rufus and I had arranged to meet in the hotel lobby. I waited and waited, and when I feared that we would miss the start of the match, I went upstairs and knocked on his door.

He greeted me in underpants and vest, apologised that he was running late, and invited me in. We chatted as he dressed. He opened his wardrobe and took from it a beautiful white dress shirt, put it on, and buttoned it. The sleeves fastened with cufflinks, but he had none, so he positioned himself in front of the mirror and carefully rolled up the sleeves to just below the elbows. Cocking his head, he examined this arrangement, then rolled the sleeves up above the elbows.

'Which is better?' he asked, turning to face me.

'I think below the elbow,' I said.

He nodded and unrolled the sleeves very carefully, then undid the top three buttons of the shirt to reveal the thick gold chain on his chest. He looked in the mirror once more before picking up his keys.

Now he is leaving the stands and has disappeared into the offices in the rear. I follow him there after a while. The corridors are full of people, mainly middle-aged people, and Rufus is among them, receiving business cards and punching phone numbers into his cellphone. This is the scene he was imagining, I am sure, when he was dressing. If he is going to restore his legacy, it is among these people. He has not been among them in a long time. But he is broke. Is the history he shares with them enough? Will they let him back in?

While in Monrovia, I had lunch with a man called Saah N'Tow. I was lucky to have met him. Someone had mentioned in passing that they knew of a man who had lived in the Liberian diaspora in America for a long time and had come back to work with youth. I had phoned him at once.

Over lunch, Saah told me that he grew up on Twelfth Street, that he was an alumnus of William Tubman High, that he had been there in the late 1970s and early 1980s. I had not planned it, but sitting across the table was a man from both Rufus's Monrovian world and the Liberian diaspora. It was very exciting indeed.

I asked him when and why he left Liberia.

'I was unusual,' he replied, 'in that I left before the war got to Monrovia. It was July 1990. I had a Gio friend who had taken refuge in St Peter's Lutheran Church. I myself am Kissi. I was on my way to St Peter's to visit my friend when I was stopped at an AFL checkpoint. The soldier was very aggro. "If you go any further, I will shoot you!" From that interaction, I read the mood. I realised at once that I must leave Liberia. I left that week.

'I ended up in London, went to university there, and worked as a youth development person in a neighbourhood near Heathrow. I met a woman from Providence, Rhode Island, married her and went to live there. That is when I became involved with Liberian refugees, in Rhode Island.'

I immediately thought of Jacob. His every decision throughout the war took him to the heart of the violence, as if fate had decided that he was to see the very worst. Saah, in contrast, smelled blood immediately, before he had heard a shot fired in anger, and fled. To be blessed with fine instincts, I thought.

I asked Saah if he knew the name Rufus Arkoi. 'He has also been involved with youth for many years,' I said, 'and although he didn't go to Tubman High, he grew up on Twelfth Street.'

'Yes, I remember him,' Saah had replied. 'He was more involved on the soccer side of things. He started right here on Twelfth Street. What was the name of his team?'

'Roza,' I said.

'Roza. That's it. Community soccer on Twelfth Street was very important, very influential. Rufus went on to start a league in Sinkor, and a team called Sinkor Defenders. It took his work to a new level. It was an achievement. And then in New York I hear that he carried on with his soccer work among the refugees.'

I told Saah that Rufus wanted very much to come back to Monrovia, to start working in the NGO world, or the government world, that he wanted to rebuild something like the old Sinkor league, but much more ambitiously, throughout Monrovia, perhaps, or even throughout Liberia.

'Rufus has a lot to offer,' Saah replied. 'His skills, his experience in youth development. You look at the government's Poverty Reduction Strategy; there is a lot of space for the sort of work Rufus does.

'But if he comes with nothing, it will be very difficult. This is a crowded field. He must come with a project. He must raise money in the US. That is how I came. I had to come with my own project and my own money.'

'Rufus no longer has access to American money,' I said. 'He has been trying to rekindle his old associations here in Liberia from the early 1980s.'

'That will be hard,' Saah replied. 'Not that they don't like him any more. I'm sure they're pleased to see him. But a lot of time has passed. It is no longer the same as back then. Why should they accommodate him?'

Among the people Rufus meets in the VIP section of the stands is a sports presenter at Star Radio, a prominent local station. We leave the stadium less than halfway through the big match and go straight to Star Radio's studios on a hill overlooking the centre of Monrovia. Rufus is whisked into a soundproof studio, and given earphones to put on his head. Before we know it, the interview has begun.

Rufus is as eloquent as I have ever heard him. It is not long before everyone in the studio is still and absorbed in his words. He is the veteran Liberian soccer club founder, resident for many years abroad, supporting his team from America. The interviewer asks him of his plans for the team.

'My vision remains the same,' he says. 'My team is a vehicle through which young people can rebuild their lives. Every young man associated with Roza must work through his formal education up to college level.'

'That's a difficult standard to accept here in Liberia,' the interviewer says.

'It should be the accepted standard. You do not play just to win. Beyond that, you play to go to school.'

'Are you saying people must be of a particular educational standard to play for Roza?'

'You can recruit a first grader,' Rufus replies, 'but you must insist that they advance to keep playing.'

'Are you saying that every Roza player will be put on a scholarship?'

'It is not financially viable right now, but I am saying that at least a few Roza players must be on scholarship.'

He has had a few troubled years, Rufus says. He does not have the money he had a few years ago when he rebuilt Roza. But he has plans. He has relationships with American scouts. Very soon, he will be bringing two scouts out here to Monrovia, and they will choose two players to take back with them to sign professional contracts.

'Will they just be looking at Roza players,' the interviewer asks, 'or at all players?'

'Primarily Roza players,' Rufus replies.

Next, he is being questioned about government support for soccer.

'Teams are struggling,' he says. 'They are performing very poorly without backing. I am not one to point fingers, but sports must be a national priority. It is as important as building roads, as important as education, as important as health. It is *the* primary youth development tool. It has to be done. The country stands to benefit. I am not saying throw $3 million at sports. No. I am saying two people from each club, a coach and an administrator, should be on government salary. Soccer balls should be provided. Boots. Shin guards. Let us take this game *seriously*.'

The interview is over, and it is quite clear to everyone that it has gone very well. The energy Rufus conjured remains all over the studio.

'Was that live?' he asks.

'It was not,' the presenter replies. 'We recorded it.'

And now the producer has come into the studio, and he and the presenter and Rufus talk quietly in a huddle. Rufus is saying little: he is listening and nodding and smiling. When they break up, Rufus comes to me and takes me aside.

'They want US$250 to play the interview,' he says, almost casually, as if it is something to say in passing.

There is a long pause. Neither of us looks the other in the eye.

'It is a very influential station,' he continues. 'Government ministers listen to it. The top sports officials all listen to it. It is just that it is a lot of money.'

A loud cackling laugh comes from behind Rufus; it sounds like a human being imitating a machine gun. He turns to look, and in the moment he does so, I walk off in the other direction and out onto the balcony.

The station is on the third floor of a building high on a hill overlooking the centre of Monrovia. From here, the city is very noisy: a blend of car exhausts and horns and people's voices and roosters' crowing. To the right is the slum settlement of West Point, the shacks built so close together that from here they appear to be one shambling structure half a mile long and another half wide. In front of them is the Monrovia the Americo-Liberians built, a scattering of concrete office buildings once considered proud, but now very old and tired.

I am a little rattled by what Rufus said. On reflection, it is not his words alone that shook me, but the aura that surrounded him as he spoke. He walked out of the studio with the fresh and unexpected knowledge that although he had given his very best, there was another barrier to negotiate, one that he had not anticipated. I wondered whether he had just caught a glimpse of the prospect that things might always be so, that there might forever be another barrier, that the Liberia he has held in his heart all this time may not have been real. It is quite possible that, for many years now, he has been adrift in exile without knowing it.

It is early morning, before sunrise, and we have left the hotel and are heading into downtown Monrovia. I am accompanied only by Ignatius, our driver. We are going to pick up Aaron, a colleague who lives in the city centre with his wife and young child. We have an appointment in another town today, and before us is the prospect of a long drive.

It was drizzling when we left the Royal Hotel; now, as we stop outside Aaron's apartment, the rain is hitting the windscreen hard.

'Who *is* that?' I ask Ignatius.

A young man is staring straight into our headlights. He is just a few paces in front of us, straddling a motorbike, his arms folded, his feet planted firmly on the ground. A group of young men stands off to his right, on the sidewalk, in the shadows beyond the edges of the circle our lights have thrown. They are all staring at us. They are standing exposed in the heavy rain. They don't take cover. They stand there as if there is no rain at all.

The man on the bike is sitting up ramrod straight, his spine stretched as far as it will. Without blinking, he stares directly into our lights, or, *against* our lights, I should say, for his face is frozen in a rictus of defiance. The rain lashes his cheeks.

As Aaron hurries towards the car, his raincoat hood drawn low over his brow, the young man revs his bike, sending a grating roar down the street. He skids into motion, aiming straight at our car. At the last moment, he slides his bike sideways, his heel almost touching our fender. The engine growls again, and he weaves away from us, then ducks off into another street.

'Who *is* that?' I ask again.

'Don Bosco boys,' Aaron says cheerfully.

This is not my first experience of the Don Bosco boys, but I had not put the two encounters together. A year earlier, on a previous visit to Liberia, a friend, Kim, took me to a nightclub in the eastern suburbs, a place frequented, she told me as we drove there, primarily by expats: United Nations staff and foreign NGO workers like her.

The street outside the venue was jammed with parked cars. Kim circled twice before finding a spot about half a block from the club.

The moment she got out of the car she was swamped by a group of plaintive, crippled men. Some were missing an arm, others a leg; they moved around her nimbly on pairs of crutches. One was missing both an arm and a leg; he jumped around Kim on the ball of his foot with the help of a single stick.

They stood in front of her and to the sides of her, blocking her path.

She locked her eyes on one of them and asked his name.

'James,' he replied in a strong voice.

'James,' she repeated. 'Will you look after my car?'

He nodded, and Kim began to walk. The crippled men cleared a path for her and drifted off, in search of other patrons.

'They are called the Don Bosco boys,' Kim told me as we moved inside, 'because the Catholic Church once ran a programme for former child soldiers. These are a subgroup of Don Bosco boys: the amputees. The programme stopped long ago, but the name stuck. They are forever the Don Bosco boys.

'You choose one, you look him in the eye, ask him his name, ask him to look after your car. When you come out, you pay him 50 cents. If you don't do that, they vandalise your car.'

Once, Kim told me, she arrived at the club very late, and could only find a parking space two blocks away. When she emerged from the club several hours later, she discovered that the street was deserted; the cars that had been parked in front were gone.

As she made her way to her car, a crowd of amputees followed. First, one demanded money, then another; soon they had all joined in, competing with one another in growing degrees of insistence. By the time she reached her car, Kim told me, the Don Bosco boys were in something of a frenzy. She had decided that she would give money to the two most persistent among them, then drive off.

She unlocked her car, got in, locked the doors, put her handbag between the seats, and opened her window about five inches. Three or four hands reached in, feeling for her bag. She started the car and accelerated hard, watching one hand, then other, give up and vanish.

Rufus joins us later that morning. During a quiet moment, I describe as graphically as I can the young men we encountered outside Aaron's apartment.

'These people *live* on the street outside your door?' Rufus asks Aaron. 'They *live* on the street?'

'I try to treat them with respect,' Aaron replies. 'I do not look at them as if I'd like to spit on them. I try not to offend them.'

'Are they organised?' Rufus asks.

'Well, if someone grabs your cellphone and you run after him, the others will block you. But if you mean: do they have allegiance to a warlord? Could they be used to restart the war? I do not think so. They have expressed dissatisfaction with their commanders for failing to keep promises to look after them. When the Truth and Reconciliation Commission began holding public hearings, some of the Don Bosco boys turned up to testify and to complain about their commanders.'

'Why did Don Bosco stop supporting them?' Rufus asks.

'I'm not sure,' Aaron replies.

'Does the government have a programme for them?'

Nobody answers him.

'How can I meet with these boys?' he continues. 'Is there a youth department in the government I can talk to?'

I fear that he will get out of the car right now, buy a soccer ball, and head out to look for the Don Bosco boys.

'What would you do with them?' I ask.

'What would I *do* with them? Give me a small salary, not a lot of money, just enough to free my time, and I will put them all on the soccer field, *all* of them. I will start fourteen soccer leagues in this city, under-nine to under-sixteen, boys and girls. I will field a team called Roza in each and every one of those leagues. And everybody who puts on a soccer uniform will be required to go to school. If necessary, they will receive a scholarship to go to school. We will raise money for that far and wide.

'Educators would be linked to each soccer club. Every child who plays soccer would be mentored through school. It doesn't take a miracle. It takes a few dedicated adults to be around them, to listen to them, to guide them in simple things.

'Do you see what I am seeing? Put down a soccer ball, and young people will gather around it. Once they have gathered, you can *do* something with them. You can *heal* a country. The adults are too damaged, man. The war has made them sick. But the youth: that is another story entirely. I have seen it on Staten Island. I have met kids who have seen and done the very worst. With the right guidance, they can be okay. They are *young*.

'And if it works in Monrovia, why not take it to the rest of Liberia? Why not? You could reach every young person in this country. All I need is to knock on the right door, to get a five-minute audience with the right official. Where will I find this official? Who *is* the right official? As I told you and Junior the other day, I am too old for business as usual.'

Duazuahplay

In Liberia, I also visited Duazuahplay, Jacob's village.

Now, on his desk in his apartment, Jacob slides my compact disc into his laptop and clicks his mouse. On his screen a still image appears. The frame is filled with faces: young boys, an old woman in a cotton dress, a man in a blue-and-white soccer jersey. They are all staring intently into the camera. In the background is the mustard-coloured wall of a mud house, its window a bare hole covered by a blind. This is the first Jacob has seen of his village since he last set foot there in 1989.

He clicks the mouse again, and the people on the screen begin to dance: a slow, swaying of shoulders and arms, a gentle thrust of hips. The sound of their singing fills the apartment. It is a song with one short verse sung over and over.

Jacob stares and smiles and says nothing. Then his face turns grave. The clip lasts less than half a minute. He plays it again. On the third playing, he begins to sing along quietly under his breath.

You have to walk several miles through rainforest to reach Jacob's village, for the road, destroyed in the early years of the war, has never been mended. We were a party of four: Jacob's younger brother, Quegbaye, our driver and his mechanic, and me. We walked out of the forest into a large clearing. At precisely the same time, it seemed, a squiggly, noisy snake of people emerged from the other end. It grew longer and longer as it came closer. By the time the entire snake emerged, it was eighty or ninety people long, singing and ululating. Our bags were taken from us, and our hands were shaken, and children tugged at our trousers. And then the snake turned around and took us winding between the huts and into the village square.

I retrieved my bag and took from it a large photograph of Jacob; he wore a baseball jacket and had a rucksack strapped to his back, and he gazed with ease and supreme confidence into the camera, the blur of a brilliant green plane tree behind him. The picture was passed from hand to hand: men stared at it and slapped Jacob's face lightly with the backs of their hands; an old woman kissed Jacob gently on the cheek; another laid her hand on his brow. As the photograph moved from one person to the next, somebody took up the song again, and everyone stood up and danced. This time they formed a tight circle, and the circle began to revolve, slowly, steadily, around and around. Jacob's photograph was raised aloft, and it bobbed round and round the village square, the New York oak tree in the background growing stranger and more foreign with each moment.

The picture of Jacob I took with me to Duazuahplay.

Jacob picks faces out of the crowd.

'I only recognise the old ones,' he says. 'The young ones are strangers. They are strangers.

'Dennis Duazuah! My God, that's Dennis Duazuah! Did you give him the torch I sent with you? Did you give it to him?'

'I did,' I reply.

'And how did he respond to it? Was he amazed? He would never in his wildest dreams imagine a torch that doesn't need batteries. Was he amazed by it?'

'He was very pleased.'

'Yes, but was he curious? Did he want to take it apart and see how it worked? He's a very curious man. Jonny. I was very close to that man when I was a child. I loved that man very much. What did he do with the torch? Did he shake it hard? Or gently? You know, it doesn't matter how hard you shake it. It will work the same. How long did you stay in my village?'

'Four nights, I think.'

'Did he use the torch every night?'

'He did.'

'He was carrying it when he came to see you at night?'

'Yes.'

'How hard did he shake it? Did he realise that whether you shake it hard or gently, it works the same?'

He begins to explain the physics of the batteryless torch, and he soon loses me. My mind wanders. He sees that I am not listening.

'What did you think of my village?' he asks. 'Is it very different from what you imagined?'

'Yes,' I say. 'Very different. I have never been to a place like it.'

'Really? Really? In what way was it so different?'

'I'd never been to a place where the people eat what they grow, and that is all. They buy and sell very little. They just eat what they grow. The coffee fields your father planted are gone. The only commercial crop is sugar cane, and there is only one working mill left in your village, an old, medieval-looking contraption that the teenage boys push around and around and around all day long, squeezing the sugar from the cane among all the bees. That is the main source of money in the village, as far as I could tell. People use it to pay their children's school fees. Other than that, they eat what they grow. I had never been anywhere like that before.'

'You keep repeating that phrase,' he says. '"They eat what they grow." What does it mean to you?'

'That the war has made Duazuahplay a very remote place. Monrovia is not much more than 200 miles away. But it may as well be a million miles. Because nobody ever makes enough money to travel to Monrovia.'

I repeat a story a villager called John Gongo told me. Out of the blue, the Gongos received a message from family in Monrovia. We have a space in our house. If you send one of your three daughters to us, we will take care of her and send her to school. The Gongos were extremely excited, for the school in Duazauhplay is a school only in name, and now one of their children was going to be properly educated.

I tell Jacob of how John Gongo and his wife chose their middle daughter, their twelve-year-old, 'because she is the serious one', of how they sent her to Monrovia, and had not heard word from her these last eighteen months. I was due to leave for Monrovia two days later, and it seemed churlish to do nothing, so I told John that I would deliver a message to his daughter in Monrovia. John was very pleased. He asked me to give him a day to prepare what he might say. Each time I saw him, he said that he was not yet ready; he was still composing the message in his mind. Finally, on the very brink of my departure, he came to me. We found a quiet place, and I took out my notebook. 'Study hard,' John Gongo had said. And that is all.

Jacob listens in silence.

'Tell me more,' he says finally. 'Tell me every story you can remember.'

As I scan my memory for another, I find that I am censoring myself. Sitting face to face, I see that I cannot share some of my impressions of his village with him. Not now.

For the four days I spent in Duazuahplay, I was treated with the most excruciating deference I have ever known. Whenever I emerged from my hut, people would scramble from their chairs, usher me to a table, and serve a large meal. A crowd of twenty, sometimes thirty people, would gather to watch me eat. When I walked from one end of the village to the other, a retinue of young men accompanied me; it had been decided among them beforehand who would walk closest to me, and whom furthest away. When I washed myself, a young man stood outside, his back discreetly turned, waiting to take away my dirty water. On my first day, a rumour circled the village that I was there to build a school, then that Jacob was building a school and that I was his emissary. The idea that I might leave the village unchanged seemed unthinkable.

When my trip was almost over, and it was clear that I would not be leaving behind something substantial, a tone of irritation slipped in and mingled with the deference, at least among some of the people I had met. One of Jacob's brothers demanded that I leave my torch. Several people cornered me when I was alone and said that I must leave money with *them*, not with the chief, for they needed a new guitar, new zinc for their roof, and that I had all these things, and they didn't, and that if I wasn't going to leave them money, then at the the very least I ought to leave them my shoes, for I had a car to ferry me back to Monrovia, whereas they had to walk.

In its relation to me, I glimpsed something of this village's relation to the world. For decades, Jacob's father, the late Duazuah Massaquoi, linked these people to Liberia's centres of power. He was the one who came back to the village with the strange-sounding name and with a dozen connections to important people in Monrovia, in Ganta, in Gbarnga. Through him, children were sent to live in Congo homes and to attend school, and young men got jobs in the army.

And then, Duazuah Massaquoi's patrons in Monrovia were overthrown, and the capital city provided no more. The village was cut off and went hungry. And so some of the men of Duazuahplay joined a rebel army, Charles Taylor's army, and went to Monrovia to find booty. Their new patron lost, and lost badly. Now, they are being punished for the role they played – the name 'Butuo' is synonymous with the beginning of the war – and they are still cut off, perhaps for ever this time. They are waiting for another powerful man to emerge from the forest to save them.

In the village square, they raise Jacob's photograph high in the expectation that tomorrow Jacob himself will stand there, that he will bring a piece of America back with him.

When I leave Jacob that night he is pensive. He sits quietly and pushes back his cuticles with his fingers.

'I can stay,' I tell him. 'We can open another bottle of wine and talk, or just sit quietly together. If you don't feel like being alone, I can stay.'

'No,' he replies. 'I am just sad. That is all.'

Several days later my mother fell very ill in Johannesburg and I left the United States suddenly and for an extended period. Six weeks passed before Jacob and I saw one another again. We arranged to meet outside his apartment block on a Tuesday evening. It was mid-October. He was standing in the entrance to the building, waiting for me, and he smiled when he saw me coming and waved briefly. He was wearing a long-sleeved T-shirt and no jacket. It was unseasonably warm. Instead of leading me upstairs to his apartment, he turned right on entering the building and headed for the long ground-floor room that housed his youth centre.

The scene that greeted us was as unexpected as it was lovely. At least a dozen little children filled the space, far younger than the ones I'd seen when the two tall sales executives were there. They were six, seven years old, and they were running and shouting, all at once, all in different directions, each, it seemed, disassociated from the next: a frenzy of unconnected worlds. In the midst of them was a young man and a young woman, both white and very pretty and very well groomed. They were interns, I learned: one was an undergraduate student at the public health school at Columbia, the other at the psychology department at NYU. The woman had very long, very straight hair, and three of the children were brushing it at the same time, as if she was a horse in a stable. She allowed this quite happily. Three other children were sitting around her; she was reading them a story.

A little boy ran across the room, as fast as his legs would carry him. His foot caught between the straps of a satchel lying on the floor, and he flew forward, his entire body airborne. His knees and forearms hit the linoleum with a heavy thwack, sending shivers down my spine.

He lay there a moment, winded, searching for breath. And then he was up, in one swift movement, his smile back on his face as if he had been keeping it intact behind his back.

It was only some time later, as we were leaving, that I saw how much the boy's fall had upset Jacob. We were walking away from the centre when he stopped and turned.

'They are playing so rough,' he said. 'One of them will get hurt.'

'It wasn't so rough,' I replied. 'They are kids. They run and fall.'

He looked at me, and then through me, his countenance a picture of worry.

'I should go back.'

'There are two adults there already,' I said.

He looked at me doubtfully.

Jacob said he was too tired to cook tonight and that we should go to a Liberian restaurant down the road for takeout. We began making our way up Park Hill Avenue.

'There was another shooting here last night,' he said as we walked.

'Where?'

'Right here. Right outside 140.'

'What was it about? Drugs again?'

He scanned the street in front of him, then turned around and looked behind him.

'I'll tell you when we are at home,' he replied.

We walked in silence a while.

'I want to tell you,' he said, as we turned out of Park Hill Avenue into Sobel Court, 'that I have suspended writing my memory diaires. For three weeks I have written nothing. It was because I was getting flashbacks whenever I wrote.'

'To April 6?'

'Yes, to April 6. And to the time I left Monrovia. The flashbacks leave me . . . they disable me. They stop me from functioning. So I have put my writing aside for the moment.'

'Have you spoken to Jack?' I asked.

He smiled, a little mockingly, I thought.

'Jack's a shrink,' he replied. 'You know what shrinks say. *You* could tell me what Jack will say.'

He was distracted. He was casting his eyes all around us. 'Look how empty the street is,' he said. 'It isn't a cold night. It isn't late yet. Do you think people are scared because of the shooting?'

Suddenly, his head spun to his left and I followed his gaze; the heels of a pair of sneakers disappeared into the entrance of a building.

'I know who that is,' Jacob said.

He said nothing for a while.

'Why do I stay here? I might get shot one day. Maybe I should move. Maybe I should take African Refuge out of here too.'

'I don't think it's unsafe here, Jacob,' I said. 'I have never felt unsafe walking down Park Hill Avenue, even after midnight. When there is shooting, it is always over drug turf. It is soldiers shooting at soldiers. I have never known anybody who isn't involved in selling drugs getting shot here.'

'I could be unlucky,' he replied. 'I caught get caught in the cross-fire.'

We bought our food and walked home, and as soon as we were inside the apartment, Jacob took me over to the window.

'You see that spot,' he said, pointing his finger into the street below. 'A few months ago, I was standing right here, late, late at night, and I saw a man take a Kalashnikov out of his trunk. He shoved in the magazine, aimed. Bah. Bah-bah-bah. Bah. Do you know what a Kalashnikov is?'

'An AK-47,' I said.

'Yes. Alexander Kalashnikov. Ha!'

'These New York gangsters think they are soldiers,' I said. 'But they don't know about war. Not like you do.'

He said nothing.

We sat down and ate and drank, and at some point during the meal, Jacob said: 'I don't want what I am about to tell you to make you feel bad. It is not your fault. I have been watching the videos you took in my village. They have made me depressed. The feeling that comes over me, it is similar to the flashbacks I have about April 6. I told you that I have suspended work on my diaries. But it is more than that. I have had to delay a doctoral module. Just the other day, there was a deadline looming, and I found I could not work, I just could not work. I called my adviser and explained. Explained that I was struggling, I was having flashbacks to the war.

He has given me another six weeks. And my work at African Refuge, too. It has slowed down.'

'You get distracted and can't work?'

He nodded.

'What is it that upsets you when you see the video footage?' I asked.

'All those people, Jonny. They are old. Soon they will be dead. You told me you gave Dennis Duazuah the torch. Did you really? Can you promise me? You had just met everybody. Maybe you gave it to the wrong old man.'

I said nothing.

'Jonny, I am facing a big choice. Why finish my PhD when the price is not helping my people? It will take me a long time to finish. Maybe until 2012. All the ones in the video might be dead by then. Can I be so selfish?'

'What do you want to do for them?' I asked.

'I want to raise $10,000 and go home next year: $2,000 will be for the air ticket, $8,000 to build a school.'

'And the school's recurring expenses?' I asked. 'Teachers' salaries?'

'I must establish a foundation here in America, one that will keep providing. I have the connections here. It is possible.'

'I am trying to understand,' I said. 'A school is for young people, not the old people in the video. Are you saying that you must help while they are alive so that they can witness your help? So they can see you do good?'

He stared at his hands for a time. 'Jonny,' he said, 'can you imagine going home after a long absence to find that everyone you once knew is dead, that the people here are all strangers?'

We spoke of other things for a long time, and ate many roasted chicken wings and lots of rice and drank a bottle of wine. I am not sure how the conversation turned to this, but at some point much later in the evening Jacob said that he wanted to visit South Africa one day, and Antarctica, too. He asked how long it would take to get from the southernmost point of South Africa to Antarctica, and I said that it was very far. He wanted me to show him, but there was no atlas or globe in the apartment, and so Jacob took down a big, oval basket, and we pretended that it was the world. We discussed the poles and the equator, and the earth spinning both on its axis and around the sun, and how the first accounted for day and night and the second for the seasons. We discussed, too, why the equator is hot and the poles cold.

I did most of the talking. Jacob listened as if he was hearing these things for the first time, which was odd, because he knew a great deal more about these principles than me. Perhaps he was testing my knowledge. Perhaps he merely felt like listening. I don't know.

'How big is the sun?' Jacob asked.

'I'm not sure,' I replied. 'Much bigger than earth.'

'It is a huge ball of fire?'

'Yes.'

'Some say that the sun will die.'

'It is dying,' I said.

'It *is?*'

'By definition. Its life is finite. Just like you and I are dying.'

'That is scary,' he said. 'Without photosynthesis, all life on earth will die.'

'Yes.'

'That is scary. The implications. Do you believe in life after death?'

'It's funny you ask,' I said. 'I told you that my mother died last month.'

'You have my sympathy.'

'I watched her die.'

'You watched her? You watched her when she died?'

'Yes.'

'That's hard. I watched someone die.'

'In the war?'

'In the hospital. All through the last hours of his life, he was struggling. He was struggling to breathe.' Jacob imitated a death rattle. At first it did not sound right. He started again and corrected himself, and this time it was remarkably accurate, his mouth quite still, a deep gurgling and rattling coming forth from deep in his throat, as if there was a box of rusted nails inside him. 'He was tormented. He really didn't want to die. It was traumatic to watch.'

'My mom was the opposite,' I said. 'She was very sick and she had been told that she would never get well again. Once she heard that news, she wanted very urgently to die.

'Anyhow, what I wanted to tell you was this. When she died, we decided that the body must stay with us for twenty-four hours before the undertaker came.'

'Why! The undertaker wouldn't come?'

'It was our decision. She died at my sister's house. We were not ready for her to leave.'

'You decided? Who decided? Are you the oldest?'

'We all decided. I've always been agnostic about life after death. How can I know, after all? But watching my mother die, then sitting with her corpse for twenty-four hours, that experience made me believe so strongly that there is nothing after death, nothing at all. That you no longer exist. Maybe one day I will be unsure again, but sitting there with my mother's body, I was sure.'

My words woke something in him, something that had been sleeping all through the evening, and perhaps for much longer.

'You are wrong,' he said. He thumped his fist on the table, not in anger, but with urgency. He was strident, alive, his eyes bulging with the significance of what was at stake. The melancholy he had carried with him the last few hours seemed suddenly to have evaporated. He began telling me a story about Albert Einstein, about how Einstein was a doubter his whole life, but that towards the end, he discovered with absolute certainty that there must be something much bigger than us.

I lost track of his tale. I was distracted by the change that had come over him. It seemed that time had reeled back to the first evening I spent in his apartment, when he had been absorbed with all his being in Obama's victory over Hillary Clinton. That night, I saw before my eyes the boundary between Jacob and the man on the screen blink and disappear. They became one and the same.

He had been then, and was again, now, an arrow aimed at the future. And that was all there was in the world.

Epilogue

In early November 2009, a year and ten months after arriving in New York, I printed two copies of the manuscript of this book, posted one to Jacob at African Refuge and handed the other to Rufus over lunch at a Thai restaurant in midtown Manhattan. To Jacob's copy I attached a note proposing that 50 per cent of the book's royalties should go to him and Rufus, to spend jointly on a community project of their choosing. I made the same proposal to Rufus at the restaurant. He listened carefully, nodded, shoved the manuscript into his bag, picked up his fork, and continued with his meal in silence.

'Do Thai people always eat such small portions of rice?' he asked politely.

'We can order more,' I replied.

He shook his head. 'No, leave it. This is an excellent meal.'

I watched him eat. The air between us was leaden. When you have worked with a man for twenty-two months, followed him to his home and his work, to a dozen soccer fields in several states, and across the ocean to the land of his birth, you hope, when you finally hand over the product of this work, for at least a hint of ceremony.

'Will you read it in the next month?' I asked. 'That way we will still have time to speak about it before I leave New York.'

He nodded.

'If there are things you disagree with,' I continued, 'not just matters of fact, but of perspective, about your fight with Jacob, about your vision for Roza, about your trip to Monrovia, please share them with me.'

He nodded again.

My mind drifted. I felt anxious. I found myself wondering whether I could ever know much about this man's experiences without being there, next to him, as they unfolded. And even then . . . I am not sure why, but I imagined him on the night before he left for the United States for the first time. What did he do that night? Whom did he see?

'When you left Monrovia in 1986,' I asked, 'did Roza throw a party for you?'

'A party?'

'Did they give you a send-off?'

He frowned, absolutely astonished. 'No. No, they did not. I left in secret. I went to watch the Sinkor Defenders that afternoon, came home, picked up a small bag, got into a taxi to the airport.

'Next day: "Where Rufus? He was just here. Where he gone?" "Rufus in Newark, New Jersey, man." "What? Newark, New Jersey? You're kidding me. But he was *here*, just *yes-ter-day*."'

He scooped up some more rice with his fork, then chewed slowly.

'You don't tell people you going to *America*, man. They use voodoo on you. They *kill* you.'

Encouraged by his sudden animation, I pressed on. I asked him about his first hours, his first days in America, what he saw, what he smelled. But his flourish was over. His head was back in his rice. He had closed down once more.

We paid and left and walked towards the subway station at Columbus Circle.

'These royalties,' he asked tentatively. 'How much are they?'

I told him where I had sold the book and where I hadn't, and how much it might all add up to.

'Yeah,' he said. 'Yeah, that sounds *real* good. Roza is broke, man. Broke. You more comfortable giving me soccer balls than cash, I take soccer balls. Anything, man.'

A week later, I sat in Jacob's apartment, the manuscript I had sent in the post strewn about his living room. Some pages were greasily thumbed, others folded in half. Most were covered in green, pink and yellow highlighter. Some had scraggly columns of ballpoint marginalia running down both sides.

Jacob was pacing his living room in a vest and undershorts. He walked between the various bits of manuscript, then got onto his haunches and arranged and rearranged the pages as if he were orchestrating them to play.

'Did you expect this?' he asked. 'Did you expect this attention to detail? Have any of your other subjects been this scrupulous?'

'Some,' I said with resignation.

He frowned, clearly disappointed, thought momentarily of interrogating me further, then checked himself and returned to the papers on the floor.

He had called me four days after the manuscript arrived in the mail. His voice had been polite, but cold.

'I have read everything,' he said. 'There are very serious problems with this book: problems that will hurt family back home, other problems that will have repercussions for me here in Staten Island. And then there are still more problems I cannot discuss now. In short, there are problems.'

Reading a book-length depiction of yourself for the first time is shocking, always, for everybody who has had the experience. You have sat and spoken into a voice recorder for months, years. As you talked, you censored here and embellished there; you felt increasingly comfortable and in control; you were, in fact, writing a persona into the pages of the book that was still to be written. When you finally open the manuscript, you discover that you never were the one with the pen. The person the writer has contrived is recognisably you in the detail. But in the spirit, something is awry. The writer has cheated. He has written a you that is not you: certainly not a you that you would care to present. You have given him material that you ought to have kept to yourself, that only you should have the right to clothe and display.

Most find the experience confusing. Something is wrong, but how to put one's finger on it? Where does one's complaint begin?

If Jacob had been confused on first reading, he had acquired extraordinary lucidity by the time I went round to his apartment. He had organised his complaints into crisp categories: errors of fact; facts that were true, but whose publication would be damaging; other facts that were true but that one ought never to write down; and, finally, facts that I had used inadmissibly.

'What is the protocol in your business?' he asked. 'Sometimes, we were speaking with the recorder on. That was for the book. Other times, you came around and hung out, and I told you stuff because I wanted to tell you as a person, because I grew to *like* you as a friend. Now some of that stuff is in the book. What's the protocol in your business? You can use that stuff? Because the book you have written: I did not expect you to write this book. It is very close, very private. It is the sort of book you publish when you are old and will soon be dead. It is not the sort of book you publish when you are thirty-nine years of age.'

We went through the book page by page. The exercise took seven hours, and was accomplished over two sittings. We drank a lot of red wine and ate much rice. Jacob did not once mistake what he had said on the voice recorder with what he had said informally. They came from different rooms in his mind's abode: the one for entertaining guests, the other only for intimates. He could distinguish between them immediately.

As we proceeded, he watched my disconcertedness etch itself deeper into my face. He thanked me several times for having the courtesy to show him the manuscript before publishing. He said that I was both a gentleman and a cunning bastard.

It soon became apparent that our respective perceptions of what might go into a book came from different worlds. Jacob's conception was, to put it simply, very Liberian. His is a country plagued from its inception by the abuse of public service, a country where personal greed has become synonymous with warfare, where anybody's claim to represent people is assumed to be a cover for empire-building. It is also a country where many people have given expression to personal instability on a public stage, in the form of atrocious violence, persistent unreasonableness and a will to destroy. The 'Jacob' he wanted me to present in this book was a drained and inanimate being, shorn of personal ambition, of self-regard, of anger, of intemperance, and, above all, of any thoughts at all about his future.

'You do not share your plans for the future with whoever happens to pick up this book,' Jacob said. 'Do you understand Liberia? Do know what it means to have personal ambition? I do not want anything in this book which has me thinking about the future. Even the fact that I am studying for a doctorate . . . Talk about my MBA; that is in the past.'

'I cannot write about such a person,' I replied. 'And nobody will want to read about him. He is too boring. A person only becomes a human being by imagining his future. You are asking me to make you less than human.'

'You do not understand how some people will see it,' he countered.

'And you don't understand how sympathetic your ambition is,' I replied, 'how incredibly admirable it makes you. You have been through hell and come out the other side. Your ambition is part of that story. It is also bound to your curiosity, to your reception of new ideas. It is as much a part of you as your fingers and your toes.'

In any event, as his demands accumulated, I saw that I would lose little by acceding to many of them. The book would in fact probably end up being the better for it. He was scraping away this piece and that, when his personality had saturated everything. He had no means to drain it from the manuscript. He was beavering away with the wrong tools.

On the matter of his fight with Rufus, he was furious and indignant. 'Africans come to live in New York, and what do you write about? That they fight one another likes brutes, like animals. This aspect of your book is neocolonial.'

He eyed me nervously as he said it, his heart not in it at all.

'And as for your offer of royalties, I will have to think about it. I am not a prostitute. Paying for it does not make it okay to depict African men fighting.'

'Are you saying that writing about the fight was racist?' I asked.

'Yes.'

'That as a friend of Africans, I should have pretended that it didn't happen?'

'There are many other things to write about.'

'You are saying that to represent you as an African, I must airbrush out a significant episode in your life, one that consumed you? That you can only be represented as an African once conflict is hidden away?'

'It is not the fight per se,' he replied. 'It is how you depict me in the fight. Like I am a destroyer, a disrupter, a greedy person who knows only about subversion and destruction. When I read about myself arriving in New York, it is not me. You do not show the reader what I saw, what made me do what I did.'

'I used the material you gave me, Jacob,' I said. 'What else did I have to work with? I asked you countless times about what you saw when you came to New York. You closed up each time.'

'Of course I closed up. My feelings about these things are . . . they are mine. They are for my use, not yours.'

His words stopped our conversation. I had no reply to that, none that would not be blunt and violently self-serving. CNN flickered silently on his television screen. We both watched.

'Why, then,' I finally asked, 'did you consent to be written about? It seems you had a plan. What was your plan?'

He stared at the television. 'That is something else I will not tell you,' he said quietly.

'Let us set another time to meet,' I said. 'I will come with my voice recorder. We can talk about your arrival in New York. I will undertake to rewrite the chapter about how your fight with Rufus began.'

'I do not want to do that,' Jacob said.

'Then I have no material with which to change what I've written.'

He rubbed his eyes with the backs of his hands and stifled a yawn. He had become enormously weary.

'I could just wash my hands of this,' he replied. 'The book is published. Some journalist calls me. Asks for comment. I say: "No, this guy is just dodgy. He is a dodgy character. I endorse nothing that he has written."'

I returned to Jacob's apartment four days later. For just under an hour, he spoke into my voice recorder about his arrival in New York. He did so reluctantly, like I was stealing from him, or torturing him, but he nonetheless spoke with feeling and with clarity. He talked of how terribly vulnerable he had felt on arrival in this foreign land, alone, with his shortened leg and his visitor's visa; of how he was called upon when he slept by nightmares of Charles Taylor's goons; of his shock and sense of hurt when he discovered that no Liberian in New York was going to assist him with getting asylum, that the Liberians here seemed either to be helpless or cunning; of his epiphany that his countrymen had fashioned a Little Liberia on Staten Island, the same rottenness carried across the ocean. He thanked God for his education, for his ability to distill and to analyse, and thus to identify the political roots of his very personal experiences in the United States.

The more I listened, the more incompetent I felt. I had shadowed him for nearly two years. And yet he had decided from the start to keep hidden a sacred piece of him, a dialogue he had been having with himself about matters of the greatest personal import.

'The writer of fiction,' one of America's most thoughtful journalists has mused, 'is the master of his own house and may do what he likes with it; he may even tear it down if he is so inclined. But the writer of non-fiction is only the renter, who must abide by the conditions of the lease.'

A week after Jacob recounted his arrival in New York, I left the city for good. I had undertaken to rewrite the inception of his fight with Rufus and to email him the result. We hugged goodbye with warmth and sadness; that we had grown to like one another very much was unerasable. But as renter and tenant we were both dissatisfied, he by what I had done with the room he had leased to me, I because the room was too bare, the household treasures taken away and stored elsewhere in anticipation of my arrival. I had threatened to show this bare room to the world. And so, with reluctance, he had chosen one or two items of value, and put them back.

Throughout November and the first half of December, I telephoned or emailed Rufus once a week to ask how he was coming along with the manuscript. In truth, he was enormously busy. His trip to Monrovia had fortified his resolve to abandon New York for Liberia. On his return to the United States, he gave up his adult literacy students, his after-school programme and his space in Fox Hill. His evenings were now reserved for study. At the start of the fall semester, he enrolled for a masters degree in education at a college in downtown Manhattan. Classes were held three evenings a week. All of Rufus's other evenings were set aside for home assignments. Even Roza would have to do with far less of him. He would attend their matches, and occasionally show his face at practices.

As with most of his plans, this one was a gamble. Liberia's next presidential election was scheduled for 2011. George Weah, who had lost to Ellen Johnson-Sirleaf in the 2005 elections, would stand again. Early signs were that he would make a strong candidate. Were Weah to win, he was bound to fill the ranks of his administration with those who had peopled Liberia's golden age of soccer in the early 1980s.

'If you consider the history I have with such people,' Rufus told me, 'they would have to think very hard before refusing me a position developing youth through sports. My ideas about soccer have been brewing for twenty years. They will understand my ideas.'

To improve his chances, he would arrive home with a freshly acquired graduate degree in education from an American university.

I wondered about Rufus's judgement. In his imagination, the early 1980s had been lifted from the world and preserved somewhere quiet, perhaps in chloroform or some other age-defying substance, waiting for the right moment to return. Its heroes would be older, greyer and far chubbier, but their spirit would remain the same.

I arranged to meet him outside his college one night after classes. That afternoon, I finally received an email from him about the manuscript. 'Dear Jonny,' he wrote, 'you did a great job with most of the research work but there were some mistakes and corrections that should be made. I am listing those areas I found problems with . . .' I had misspelled his wife's maiden name, gotten the age at which he began high school wrong, and a couple of other things.

I do not think he cared very much about what was in the book. That was my business. His was what he might get from it. I am not sure what he imagined that would be when he agreed to work with me. It turned out to be the promise of a modest royalty. He would take that and move on.

I was waiting for him when he emerged from his college on Broadway. It was windy and cold, and downtown Manhattan was deserted. We ate at a McDonald's that was just closing, Rufus bantering with the cleaning staff, then walked towards the l train at Chambers Street, which would take us to the Staten Island ferry.

I had arranged for Rufus to give a presentation about Roza the following day at the Open Society Institute, where I had a fellowship.

'Thanks for the exposure,' he said. 'What should I talk about?'

'Well,' I replied, 'there are two programmes at OSI whose staff would be interested in your work. One deals with immigration, the other with black men.'

'Black men?'

'Yeah. Why they do so much worse than black women: at school, in the job market.'

'Black men do worse than black women?'

'You know that from Park Hill Avenue,' I said. 'Compare how Roza men do with Ladies of Prestige women.'

'Yeah. I was thinking too narrowly. I was thinking only of Liberians.'

At the intersection ahead of us, a well-groomed white man stood on the kerb and hailed an approaching taxi. The wind lifted the tails of his coat as he opened the cab door, turning it for a moment into a dramatic cape.

'Even that,' Rufus said. 'A black man stand on that corner at this time hailing a cab: he wait a long time, man, a long time.'

We crossed the street and walked into the subway station.

'You know,' he said, 'if it isn't rehabilitated, the whole of Liberia will end up like black men. If it isn't rehabilitated, Liberia may never recover from the war. The country is sick from war. You see it in Staten Island. There was no fighting on Staten Island before the war. There was one Liberian church when I arrived. Now, there are nine. In twenty years, Liberians have not accomplished anything here. They have only fought.

'First step is to admit that you are sick. You pull out a small circle of people, three or four, who admit they are sick. I myself admit it. It is the first step. You can do this with the young, not the old. With the old, it is too late.'

By now, we were on the subway heading for South Ferry.

'One of the reasons I wanted to meet you tonight,' I said, 'is that I have a simple question to ask. I've been writing about you, and yet there is this question I can't answer. Most people, when they get to forty-five, fifty, they start slowing down a little. They stay still, start building around where they are. You are the opposite. You want to go home and start fifty Roza teams, reach every kid in the country, run for president. You want more than anything to leave your mark on the world, to have changed something permanently by the time you die.'

He dropped his chin and smiled into his chest. He liked the question very much.

'Others have asked me the same thing,' he replied, 'about my ambitiousness. I wouldn't call it ambitiousness. I would say that I have unfinished business. I had seventeen Roza teams. That business was interrupted.'

'By the war coming to New York, the sickness . . .'

'Yes. The sickness. The war.

'Sport is my world. Other worlds are not mine. You are a writer. That is your world. I play in your world, I am not being honest with myself. In Liberia, if you're educated, you go into politics. That is not my world either. Mine is sport. That is where I belong.'

I waited with him at the ferry terminal, and when the ferry arrived we shook hands and said goodbye, and I walked back to the subway. Making my way uptown, it occurred to me that the Liberia he had just described was really a description of the difference between his interior world and the world outside. He spoke of adults versus young people, then of politics versus sport. Adults and politics are sullied and useless; you cannot work with them for you cannot change them; they are stubborn; they are difficult; they require too much negotiation, too much manoeuvring; they tire you out and depress you. But young people, a ball, a football field: this is what holds one's spirit. It is a brightly lit place peopled by heroic figures and cheering crowds. It is a place of the imagination. As such, it is devoid of reason; in this world, you can wish away all paradoxes and contradictions. You do not have time to stop to consider whether things make sense. Above all, it is a transferable world. You can moor it down to Monrovia in the early 1980s, roll it up, take it to New York and hammer its pegs into Staten Island. When the old people and the politics threaten to ruin it there, you can take it back across the ocean once more.

Rufus's interior world, it struck me, was tailor-made for exile. In the moment of departure you gather every last detail of the place you are leaving, infuse it with all your wishes and desires, and carry it with you, like a great living ornament, wherever you happen to go.

Notes

Page 35. 'The whole commerce between master and slave . . .' Thomas Jefferson, *Notes on the State of Virginia*, Chapel Hill: University of North Carolina Press, 1955 (first published in 1784), p.146.

35. 'Deep rooted prejudices . . .' Jefferson, *Notes*, p.138.

35. 'brought up, at the public expense . . .' Jefferson, *Notes*, pp.137–138.

36. 'blacks will never be a people until . . .' cited in James T. Campbell, *Middle Passages: African American journeys to Africa, 1787–2005*, New York: Penguin, 2006.

36–37. 'The newcomers from America . . .' Ryszard Kapuściński, *The Shadow of the Sun: my African life*, London: Penguin, 2002, pp.239–240.

41. 'They all have high-sounding titles . . .' William Nesbit and Samuel Williams, *Two Black Views of Liberia*, New York: Arno Press and New York Times, 1969, p.15; '*cannot read*, and are totally ignorant . . .', p.34; 'As in [America, where] the slaves occupy small buildings . . .' p.39.

44. 'most of the income earned from trade . . .' Amos Sawyer, *The Emergence of Autocracy in Liberia*, San Francisco, Institute for Contemporary Studies, 1992, p. 161.

45. 'Frontier force soldiers, their salaries years in arrears . . .' Campbell, *Middle Passages*, p.244.

62–63. 'taking regular lessons in English . . .' Gus Liebenow, *Liberia: the quest for democracy*, Bloomington, IN. Indiana University Press, 1987, pp.203–4.

124. 'more resembled a street-corner hustler . . .' Stephen Ellis, *The Mask of Anarchy: the destruction of Liberia and the religious dimension of an African Civil War*, 2nd edition, NYU Press: New York, 2007, p.xxi

264. 'The writer of fiction is the master of his own house . . .' Janet Malcolm, *The Journalist and the Murderer*, New York: Vintage, p.153.

Further Reading

The following books and articles all played a part in shaping *Little Liberia*.

Stephen Ellis's *The Mask of Anarchy: the destruction of Liberia and the religious dimension of an African civil war*, 2nd edition (New York, 2007) is the standard work on the Liberian civil war and was an indispensable aid throughout this project. Those interested in Ellis's thoughts on the role of religion in the war might also want to consult his book *Worlds of Power: religious thought and political practice in Africa* (Oxford, 2004) co-authored with Gerrie ter Haar. James Youboty, *A Nation in Terror: the true story of the Liberian civil war* (Philadelphia, 2004) is a richly observed, albeit sharply biased, guide to the war.

There are many excellent eyewitness accounts of various episodes of the war. Henrique F. Topka, 'Cuttington University College during the Liberian Civil War: an administrator's experience', *Liberian Studies Journal*, XVI, 1 (1991), pp.79–94, is a perceptive account of the conduct of NPFL forces at the beginning of the war. Mark Huband's book, *The Liberian Civil War* (London, 1998) is impeccably researched and profits enormously from the author's misfortune of having been kidnapped by NPFL forces. Denis Johnson was also kidnapped by the NPFL. For his valuable reportage on his experience, see 'The Small Boys Unit: Searching for Charles Taylor in a Liberian Civil War', in *Harper's Magazine*, October 2000, pp.41–60. It is also worth consulting the essay on Liberia in Bill Berkeley, *The Graves Are Not Yet Full* (London, 2002). Africa Watch diligently chronicled the first half of the war in periodic reports, all of which are available on the Human Rights Watch website.

I profited enormously from Amos Sawyer, *The Emergence of Autocracy in Liberia: Tragedy and Challenge* (San Francisco, 1992), a magisterial history of Liberian political economy and statecraft from the early nineteenth to the late twentieth century. On what being black and living in Africa meant to the Republic's Americo-Liberian founders, Wilson Jeremiah Moses, *Alexander Crummell: A Study of Civilization and Discontent*, (Oxford, 1989) is excellent. On the long arc of Liberia's history since Americo-Liberian settlement, see also Jeremy Levitt, *The Evolution of Deadly Conflict in Liberia: from 'paternaltarianism' to state collapse* (Durham, N.C., 2005); Elwood E. Dunn, *Liberia* (Oxford, 1995). James T. Campbell, *Middle Passages: African American journeys to Africa, 1787–2005* (London, 2006) contains several masterful essays on African-American involvement in Liberian statecraft. The essay on W. E. B. Du Bois's visit to Liberia in 1923 is especially remarkable. Many thanks to Charles van Onselen for insisting that I read Campbell's book.

The youthful Graham Greene's travelogue, *Journey Without Maps* (London, 2006) is a perceptive account of Americo-Liberian rule in the hinterland in the 1930s, and ends with a brief but powerful portrait of Monrovia. Merran Fraenkel's ethnography of Monrovia in the late 1950s, *Tribe and Class in Monrovia* (London, 1964) is a gem, capturing the city's complexity in simple, lucid prose. Fraenkel also observes the style of President William V. S. Tubman's rule and the vocational milieu of Monrovia's elite. Hans J. Massaquoi's memoir *Destined to Witness: Growing Up Black in Nazi Germany*, (New York, 1999) contains an interesting portrait of Tubman and of Americo-Liberian culture in the immediate post-World War II period. Helene Cooper's memoir, *The House at Sugar Beach: in search of a lost African childhood* (London, 2008) has a superb account of Monrovia's elite in the late 1970s.

Far too little has been written about either the student movement in which Jacob was involved or the world of football that so absorbed Rufus. Togba-Nah Tippoteh, *Democracy: the call of the Liberian people* (Tofters Tryckeri, 1981) gives some sense of the student movement. The best portrait of Doe I have read is by Emmanuel Bowier, who knew Doe well, and is published in Tim Hetherington, *Long Story Bit By Bit: Liberia Retold* (New York, 2009). My interpretation of the relationship Jacob's family forged with the Americo-Liberian elite leaned a great deal on work of the anthropologists Caroline Bledsoe and William Murphy. See Bledsoe, '"No Success Without Struggle": Social Mobility and Hardship for Foster Children in Sierra Leone', in *Man* vol. 25, no. 1, 70–88, 1990. And Murphy, 'The Rhetorical Management of Dangerous Knowledge in Kpelle Brokerage', in *American Ethnologist*, vol. 8, no. 4, November 1981, pp.667–685; Murphy,

'Secret Knowledge as Property and Power in Kpelle Society: Elders Versus Youth', in *Africa*, 50 (2), 1980, pp.193–207. The book that most influenced Jacob's thinking about Liberia during his student days was almost certainly Robert Clower *et al*, *Growth Without Development: an economic survey of Liberia*, (Evanston, IL., 1966).

Amos Sawyer, *Effective Immediately: dictatorship in Liberia, 1980–86, a personal perspective* (Bremen, 1987) is illuminating on Doe's Liberia. Ellen Johnson-Sirleaf, *This Child Will Be Great: memoir of a remarkable life by Africa's first woman president* (London, 2009) is interesting on Doe, but disappoints for the fact that it is more a politician's electoral pamphlet than a work of self-reflection. One hopes that Sirleaf puts pen to paper again some time when the stakes are not quite as high. Gus Liebenow, *Liberia: the quest for democracy* (Bloomington, IN., 1987) is a very good survey of Liberia from the post-World War II period to the mid-1980s.

Surprisingly little has been written on Africans in New York. Paul Stoller, *Money Has No Smell: the Africanisation of New York City* (Chicago, 2002) is a fascinating account of West African street traders on 125th Street in Harlem and on Canal Street, but it isn't reflective of the Liberian experience. In Edwidge Danticat's novel, *The Dew Breaker* (New York, 2004) Haitian immigrants in Brooklyn encounter a fellow countryman who tortured them and others back home; the novel invokes the atmosphere of unfinished and unspoken business that pervades *Little Liberia*. See also Andrew Rice, 'The Long Interrogation', in *The New York Times Magazine*, 4 June, 2006, in which an Ethiopian woman encounters a man in Atlanta she claims tortured her back home. Tracey Kidder, *Strength in What Remains* (London, 2009) contains a brilliant account of a Burundian refugee's first weeks and months in New York. Mary C. Waters, *Black Identities: West Indian Immigrant Dreams and American Realities* (New York and Cambridge, Mass.) is in part about the relationship between African-Americans and black immigrants in New York.

Dave Eggers, *What is the What* (San Francisco, 2006) is, among many other things, a stunning depiction of the experiences of an African refugee in the United States. Joan Didion, *Miami* (New York, 1987) and David Rieff, *The Exile: Cuba in the heart of Miami* (New York, 1993) are both fine observations of the bubble of collective exile in an American city.

Acknowledgements

On a September evening in 2006, I sat with an old friend at a cocktail bar in Cape Town watching the sun sink into the Atlantic Ocean. The old friend was Graeme Simpson. He was visiting from New York. He told me that he had recently spent an afternoon speaking to the representatives of a community of Liberians living in a Staten Island housing project. It was a remarkable afternoon, he said, for although these people resided in New York in 2006, it appeared to him that in their mental lives they inhabited another time and place; from what they were saying, he believed that they were frozen in the moment of their flight from wartime Liberia.

Graeme's description of this community stuck in my head and refused to budge, so much so that the following April I went to Staten Island where I met Rufus Arkoi and Jacob Massaquoi. The rest of the story is the one you have just read. It would most certainly not have been written in the absence of that conversation with Graeme. Many, many thanks.

I am also certain that I would not have written this book without the help of Dinni Gordon and Todd Clear who, motivated entirely by generosity and goodwill, secured a position for me as a visiting scholar at the City University of New York's John Jay College, without which I would not have acquired the legal status permitting me to work in New York.

I was supported, while working on this book, by a grant and a fellowship. The grant was from the Harry Frank Guggenheim Foundation. Many thanks to Karen Colvard, who gave wonderful support, not least by taking me on a trip to Monrovia to meet with Liberia's Truth and Reconciliation Commission. Thanks, also, to Shelby Grossman, whose commitment to, and knowledge of, Liberia was both salutary and a great pleasure to imbibe.

The fellowship was from the Open Society Institute from whose offices I worked throughout 2009. Thanks to Lenny Benardo, Bipasha Ray, Steve Hubble, Sasha Post and Lisena DiSantis for all their support.

I thank everybody on Park Hill Avenue who gave of their time, but should single out Amelia Wood and Tylah Davies. I spent many an hour with both, and intended to write their stories. That did not happen in the end, for various reasons. I learned a great deal from both of them.

Thanks, too, to those in Monrovia and in Nimba County who lent me their time. I owe a special debt of gratitude to Lizzy Goodfriend, Quegbaye Duazuah, Kanio Gbala, Aaron Weah and Ignatius Weah, who shared their wisdom, their knowledge, and their candid feelings.

Ruthie Ackerman, who was herself immersed in Park Hill matters for the duration of my project, became an interlocutor and a friend.

Thanks to Dan Franklin and Tom Avery at Jonathan Cape, and Jeremy Boraine, Anika Ebrahim and Francine Blum at Jonathan Ball, and to my former agent, Isobel Dixon, who worked with passion and conviction on behalf of my books and their author for seven years.

The thanks I owe to Jean and John Comaroff are long overdue. The warmth of their spirit and the volume of their energy are unrivalled. They have used these qualities, along with their intellectual authority, to advocate on behalf of my work far more widely than I ever imagined, giving my books an audience I scarcely deserve.

I am grateful to those who read drafts of the manuscript. Antony Altbeker, Dinni Gordon, Steve Hubble and Mark Schoofs generously took time from their busy lives to read and comment on my work. I owe a special debt of gratitude to two people who did considerably more than read drafts. What I have learned from Dedi Felman has so permeated my thinking that it has become immeasurable. She read most of the manuscript twice, free of charge, and helped decisively to shape its course. Many, many thanks. Mark Gevisser read much of the manuscript three or four times, exercising remarkable grace and patience all the while. You are a masterful reader; I have been very lucky to have you.

I have been lucky, too, to have Lomin Saayman, who took a leap of faith and accompanied me on this adventure, making it all worthwhile.

I dedicate this book to my mother, Sheila Steinberg, who died while I was writing it, and whom I miss a little more each day.

Index

penguin.co.uk/vintage